Praise for Rosemary Mahoney's

DOWN THE NILE
Alone in a Fisherman's Skiff

"This intriguing book encompasses far more than Rosemary Mahoney's hours on the Nile and a delicious recounting of the river's history. . . . In a culture so at odds with her own, the author is vexed and perplexed and bemused—all of this rendered in gorgeously vivid prose. . . . Mahoney has a gift for revealing apparently unremarkable moments in such a way as to make them utterly engrossing."
— Lisa Fugard, *New York Times Book Review*

"Rosemary Mahoney is a traveler in the intrepid tradition of Gertrude Bell, Isabella Bird, and Florence Nightingale, and she prefers to go it alone. . . . *Down the Nile* is thus as much about perseverance as it is about crocodiles and currents. It is also a book about respecting different cultures while holding on to your own."
— Susan Salter Reynolds, *Los Angeles Times Book Review*

"Great travel writing is like a classic film: the author reels us in and offers us the sights and sounds of an exotic place without requiring us to leave our chairs. From Mark Twain to Bill Bryson, America has produced scores of restless souls eager to see the world and just as eager to report back. Rosemary Mahoney is one such writer, and she has a knack for injecting herself into unusual situations in faraway places and turning her adventures into riveting prose. . . . Her language is so evocative, her descriptions so vivid, that the reader is carried along as if in a boat on a slow, smooth river. . . . Mahoney's rich, knowing voice conveys an understanding of the fundamental cultural differences between modern Egypt and the modern West and, at the same time, a sense that we are all human, despite the differences that divide us. . . . Surpassing obstacle after obstacle, she makes her way from Aswan to Quna with readers eagerly in tow. Traveling along with her, we almost forget we're reading."

—Charles Gershman, *Miami Herald*

"Riveting. . . . The trip would be no more than a gutsy stunt if Mahoney were not such a beautifully precise writer and such a compassionate observer. It is easy for her to empathize with Amr Khaled, the grave, bighearted boatman who accompanies her on the first leg of her journey and whose humanity will engrave itself in your memory. . . . In the course of her trip, Mahoney traversed just 120 miles of the world's longest river; by the end of her brilliant travelogue, you'll wish she'd tackled the whole length."   —Jennifer Reese, *Entertainment Weekly*

"On the water, Mahoney's flair for description coaxes reverence and wonder, at once delicate, opalescent miniatures of her surroundings, though with the chew and savoriness of nougat. She also displays a felicity for drawing history into the mix, flashing sequins of background color."

—Peter Lewis, *San Francisco Chronicle*

"Disguised in a white shirt and loose pants, Mahoney passes for an Egyptian fisherman for most of her Nile adventure. Her compelling chronicle makes clear it was worth playing the spy: following in the steps of travelers like Gustave Flaubert, whose writings complement her story, she experiences a rare view of a timeless culture of mud houses and stone ghats. Mahoney confesses that, like any anthropologist, she tried to grasp the sense of 'being let in on a secret.' Grasp it she does, and *Down the Nile* is a first-rate report on her mission."

—Michelle Green, *People*

"A loner, adventurer, and avid rower, Rosemary Mahoney defied history, tradition, and even death in Egypt by boating in a skiff *Down the Nile* because, she writes, 'I had never seen a river flowing northward and therefore must not have believed in my heart that it was truly possible.' Captivated reader—believe!"
— *Elle*

"In her page-turning memoir, Rosemary Mahoney defies naysayers, Egyptian police, and a fear of crocodiles to row down the Nile alone."
— Rebecca Barry, *More*

"Helen of Troy went up the Nile. So did Hadrian and Plato. Julius Caesar and Napoleon sailed upon it in conquest, while Mary, Joseph, and Jesus are said to have fled along its waters. Among all the figures to float along the Nile, none came home with a story like that of Rosemary Mahoney. . . . A shrewd, funny, and determined adventurer, with a style as lissome as the river itself. . . . Mahoney's *Nile* is worthy of awe. . . . The book unfurls a poetry of perception."
— Karen Long, *Cleveland Plain Dealer*

"What is evident throughout Mahoney's captivating narrative is that we are in the presence of a ferociously independent and restless spirit, someone who cherishes nature and history and travel and adventure, and who bristles at the restrictions placed on women all around the globe."
— Elaine Margolin, *Denver Post*

"A travel-minded memoir guaranteed to transport you."
— Megan O'Grady, *Vogue*

"This is travel writing at its most enjoyable: the reader is taken on a great trip with an erudite travel companion soaking up scads of history, culture, and literary knowledge, along with the scenery."
— *Publishers Weekly* (starred review)

"Mahoney's book is hard to put down both because of the stickiness of a woman rowing the Nile, alone, and because of the evocative beauty of her prose."   —*Harvard Magazine*

"You might call Rosemary Mahoney a writer of travel books. But the label hardly does justice to her remarkable gifts for scene, setting, dialogue, characterization, and thoughtful cultural overview. . . . She makes use of the tools of fiction to sharpen and refine her observations."
                                             —Dan Cryer, *Boston Globe*

"Fascinating stories that hold lessons about our world. . . . The most memorable part of Mahoney's adventure was the Egyptians themselves."   —Bill Marvel, *Dallas Morning News*

"Essential to the success of *Down the Nile* are Mahoney's quicksilver intelligence, her sharp eyes, and her slightly astringent voice. Yet at the same time she is patient and generous enough to allow people and things to show her their best—and they frequently do. . . . *Down the Nile* is studded with small, sensitive portraits that reveal much about the land beyond the landscape."
                                       —Marjorie Kehe, *Christian Science Monitor*

"Wicked vivid. . . . Spiced with a hearty does of cultural context, history, and dry humor."   —*Bust*

"With humor and grace Mahoney takes us to see things we could never see, meet people we would never know, make connections that would never occur to us—all in sentences as sharp and revealing as a camera lens, or as soft as a lover's caress. . . . Nothing you will ever learn about Egypt will strike you as being as honest and true as the portrait that emerges from this strange journey by an enormously gifted writer."
                                             —Doug Riggs, *Providence Journal*

"Mahoney's determination to pull this off, in a society where women are routinely held back in myriad ways, is the central premise of her sparkling travelogue. . . . Mahoney writes with a keen understanding of the joys of travel."
—Mary Houlihan, *Chicago Sun-Times*

"I think Rosemary Mahoney is the best travel writer since Freya Stark, and since Stark is dead, Mahoney is singular in her field. . . . Wherever Mahoney is and whatever she is doing, she is a congenial companion and her narrative fascinates. . . . History, literature, and adventure combine to make *Down the Nile* a treasure."
—Laura Wadley, *Provo Daily Herald*

"Mahoney's challenge as an American woman is persuading one of Egypt's endearingly sexist, dirt-poor tour-boat operators to sell her a rowboat. . . . Mahoney is such an alluring storyteller and intelligent companion, she makes this a trip worth taking."
—Jocelyn McClurg, *USA Today*

DOWN THE NILE

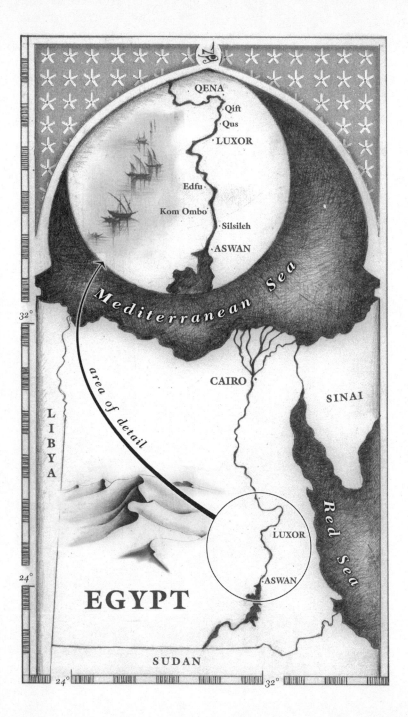

QENA

Qift

Qus

LUXOR

Edfu

Kom Ombo

Silsileh

ASWAN

Mediterranean Sea

area of detail

32°

LIBYA

CAIRO

SINAI

Red Sea

24°

24°

32°

EGYPT

LUXOR

ASWAN

SUDAN

DOWN THE NILE

Alone in a Fisherman's Skiff

ROSEMARY MAHONEY

BACK BAY BOOKS
Little, Brown and Company
NEW YORK   BOSTON   LONDON

Back Bay Books / Little, Brown and Company
Hachette Book Group
237 Park Avenue, New York, NY 10017
Visit our Web site at www.HachetteBookGroupUSA.com

Originally published in hardcover by Little, Brown and Company, July 2007
First Back Bay paperback edition, September 2008

Back Bay Books is an imprint of Little, Brown and Company. The Back Bay Books name and logo are trademarks of Hachette Book Group, Inc.

To protect the privacy of individuals, some of the names used in this book have been changed.

Excerpts from Flaubert in Egypt: A Sensibility on Tour, by Gustave Flaubert, translated by Francis Steegmuller, are reprinted with permission of McIntosh & Otis, Inc. Copyright © 1972 by Francis Steegmuller; excerpts from Letters from Egypt: A Journey on the Nile, 1849–1850 (Grove Press, 1988) by Florence Nightingale courtesy Grove/Atlantic, Inc.

Library of Congress Cataloging-in-Publication Data
Mahoney, Rosemary.
    Down the Nile : alone in a fisherman's skiff / Rosemary Mahoney. — 1st ed.
        p. cm.
    Includes bibliographical references.
    ISBN 978-0-316-10745-7 (hc) / 978-0-316-01901-9 (pb)
    1. Nile River—Description and travel.   2. Egypt—Description and travel.
I. Title.
DT116.M35   2007
916.204'55—dc22   2006034168

10 9 8 7 6 5 4 3 2

RRD-IN

Book design by Iris Weinstein
Map designed by John Barnett

Printed in the United States of America

FOR MADELEINE STEIN

CONTENTS

DOWN THE NILE

The River That Flows the Wrong Way

O N THE DAY that I hoped to buy a rowboat in Luxor, Egypt, I was awakened, as I had been every morning in Luxor, by a Koranic antiphony drifting from the Islamic boys' school next door to my hotel. With all the zeal of a Baptist preacher's, a young boy's amplified voice shrieked repeatedly in Arabic, "There is no God but God, and Muhammad is his witness!" and a shrill chorus of his schoolmates howled the words back at him. I got out of bed and went to the window—at 7:00 a.m. the glass was already warm as an infant's forehead—and discovered that during the night many colorful cloth banners had been strung above the corniche, Luxor's Nilefront boulevard. In hand-fashioned Arabic characters, the banners read, "Welcome Mister President of the Government, Muhammad Hosni Mubarak, the Leader of Our Victorious and Progressive

Destiny." Scores of teenage Egyptian soldiers in black uniforms, woolen berets, and white plastic spats lined the avenue in the ninety-eight-degree heat, more or less at attention, rifles at their sides, evidently awaiting the president's arrival. Profiting from a police barricade, the usually hectic street was, for once, mercifully quiet. Across the glittering ribbon of the Nile, the Temple of Hatshepsut and the Valley of the Kings lay blanketed in the pink morning light.

I dressed and went downstairs to the lobby, where the hotel manager and two of his employees sat shoulder to shoulder on a couch before a flickering television. All three men wore white turbans and gray gallabiyas, the traditional Egyptian gown, and, in one of the more baffling manifestations of traditional Egyptian fashion, heavy woolen scarves wound around their necks, as if against an arctic wind. No matter the time of day, the lobby of this hotel was always exceptionally dark, and through the gloom the three men looked like consumptives recuperating in a sanatorium. They were watching an American film in which jeering, sweaty-faced Confederate soldiers were busy abusing a group of morose black slaves.

With an apology for interrupting their entertainment, I asked the hotel manager why President Mubarak was coming to Luxor that day. Without looking away from the television the manager replied, "To open new hospital and sex tomb."

I studied his long brown nose, his luxurious black mustache. Surely I had misheard him. "Sorry," I said, "to open a what?"

"Hospital and sex tomb," he said dully, scratching his chin.

The hospital sounded likely enough, but the idea of a "sex" anything being publicly celebrated by the Egyptian president was preposterous. In this Islamic nation, sex, strictly forbidden outside marriage, was not a subject for public discourse or civic celebration. Human flesh, particularly women's, was to be concealed, and though in Egypt the assumption of the veil at puberty was officially a matter of individual choice, many Egyptian women wore the *hijab*, the veil that fully concealed the head and neck, and a surprising number wore the more forbidding *niqab*, a drape that covered mouth, nose, forehead, sometimes even eyes. Chaste Egyptian women were reluctant to have their photograph taken, because multiplying and displaying their image in this way was considered unseemly. Before my first trip to Egypt, I had been counseled to keep my arms and legs covered, not to wear shorts, and never to touch a man in any way except to shake hands. I had been endlessly informed by people who had experience in the matter that purity, chastity, and piety were Egypt's prevailing sentiments, and that foreign women who came to Egypt and dressed in a provocative way (there are, in fact, many who do) would be considered promiscuous, unprincipled, fair game for harassment and disrespect.

And yet, having spent a total of three and a half months in Egypt on three separate visits, I could not deny that, although I always wore long trousers and long-sleeved shirts and conducted myself as decorously and seriously and modestly as my reasons for coming here would allow, I had never visited any country in which sex had so often arisen as a topic of conversation; had never witnessed more bald nudity (including not one but two men openly masturbating on city streets, dozens of bare breasts proffered at the howling mouths of infants, men and children freely relieving themselves wherever the need struck them); had never received so many offhand proposals of marriage and professions of love from mustachioed strangers, more swaggering requests for a dance or a kiss, more offers of romantic dinners; had never been the target of more wolf whistles and catcalls and distinctly salacious whispers emanating from behind dusty clumps of shrubbery. Nowhere else in the world had a smiling stranger approached me and a friend on a busy street and said, "I want fuck you," with the idle geniality one might extend in saying, "Looks like rain."

On the hotel television a mounted Dixie soldier rattled his musket at a handsome slave and jeered, "Git workin', boy! This ain't no holiday."

The three Egyptians stared at the screen in slack-jawed wonder. Their bulky turbans were silvery in the electric blue twilight. I saw that it would be futile to try to get to the bottom of what the hotel manager was telling me about the president's visit to Luxor and went out the front door into the stunning Egyptian sunlight.

〰〰〰

I HAD COME to Egypt to take a row down the Nile. My plan, inspired by a love of rowing, was to buy a small Egyptian rowboat and row myself along the 120-mile stretch of river between the cities of Aswan and Qena. This was a trip I'd been considering for more than two years, since my first visit to Egypt when I caught a glimpse of the Nile in Cairo and realized in a moment of deep disorientation that it flowed northward. At 4,163 miles from its southernmost source—a spring in a tiny village in Burundi—to its debouchment in the Mediterranean Sea, the Nile was the longest river in the world. It rubbed against ten nations. Some 250 million people depended on it for their survival. It had fostered whole cultures and inspired immense social and scientific concepts: astronomy, height measurement, square measurement, mathematics, law and equity, money, civic order, and police. And it flowed north, which truly surprised me. That it surprised me was equally surprising. For years I had known about the many explorers—John Hanning Speke, Richard Burton, David Livingstone, and all the rest—who had headed *south* into deepest Africa searching for the Nile's *beginning*. For years I had known that the Nile flowed *into* the Mediterranean Sea on the north coast of Africa and not *out* of it. The only explanation I can offer for my astonishment at the sight of the Nile flowing northward is a simple touch of obtuse provincialism: I had never seen a river flowing northward and therefore must not have believed in my heart that it was truly possible. (I was later comforted to learn that Pharaoh Thutmose I, who had spent years ruling life along the Nile, was exactly as obtuse and provincial as I. When he traveled to Mesopotamia in the sixteenth century BC and saw the south-flowing Euphrates River, he was stunned, describing it in his notes as "a river that flows the wrong way, so that boats go northward when they sail upstream." Similarly, he dismissed the entire Persian Gulf with the epithet, "the sea of the river that flows the wrong way.")

The north-flowing Nile that I saw in Cairo was wide and coffee colored and dumpy, with piles of trash spilling down its eastern bank with the distinct look of having been recently unloaded from a municipal truck. Some of the trash was on fire, sending into the air slender strings of fishy-smelling yellow smoke. This urban strip of river—crowded with powerboats, ferries, tour boats, private yachts; spanned by four or five great bridges; and lined with skyscrapers and luxury hotels—was nearly the very end of the great Nile River. It was understandable then that it looked worn out, congested, and a bit abused. For all its fame and legend, it looked no more or less majestic than the Ohio River creeping through Pittsburgh.

My romantic impression of the Nile had been informed by the paintings of David Roberts, the nineteenth-century Scottish artist who depicted the Egyptian Nile as a lagoonish idyll of soft-sanded banks, mirror-still coves, stands of tasseled reeds, oxen lazily grazing in the shade of slender date palms, barefoot women balancing water jugs on their heads, and sails flushed pink by a tropical sun setting enormously in the distance, which distance was always punctuated by either a colossus, an obelisk, a minaret, or a pyramid. Roberts had depicted the Nile that way because that was the way the Nile looked when he saw it in 1838.

On that first trip to Egypt, in 1996, I boarded a cruise ship

in Luxor, steamed southward up the river, and found on the
second day out that, without my having registered the grad-
ual change, we had somewhere along the way shed Luxor's
modern urban shabbiness and glided into the precincts of a
David Roberts canvas. From the luxurious deck of the ship, it
struck me one evening that I was looking at an ox, palm trees,
sandy banks, mirror-still coves, water jugs on women's heads,
pink sails in an archaeological distance. I saw flamingos and
storks, soft colors, an explosive sunset, obelisks and minarets, and now and then a ruined pharaonic temple. I saw no
skyscraper and only several buildings that could be truly
termed modern. But for a few power lines threading in and
out of the tops of palm trees, an occasional plastic water bottle bobbing on the current, a motorized water pump, and a
handful of water jugs made not of clay but of aluminum, there
was little in the rural Nile landscape to suggest that nearly
two hundred years had passed since David Roberts visited
Egypt. Beyond Egypt's cities, the Nile was much as I had always envisioned it—a rare instance of a fantastical precon-
ception matched by reality.

I was charmed. With a score of middle-aged Spaniards sunbathing on the large deck behind me, I leaned against the
ship's railing and watched, entranced, as the Nile slipped by.
The wide river and its green banks looked old and placid, in-
scrutable and inviting, and yet it was all as distant and inaccessible to me as it had always been. Unable to leave the ship,
with its planned itinerary and guided tours, I realized I might
as well be watching this wonder from behind a glass wall.
What I wanted, really, was not just to *see* the Nile River but to
sit in the middle of it in my own boat, alone.

〰〰〰

I BEGAN ROWING some ten years ago when I lived on a small
island in Maine. Forced to ferry myself over the water, I found

that I enjoyed the task. Rowing was a peaceful, meditative activity, and the constant movement—the inherent mobility—of the water was enthralling. Land was stationary and always belonged to somebody. Water, on the other hand, was free. It moved and shifted and traveled. It was volatile, and when aroused it could be unforgiving. I found it frightening and a little bit thrilling to think that the water that throws itself against the coast of Kennebunkport in July might feasibly be the same particular water that laps at the crab-covered rocks in Bombay Harbor the following March. And it pleased me to realize that I could sit in a small boat and propel myself across all this hugely moving water with an engine no more powerful than my own two arms. One day I told the woman who owned the island I lived on that I planned to row across Penobscot Bay to another island two or three miles away. She protested, said it was impossible, made me promise her I wouldn't try. I promised, then did it anyway, and having successfully done it, I wanted to do more, to go farther, to row elsewhere. I rowed wherever I had a chance—in Boston Harbor and Central Park and a lake in southern France. I rowed on the Charles River in a carbuncled dinghy, while the elegant fours and eights speared by like airborne swans. I rowed on the Aegean Sea and on a pond in Oregon.

These days I live at the edge of Narragansett Bay. I row here too—up the Seekonk River one day, down to Occupessatuxet Point the next. Often I row my boat into the middle of the bay, ship my oars, and sit back to see where the tide and the current will take me. I do this, I know, not because it's peaceful but because there's an edge to it—it can be peaceful, yes, but it is never truly relaxing. I do it because there's an element of surrender in the exercise, an active acknowledgment of how breathtakingly tiny and helpless I am in the greater scheme of things, a condition that I spend the rest of my day ignoring, denying, scorning, or forgetting. It is frightening yet also liberating to admit a force far larger than our own.

〰〰〰

I SHOULD SAY, before you get the wrong idea, that I have no desire to die. I do not want to die even if it be peacefully in my sleep in my own bed. Less do I want to drown to death or burn to death or choke to death or crash to death or have any body part of mine maimed or disfigured or messed with in any way (and especially not by a crocodile, more about which later). I am, in fact, a woman who can be driven witless with discomfort and frustration by the merest splinter, wart, cold sore, sty, hangnail, or personal insult. I am not afraid to die; I simply do not want to. Nevertheless, I am also a person who is drawn to doing physically difficult and sometimes even dangerous things. I cannot deny that I like to find myself in sticky situations, with the feeling that I've really gone and done it this time, that I'm finally sunk, that there's no turning back and possibly no tomorrow. As regards my aversion to death, I think this impulse makes sense. Death — or dread of it really — has always seemed to me to be the subtext, if not the downright text, of all physical adventure. It's a calling forth of the despised thing in an effort to stare it down, a test of how far life can push itself into death's territory without getting burned, and ultimately an effort to become inured to the inevitable prospect. Contrary to what we might expect, acceptance of our limitations and of all that lies beyond our control assuages the anxieties that arise from the misplaced responsibility we habitually and rather grandiosely depute to ourselves.

Returning home from my first visit to Egypt, I took my boat out on Narragansett Bay and imagined myself gliding alone down the Nile among the flamingos, reeds, and palm trees. For months I imagined this. On winter days, when the Rhode Island sky was gray and cold, I pulled myself across the bay and conjured what I had seen along the Nile. I fantasized about returning to Egypt, finding a boat, and heading off down the river on my own. On that first trip to Egypt, whenever I mentioned my Nile rowing idea to Egyptian people they had all said with real disbelief, *Impossible! You are a woman! The river is big! Not mentioning any crocodile! And dangerous ships! And the fisherman who can become crazy seeing a woman alone!* Egyptians generally thought the plan was idiotic, pointless, and dangerous, and seemed to find it inconceivable that anyone at all would want to row a boat on the Nile for no pressing or practical or, above all, lucrative reason, let alone a foreign woman, and especially when you could make the same trip lounging on a comfortable tour boat with your feet up and a drink in your hand. But sitting in Narragansett Bay, I earnestly wondered why such a trip should be impossible. The Nile was a consistent, stately river that flowed up the continent from the south while the prevailing winds came out of the north, a rare phenomenon that for centuries had allowed easy passage in both directions. Why should its location in Egypt make this river any more forbidding, inaccessible, or unrowable than any other?

A year passed, and my fantasy failed to fade. I found myself spending afternoons in my local library, pawing through books about Egypt and the Nile, studying photographs, gathering information about the river and about others who had traveled on it. Millions of people—including thousands of foreigners—had traveled on the Nile, among them the obvious centuries of Egyptian fishermen, farmers, and pharaonic slaves who daily went up and down the river as a matter of survival. Hadrian went up the Nile. Herodotus did it too. Plato did it. So did Helen of Troy. Julius Caesar and Cleopatra went up the Nile. So, reportedly, did Jesus, Mary, and Joseph. Napoleon and his ill-fated soldiers did it in 1798, and along with them went Dominique-Vivant Denon and twenty-one mathematicians, three astronomers, seventeen civil engineers, thirteen naturalists and mining engineers, thirteen geographers, three gunpowder and saltpeter experts, four architects, eight draftsmen, ten mechanical draftsmen, one sculptor, fifteen interpreters, ten writers, and twenty-two printers, all sent to record and analyze every possible fact about Egypt, its monuments, its culture, and its people. The result of their efforts was the *Description de L'Egypte,* published between 1809 and 1828, an enormous nineteen-volume summary of the country, complete with highly detailed measurements, etchings, and drawings. The international publicity and huge number of maps the *Description* brought with it eventually inspired the world's curious to flock to Egypt in droves. (Thanks to Napoleon's expedition, by 1820 Egypt was the best-mapped country in the world.) The country that had been lost to the rest of the world by a thousand years of Arab rule, which had essentially barred foreign travelers from the Nile Valley, quickly became the favorite destination of explorers, scientists, tourists, and notables alike. When Victor Hugo wrote in his preface to *Les Orientales* in 1829, "We are all much more concerned with the Orient than ever before," the statement was directly due to Napoleon's fact-gathering expedition and the long-locked door it had opened. Edward Lane, Edward Lear, Lord Byron, William Makepeace Thackeray, Percy Bysshe Shelley, and William Cullen Bryant all went to Egypt in the first half of the nineteenth century. Florence Nightingale went in 1849. So did Gustave Flaubert. Herman Melville went, as well as kings and queens of numerous nations, the Prince of Wales, Émile Zola, Winston Churchill, and William Golding. In the 1950s, three men in kayaks, John Goddard, Jean Laporte, and Andre Davy, together paddled nearly the full length of the Nile, from the Kagera River to Alexandria, and in 2004, a team of explorers led by Pasquale Scatturo rafted the length of the Blue Nile from its source in Ethiopia to the Mediterranean Sea.

It has never been the custom, however, for foreign visitors to operate their own craft on the Egyptian Nile, and in modern times the government actively discourages such journeys. Tourists opt instead for the cruise ship or, less often, hire an Egyptian sailor to captain a felucca, the traditional lateen-rigged sailboat ubiquitous in Egypt. In my first four weeks in Egypt, I had neither seen nor heard of any foreigners on the river unaccompanied by an Egyptian captain or of a single woman, Egyptian or otherwise, operating a boat on the river. Still, I saw no truly persuasive reason that the trip I had in mind should not be possible for me. Narragansett Bay was a body of water complicated by altering tides, sometimes large waves, sudden violent weather, scores of international shipping tankers powered by propellers the size of houses, and speedboats occasionally operated by reckless drunken drivers. In Egypt, though the Nile did indeed have its own peculiar set of hazards, there would be none of that. The Egyptian Nile was hardly a wilderness: more than fifty-five million people lived alongside it; there were no ferocious animals left there to speak of; and I knew that a desperate traveler armed with a little bit of money could find her way off the river, one way or another, at any time.

The more I learned about the Nile, the less forbidding it seemed. I had so often imagined rowing on the Nile that doing so had begun to feel less like a fantasy and more like a memory that only wanted its corresponding action rightfully exercised.

Two years after my first visit, I returned to Egypt, determined to find a boat and make my trip on the Nile. In an effort to acquaint myself with the stretch of the river that I was interested in rowing, I once again spent four days on the deck of a cruise ship, traveling—this time from Luxor to Aswan—with a pair of binoculars pressed to my face, examining every island and shoal, observing the currents, trying to gauge the swiftness of the river's flow, watching fishermen at sunrise laying their nets. When rowing upriver, the fishermen hugged the shore, where the current was less intense and occasionally even eddied in reverse. Their boats sat low in the water, were flat bottomed, were made of steel, were on average twelve to fourteen feet long and three feet wide, and were roughly the shape of a Turkish slipper, narrowed at both ends but slightly higher and finer at the bow. As oars they used long, coarse, bladeless planks that resembled nothing so much as clapboards ripped from the face of a derelict house. They used not the U-shaped metal oarlocks I was accustomed to, but vertical pegs of wood or steel to which the immense oars were lashed with a length of prickly twine. The current never appeared swift enough to vex or deter these fishermen. They maneuvered their boats with breathtaking precision and finesse, making sudden one-hundred-eighty-degree turns with a simultaneous and contrariwise two-wristed snap. From Aswan to Cairo, the Nile bed falls little more than five inches per mile, which means the river offers a relatively slow, peaceful ride. In my observation, the current was swift but never roiling; there were no rapids to speak of other than those tossed up by the boulders of the first cataract above Aswan; and while there were shallows treacherous enough to stop a misguided cruise ship, none was shallow enough to prevent a small, light, flat-bottomed boat from smoothly proceeding. As for the dangerous ships Egyptians had warned of, there were no ships on the Nile that I could see, other than the plodding, festively lit cruise boats equipped with swimming pools and dance floors and packed with vacationing Europeans. (The size of these cruise ships was trifling compared to the hulking tankers I regularly marveled at on Narragansett Bay.) There was never a threat of rain. There was the possibility of a *khamaseen,* a hot southeasterly wind that whips dust out of the Sahara and renders the air a stinging, opaque mass,* but this was April and just in advance of the season for that. There was a

* According to Herodotus, an Egyptian sandstorm could be bad enough to bury an entire army. The Persian King Cambyses sent fifty thousand men into the desert, "but," Herodotus wrote, "they never returned . . . As they were at their midday meal, a wind arose from the south, strong and deadly, bringing with it vast columns of whirling sand, which entirely covered up the troops, and caused them wholly to disappear."

large lock at Esna that looked complex and possibly like trouble for a small boat, and a few bridges that did not. As for crocodiles, there were, the captain of my cruise ship had dismissively confirmed with a dry laugh, no crocodiles whatsoever in the Nile below the High Dam.

In planning my rowing trip, among my greatest worries was unwanted attention from the Egyptian police. In terms of freedom and accessibility, the Nile was a far cry from an American river on which any psychopath could, without hindrance or permission, indulge in any half-baked boating scheme he was capable of devising. I had been told that in order to travel alone on the Nile, I would need police permission, that such permission was not likely to be granted, and that if by some miracle permission *was* granted, weeks of bureaucratic wrangling would follow; I would have to come up with a considerable amount of money in fees; and that, in the end, if they let me go, the police would insist on sending an officer with me for my protection.

Since the 1997 massacre of fifty-eight tourists at Luxor's Temple of Hatshepsut (an act of terrorism euphemistically referred to in Egypt as "the accident") and several other slightly less devastating terrorist attacks perpetrated by the extremist Islamic group *Gama'at Islamiyah,* the Egyptian government has at times elevated its tourist protection operations to levels worthy of visiting heads of state. A country of sixty-two million people whose chief source of income is tourism cannot afford another "accident." Groups of foreign visitors who want to venture off the beaten tourist paths must now, in theory at least, be accompanied by a police convoy. Sightseers are often trailed by soldiers toting semiautomatic rifles, their sagging pockets stuffed with bullet cartridges bulky as bricks. More often than not, the soldiers are skinny, vaguely staring pubescents who carry their guns slung over their shoulders like cumbersome schoolbags, wear flip-flops for shoes, and spend a lot of time napping on the job. Security points have cropped up at important tourist sites—a show of outdated metal detectors and young guards rummaging halfheartedly through visitors' handbags. At other times the security effort seems a mere rumor. "If you go to Fayoum, you'll have to have a soldier in your car with you once you get there." I went to Fayoum. There was no soldier. At the Temple of Hatshepsut, where tourists had not long before been shot and hacked to death with machetes, I found the primary guard fast asleep in his guardhouse, slumped heavily in his chair, mouth hanging open, arms dangling at his sides—so unconscious was he that even when I put my camera eight inches from his face and snapped his picture he never awoke.

The Egyptian efforts at security are designed as much to make tourists *feel* safe as to actually frighten or deter militant Islamic terrorists intent on damaging the secular, West-tending Egyptian government. Fanatical terrorists could probably not be deterred, but vacationing tourists could be soothed and assured by the sight of Mubarak's soldiers. As for the river police, I had seen a few police boats at Aswan and Luxor manned by large groups of young men, but nowhere else. If I asked the Egyptian police for permission to row a boat down the Nile, I would undoubtedly have to take them with me and perhaps endure at their hands the very intrusions and harassments they were supposedly there to protect me from. If I didn't ask, I was on my own. The latter seemed preferable.

As for random crime unrelated to terrorism, the rate of personal crimes against foreigners in Egypt was low because the consequences for perpetrators were dire. But for the violent period of Gamal Abdel Nasser's nationalist revolution during the 1950s, when anti-European feeling was high, since the days of Napoleon's invasion and the subsequent rule of Muhammad Ali, the average foreigner in Egypt has generally been accorded civil rights and a moral status superior to that of the native Egyptian. In the early nineteenth century, if a foreign visitor was murdered, every Egyptian within walking distance of the event would, without trial or investigation, be put to death as punishment. If a foreigner complained of having had his money stolen by one Egyptian, some thirty Egyptians would be jailed for a month. In 1849 Florence Nightingale observed, "The police which Mehemet Ali instituted . . . have effectually cleared the country and secured the safety of Europeans. No pains are taken to investigate who is the offender; when an offence occurs, the whole village suffers to save the trouble of inquiring who's who . . . If you miss a pin now, the whole village is made responsible for it, and the whole village bastinadoed." And as late as 1872 Amelia Edwards, a British writer who traveled up the Nile, recorded an incident in which a member of her boat party, while hunting for fowl, accidentally grazed the shoulder of a child with his buckshot. Properly incensed, the local villagers grabbed the man's gun from him, struck him on the back with a stone, and chased him back to his boat. Edwards's party filed a complaint against the village. In response the governor of Aswan promised that "justice would be done," arrested fifteen of the villagers, chained them together by their necks, and asked the hunter in what manner he would like the scoundrels punished. The hunter confessed that, not being familiar with Egyptian law, he had no idea what would be fit. The governor replied, "Whatever you want is Egyptian law." The hunter stated that his aim was simply to "frighten [the villagers] into a due respect for travelers in general." In turn, the governor assured the hunter that his only wish was to be agreeable to the English and averred that the entire village should have been beaten "had his Excellency [the reckless and obviously not too bright hunter] desired it."

The foreigner's word was rarely questioned in Egypt, and the essence of that custom remains even now. One day while walking in Cairo with an American friend, two young boys called out to us, "Give us money!" When we didn't reply, one of them threw a stone at us. In an offhand way my friend told an Egyptian man what had happened, and immediately the man summoned a police officer who swiftly collared the two boys and, to our dismay, beat them silly with a bamboo stick. Neither man had witnessed the event, neither had questioned whether our story of the thrown stone was true. The foreign tourist, protected by Egypt's dependency on her cash, enjoys an unwarranted elevated status. In 1849 Flaubert wrote, "It is unbelievable how well we are treated here—it's as though we were princes, and I'm not joking." That particular social luxury had altered only slightly in a hundred and fifty years.

The truth was that the biggest obstacle to my trip would not be political, natural, or criminal, but cultural. My attempt merely to purchase a boat would prove nearly more arduous than the trip itself. Had I a boat of my own with me, I would have simply put it in the water and slipped away, taking my chances as they came. But I had no boat, and I knew that finding one in Egypt would involve dealing with a succession of men who would wonder why a female foreigner wanted such a thing, would try very hard to dissuade me from my intentions, and would eventually suggest that instead of rowing down the river I should spend my time in Egypt dancing and dining with them.

The Egyptian temperament—invariably gregarious, humorous, and welcoming—is also spiked with a heavy dose of intrusiveness. Curious and paternalistic toward foreigners, Egyptians watch over their visitors with elaborate concern—a sweetly self-important trait, as though one could not possibly survive without their attentions and advice. On seeing a pen tucked in my shirt pocket a gentleman says with genuine alarm, *Madame! Be careful not to lose your pen!* As I leave a hotel another says, *Oh, lady! Please be sure to close your bag tightly for safety.* Without asking if I want him to, a delightfully friendly shop-keeper with mahogany-hued teeth and one pinkish, weeping eye, takes proprietary hold of my backpack, tamps at his tongue with a greasy crumpled cloth, and rubs dust from the pack with his plentiful saliva, saying, *Better this way!* When I put my ho-tel room key under the leg of my breakfast table to keep the rick-ety thing from wobbling, a waiter hurries over, plucks up the key, and says with regal self-congratulation, *You dropped your key, madame. You must be careful!* Once more, surreptitiously, I tuck the key beneath the table leg; dramatically he picks it up again. If I stand before a shop window full of wristwat-ches, within thirty seconds a passerby will put his nose to mine, point to what I am looking at, and inform me with the patronizing indulgence of a kindly professor instructing a barefoot hillbilly, "This is wristwatches, you see." And it is nearly impossible for a foreigner to proceed down an Egyptian street without having to answer the same dozen investigative questions shot from the mouths of six dozen people within the span of, say, five minutes: *What your name? Which your coun-try? You are alone? Married? Children? Where you went today? My God, you shouldn't go there. What you did last night? Oh, my God, I will tell you something better to do. What you want? No, no, you do not want that. You will want this better thing more. Do not walk that way. There might be a wolf/snake/bad man. Look out, my God, for the traffic.*

In Egyptians, this trait seems derived not only from a wish to try out the few English phrases they've learned but also from a particular conviction that they know far better than you do what's good for you. Confronted with foreign tourists, Egyptians become noisy and nosy, bossy and brash, intrusive and terribly friendly.

Not comprehending my wish to row myself down the river alone, well-meaning Egyptian men, I knew, would try to stop

me or, alternatively, would offer a crippling degree of help.
And so, as I began my search for an Egyptian rowboat, I resolved to take a slightly Fabian approach, to move slowly,
evade questions, and tell no one exactly what it was that I
wanted to do.

Aswan

M Y SEARCH FOR a boat began in Aswan, the southernmost Egyptian city, the starting point of my rowing
trip, and technically the beginning of the Egyptian
Nile. I wanted a simple fisherman's rowboat, long and narrow,
with room enough to lie down in at night. I had estimated that
my trip would take five days at most. Forewarned of the possibility of scorpions and adders along the riverbanks, I had no intention of sleeping on land. For four days, I roamed around
Aswan and its islands looking for a suitable boat, searching the
riverbanks, crashing through reeds, climbing over sand dunes
and boulders, picking my way past bony dogs lying prone and
comatose in the baked dust, scouring the mud-brick Nubian
villages on Elephantine Island, asking oblique questions, fend-
ing off friendly advances, and trying, without luck, not to draw
attention to myself.

With unctuous persistence, felucca captains tried to hook my business as I walked by, dancing and clamoring around me like sheepdogs, following me sometimes for a quarter of a mile and so closely that their shoulders repeatedly brushed against mine. *Remember me?* they said into my ear, though they had never set eyes on me before. *Where you are going? Want felucca? Sailing! Special price because you are special! Five bound. Maybe later? Maybe tomorrow? Cataract. West Bank. Why no?* The phrases spilled out of them in perfectly inflected American English. At that time tourists were scarce in Egypt because of the rising fear of terrorism, and beneath the suave and chattering bravado the captains' voices had the despairing ring of the mendicant's plea. At any one time there might be thirty captains poised on a dock, waiting in vain for work. The very sight of them was coercive. Wondering how they survived, I felt a strong obligation to take their felucca rides. Whenever I declined and walked on, the captains reduced the already pathetically low five-pound fare to three, making me feel instantly stingy, though my declinations were never a matter of money.

As I stumbled through Aswan, dozens of barefoot, cinnamon-skinned children trailed me. Dressed in little more than ragged dish towels, they were big-eyed, auburn-haired, seemingly weightless, and irresistibly beautiful in the rickety, knock-kneed way that newborn calves are beautiful. They had flies in their eyes, and noses running with snot. They had long curling eyelashes and narrow shoulders and tiny, dusty ankles. They wanted money, pens, and candy. "Hello, baksheesh!" they shrieked. "Hello, pen! Hello, bonbon!" They trailed after me sometimes for ten minutes, emitting jagged moans of entreaty, twisting their faces into little Greek masks of tragedy, dancing on the hot stones, and plucking at my hips until I gave them something. Eventually I bought a large box of pens and a bag of hard candy, collected a stack of fifty-piastre notes, stuffed this various arsenal of baksheesh into my pockets, and, like

a pandering candidate passing out campaign fliers, distrib-
uted it regularly as I skulked through the town.

With a landscape unlike any other on the Nile, Aswan struck
me as Egypt's prettiest spot. Scattered with tiny green islands,
the river in Aswan has the feel of a storybook oasis. Its banks,
more desert dunes and granite cliffs than farmland, suggest the
harsh Saharan void that surrounds the town, underscoring Aswan's appeal as a cozy refuge. Between the town, on the east
bank of the river, and the High Dam just to the south of it, granite bedrock and massive boulders whip to life a river that everywhere else in Egypt moves slowly and uniformly, like an
intransigent bank of fog. Six hundred miles south of Cairo, a
mere hundred miles from the Tropic of Cancer, home to many
dark-skinned Nubians, and marking the border between Egypt
proper and its southern ethnic region of Nubia, the city of Aswan feels more African than any other Egyptian town. The
place has a sharp-edged clarity, as if chiseled and burned clean
by the sun; color glows here with greater intensity than anywhere else in the country. Because it is narrower and because
there are many more feluccas here, the river at Aswan appears
busier and more festive than it does at Cairo and Luxor. Large
white triangles of sail crisscross the river in a kind of jaunty
tarantella.

Aswan's desert air seems to caress the town with warm
promise, lending vividness and meaning to manifestations of
poverty and human struggle that would elsewhere be considered ugly. The piles of garbage, the heaps of smoldering ashes,
the scatterings of broken glass, the architectural rubble, the
human excrement, the sun-bleached plastic shopping bags and
rusted tin cans that seem to ring all Egyptian villages and be-
smirch every empty plane between them are, in Aswan, soft-
ened by the sheer volume of sun and water, color and air. Here,
fishermen's houses cobbled together out of mud bricks and
rusted tin cans appear somehow more ingenious than slovenly,

more fascinating than dispiriting. In a little village of Aswan near the Old Cataract Hotel, I stepped on a scrap of shaggy bath mat in the road and realized with a start that it bore in one of its corners a yellowed set of jaws studded with two rows of brittle teeth. In another corner it had a moth-eaten tail. It was not a mat at all but the flattened carcass of a dog, a mud-caked rope cinched around one hind leg, tongue hanging out like a twisted strip of leather. It had been there a very long time. I walked on, fine beige dust splashing up around my ankles with each step, and knew that the thing I had just stepped on would have had a considerably more disturbing effect on me in a cold and rainy climate.

Aswanians had physical freedom, if not economic. The lissome ease with which Aswanian men move seems a direct response to the bright, dancing air. Fat men jiggling up and down on the backs of trotting donkeys manage to look graceful and in control. A man riding a bicycle and carrying enough lumber on his head to build a modest dance floor turns at full speed and without mishap through a crowded intersection, squeezing between a truck and a bus, one hand on the handlebars, the other steadying his boards. He moves with the swift, elegant confidence of a bullfighter evading a bull, though his tires are strained nearly to flatness beneath the weight of his cargo.

As I walked up and down the river, I stopped each time I saw a boat I liked and struck up a conversation with its owner, and if he seemed even remotely congenial I would eventually ask if I could try the boat for just a minute. The request usually met with a derisive snort of laughter and a long string of questions and jokes. "Only if I can come with you," the men said. Or, "You don't know how. I will row you," or, "Only if you pay me eighty pounds for one hour," or just plain, "No, madame. You cannot."

One day I met a young red-haired, blue-eyed, freckle-faced

Nubian* who agreed to let me use his boat, until his father found out what he had done and chased him down the river-bank, shouting and cursing and brandishing a bamboo stick. It was a matter of money—the boy, unaccustomed to foreigners asking for rowboats, had neglected to ask me to pay for the privilege of rowing myself around in a very small circle in front of the Old Cataract Hotel. I made up for the son's transgression by paying the father, who looked as though he wanted to beat me too. In the end I didn't dare try his boat.

Another hot day in a palm-ringed cove on Elephantine Island, the largest island in the Nile at Aswan, I came upon a young man sitting in a rowboat anchored in the shade in shallow water. He was deeply absorbed in the task of sewing a rip in a dingy pair of boxer shorts and didn't notice that I had appeared on the riverbank above him. In the cockpit of a felucca anchored not two feet from him, an older man lay on his back napping, one arm slung across his face and his bare toes pointing up into the trees. I sat on a rock above the cove, listening to the smooching sound of unripe dates the size of peas falling into the water from the overhanging trees, until the men noticed me and both sprang up at once and began to shout like hounds heralding an intruder, asking me if I needed a lift across the river for a special price. I approached the men, greeted them, and after some minutes of small talk eventually asked the young one if he thought it was possible to row all the way to Cairo in the boat he was standing in.

"I have done it," he said, and as if to prove this he sat down abruptly on the thwart. "It took me three weeks to row from Aswan to Luxor."

* The result, I was several times told, of Bosnian soldiers having traveled here with Yavuz Sultan Selim's Turkish army in 1517 and mixing with Nubians. In Nubia, the southernmost region of Egypt, Amelia Edwards had been frightened by the sight of these redheads who "though in complexion as black as the rest, had light blue eyes and frizzy red hair."

In proper bantering Egyptian fashion, which had taken me
some time to get used to, I clapped a hand to my forehead with
mock astonishment and suggested that three weeks was awfully slow, that a person could drift that distance in less time,
which was probably not far from the truth.

"I think I could row it in ten days," I said, testing his sense
of humor. This needling boast was just the thing, for the young
man gave his rat-colored boxer shorts a twist and let out a yelp
of laughter, and his sleepy-eyed friend smacked the deck of
his boat and hooted, "Oh, laugh! It's fun! For you, madame?
Not possible!"

Nubian bongo drums pulsed in the botanical gardens of
Kitchener Island across the way. A curious warbler talked
loudly in a tree. The young man had a thick face and a bou-
quet of coarse black whiskers on his chin. His hair was straight
and glossy and black, and he wore it in a bowl-shaped cut, a
curtain of bangs hanging to his eyes. His teeth, which I specu-
lated had not been brushed since grade school, were the color
of unpeeled almonds. His gallabiya was torn and dirty, and
that was surprising, for in Aswan even the lowliest laborers
always looked recently washed and laundered. He sat in his
boat and smirked at me. I asked him if he would sell me the
boat. "Three thousand bounds!" he shouted. His laugh was
startling, a toy poodle's high-pitched yip.

"Magnoun," I said, and the old felucca captain hooted again.
"She said 'crazy'! She is good woman!" Standing barefoot on
the deck of his boat, one arm rakishly hugging the mast, the
captain asked what country I was from. I told him. His salt-
white mustache and handlebar eyebrows twitched with interest. "Ronald Reagan!" he said gleefully.

"Yes," I said, "and George Bush."

"John Kennetty!" he said in a trumpeting way. It sounded
like a minor challenge. I hesitated, not certain what the correct reply might be. I took a stab. "Richard Nixon."

"Ibrahim Linkum!"

Curious as to where this would lead, I said, "George Washington."

The captain fussed with his turban and pointed a crooked finger at me. Gamely he cried, "John Wayne! Beel Cleelington! Gary Coober! Charlington Heston!" categorizing presidents with movie stars in an entirely reasonable way.

In the distance the noontime call to prayer had begun, and though to me this enormous sound was always utterly arresting, like a simulacrum of God himself suddenly descending from the sky, and though it was officially imperative that all good Muslims get down on their knees and pray, the two men seemed to take no notice. I asked the young man if I could try out his boat, but, like so many men in Aswan, he had difficulty understanding what exactly I wanted until I went over, lifted an oar in my hand, and pointed at myself. He offered to row me. I said no. He offered to come with me while I rowed. I said no, I just wanted to try the boat alone for one minute. With stabbing defiance he said, "Fifteen bounds for one minute!" After a protracted wrangle, we settled on a slightly less extortionate five. The young man fell to a crouch in the bottom of his boat and began rummaging in a cubbyhole under the stern, and at the end of a lot of muttering and pawing through a jumble of possessions that clanked and thudded loudly against the hull like chains and stones and empty cans, he withdrew an English copy of *Marie Claire* magazine. Courteney Cox on the cover. He climbed out of the boat, opened the magazine, and held it up for me to see. Pointing at the English text, he said, "German?"

The magazine had the heft of a telephone book. "English," I said.

He flipped furtively through the pages, showing me photographs of women in scanty outfits, advertisements for bras and stockings, tampons and vinegar douches. Lovingly he touched the smooth thighs and burnished breasts on the pages, the glazed lips, the bare bellies, and bunchy buttocks

with his calloused fisherman's fingers. He seemed to have
fallen into a trance. He gave off the humid scent of wet hay.
His black eyes looked feverish as he jockeyed the magazine up
to my face. He wanted me to look with him. He breathed down
my neck. My presence at his side, though sweaty and dirty
and wary and outfitted not unlike a Canadian Mountie, had
clearly had an enhancing effect on what were, for him, already titillating images. And seeing these otherwise banal
ads through his goggling Muslim eyes, they looked, in turn,
weirdly pornographic to me.

"Let's go," I said, anxiety in my voice. The young man was
twice my size. He dropped the magazine into the bottom of
the boat, snatched up his undershorts, held them to his mouth,
and snapped the sewing thread with his teeth. With an awkward little one-footed hop, he tried to pull on the shorts under
his gallabiya, hooked his big toe on the waistband, stumbled,
jigged about in the sand, righted himself, and tried again. I
climbed into the boat, and he untied the painter and pushed
me off with his foot.

I rowed out to the middle of the river, which was quiet
now in the midday heat, while the two men looked on, up to
their hairy shins in water and daintily elevating the hems of
their gowns to keep them dry. They watched nervously, as if
anticipating having to catch me in a neck-breaking tumble.

Beyond the shade of the cove, the heat of the sun directly
overhead was so intense it seemed to affect my hearing, ren-
dering the swilling of the oars in the water surreally loud. In
the stark sunlight, the water was the color of mercury. Batlike
green bee-eaters darted over my head like gaudy bits of paper
caught on a wind. The fat magazine was slippery under my
feet. I gave it a kick and sent it flopping into the bow. The sun
that day seemed full of vengeance, intent on punishing every
living thing. Gusts of heat came off the dunes with the force of
a fire draft. I let myself get snagged on the river's current for a
moment, floated quickly downstream twenty feet, and climbed

back up with stiff slow pulls at the oars. The oars were long and unwieldy. The boat moved heavily. It was portly and thick planked, hard to maneuver, and much bigger than I needed. Yet it was immensely exciting to be alone, finally, in a boat on the Nile, like that dream of stepping off a towering cliff only to find that you can fly.

<center>~~~~</center>

IN THE THIRD WEEK of November 1849, Gustave Flaubert and his friend the photographer Maxime du Camp arrived at the port of Alexandria with the intention of renting a boat and crew and sailing up the Nile. Several days later Florence Nightingale and her friends Charles and Selina Bracebridge also arrived at Alexandria intending to do the same. Egypt in 1849 was still at the relative dawn of its popularity with European travelers: Thomas Cook's steamship package tours hadn't yet arrived; some Egyptians had never seen a white woman before; and for a European a trip on the Nile was still an exotic adventure. The novelty of the Nile experience for travelers like Flaubert and Nightingale is best understood in light of the fact that between the years 646 and 1517 Egypt's Islamic rulers had closed the country to virtually all outsiders. A few traders and pilgrims managed to enter the Nile Valley during this thousand-year period, but reliable information about Egypt was scarce. To the average European, the place was as arcane and mysterious as the moon. In 1517 when Egypt fell under the rule of the Ottoman Empire, it became more accessible to Europeans, and by the eighteenth century several Europeans succeeded in traveling up the Nile all the way to Upper Egypt.* The site of the ancient city of Thebes

---

* As you know, the Nile flows from south to north. Since one must travel upriver to reach the south of Egypt, the south is commonly referred to as "Upper Egypt" and the north, therefore, as "Lower Egypt."

was lost to the world until 1707 when a French Jesuit, Claude Sicard, positively reidentified it. The British adventurer Richard Pococke, the Swedish scientist Frederick Hasselquist, the Danish artist Frederick Lewis Norden, and the French naturalist Charles Sonnini all traveled to Egypt during the eighteenth century and returned to Europe with detailed accounts of what they had seen.* Constantin Volney's record of his travels in Egypt and Syria deeply impressed Napoleon and helped in part to inspire the French invasion of Egypt in 1798 and the resultant boom in Egyptology.

The sudden European preoccupation with Egypt was prompted not only by literary accounts and Napoleon's *Description de L'Egypte* but also by the rarely seen antiquities and obscure artifacts that travelers were bringing home with them. Visitors to Egypt returned with trunks full of mummies, painted sarcophagi, stone carvings hacked off walls, hieroglyphic tablets, statues of Egyptian gods, and funerary furnishings lifted from pharaonic tombs and burial chambers. Dazzled by all this rare and mysterious loot, collectors and antiquarians began hurrying up the Nile searching for more. The craze for things Egyptian grew so great that one wealthy British collector, William Bankes, bothered to have an entire obelisk uprooted from the Temple of Isis at Philae, had it dragged back to England, and propped it up in his garden in Dorset. Soon entire nations began engaging in the plunder.

Intent on modernizing the country, Muhammad Ali, who became pasha of Egypt in 1805, called on foreign experts for technical and political advice. In exchange for their guidance, foreign consuls were freely allowed to excavate Egyptian

---

* Sonnini's assessment of 1777 was blunt: "Slavery, and stupidity, its inevitable consequence, have filled the place of power and grandeur. Superstitious ignorance has succeeded to the love of the sciences, to the exercise of the arts; and perfect civilization has disappeared, to make way for brutality and savageness of manners."

archaeological sites and remove the spoils to museums in their own countries. In 1815 the Italian strongman Giovanni Belzoni went to Egypt and, under the aegis of the British consul, within a mere three years found the opening of the second pyramid, discovered the royal tomb of Seti I, opened the Great Temple of Abu Simbel, and recovered the statue of the Young Memnon. Belzoni shipped off to England every movable thing he found—as well as a few things any sane person would have considered immovable, including William Bankes's six-ton Philae obelisk. In 1821 Belzoni's collection of Egyptian antiquities was put on display at the Egyptian Hall in Piccadilly. The show was a roaring success: on opening day alone nearly two thousand people paid half a crown apiece to look at Belzoni's treasures.

Before long, people like Flaubert and Nightingale could visit the Louvre and the British Museum and see firsthand what manner of wonders the Nile Valley harbored. Jean-François Champollion's deciphering of the newly rediscovered Rosetta stone gave meaning to what they saw—until then even the Egyptians themselves had lost all understanding of ancient Egyptian writing. When Edward Lane's exhaustive *An Account of the Manners and Customs of the Modern Egyptians* was published in London in 1836, it met with such fascinated demand that its first printing sold out in two weeks. And when the enormous obelisk from Luxor (230 tons; 75 feet tall) was shipped to France and installed in the Place de la Concorde in 1833, Egypt was firmly locked into the European imagination.

By the time Nightingale and Flaubert made their journeys to Egypt, a few steamships had already been introduced to the Nile, but for most foreign travelers the custom was to head for Boulac, the port of Cairo, and select a *dahabieh,* a private cruising boat, from the many available for hire there.

By all accounts Boulac was a tumult of vermin, shysters,

hucksters, thieves, and fleas. There boats arriving from Upper Egypt unloaded exotic merchandise—hippopotamus
hides, elephant tusks, monkeys, ostrich feathers, rubber, pottery, livestock, slaves, ebony, and nearly everything else
imaginable—from the farthest parts of Africa. Passenger steamers and mail boats from Alexandria also disgorged their cargo
there; the docks crawled with stevedores, merchants, captains,
sailors, and hurrying travelers. With the hired assistance of a
dragoman—an all-purpose interpreter who would explain, in-
tercede in, and arrange all the practical matters that might arise
during the long trip on the Nile—the traveler would brave the
chaos of Boulac to inspect the boats on offer, while the *dahabieh*
captains and their crews looked on, hungrily hoping the foreign
customer would choose them and their vessel for the well-paid
three-month journey up to the second cataract on the Sudanese
border and back.

The hiring of a *dahabieh* was nearly as much an ordeal as
any other task in the long Nile journey and often took several
days to accomplish, with the most difficult moment being the
settling of the rental contract. Captains and dragomans were
famous for driving a hard bargain. Contemporary Baedeker's
guidebooks warned the traveler, "The Egyptians, it must be remembered, occupy a much lower grade in the scale of civilization than most of the western nations, and cupidity is one of
their chief failings." In a letter to his mother Flaubert wrote,
"I'm going to Bulak to see a few [boats]. It is no slight matter . . .
Most dragomans are appalling scoundrels."

The *dahabieh* of the mid-nineteenth century was similar in
design to the boats used by the pharaohs, a long, many-
compartmented sort of floating house that could be either rowed
or sailed. The largest of them reached one hundred feet in
length and twenty feet in width. At their prows they had places
for a dozen oarsmen who would row, galley fashion, when the
wind failed. The boats were flat bottomed and shallow, had two

masts and a lateen-rigged mainsail so enormous in relation to
the size of the boat that the slightest puff of wind gave it sufficient force to carry the boat against the Nile's current. The cabins were built on the deck toward the stern, and above them
was a higher deck accessed by a short flight of steps. Passengers
only were allowed on the upper deck, while the lower deck was
reserved for the usually flea-ridden crew. The kitchen, a shed
equipped with a charcoal stove, was situated toward the front
of the boat, away from the passengers' cabins.

Amelia Edwards, who traveled up the Nile in 1872 and
wrote a staggeringly detailed account of her trip, including every hieroglyph she studied, every snack she ate, and the number of steps at the Temple of Horus at Edfu (she counted 224),
offers in her book, *A Thousand Miles Up the Nile,* probably the
most thorough description extant of a Nile *dahabieh:*

A dahabeeyah [has] four sleeping cabins, two on each side.
These cabins measured about eight feet in length by four and a
half in width, and contained a bed, a chair, a fixed washing-
stand, a looking glass against the wall, a shelf, a row of hooks,
and under each bed two large drawers for clothes. At the end
of this little passage another door opened into the dining
saloon—a spacious, cheerful room, some twenty-three or
twenty-four feet long [bigger than the dining room in my
house!], situated in the widest part of the boat, and lightened
by four windows on each side and a skylight. The paneled
walls and ceiling were painted in white picked out with gold; a
cushioned divan covered with a smart woollen reps ran along
each side; and a gay Brussels carpet adorned the floor. The dining table stood in the centre; and there was ample space for a
piano, two little bookcases, and several chairs. The window-
curtains and portieres were of the same reps as the divan, the
prevailing colours being scarlet and orange. Add a couple of
mirrors in gilt frames; a vase of flowers on the table . . . plenty

of books, the gentlemen's guns and sticks in one corner; and the hats of all the party hanging in the spaces between the windows; and it will be easy to realise the homely, habitable look of our general sitting room . . . Another door and passage opening from the upper end of the saloon and led to three more sleeping rooms, two of which were single and one double; a bath room; a tiny black staircase leading to the upper deck; and the stern cabin saloon.

Though not all *dahabiehs* were luxurious enough to accommodate a grand piano, the general design of these boats was fundamentally the same, and even the most modest of them offered surprising comfort. Floating down the Nile in a *dahabieh* was a bit like floating down the Nile in a brownstone.

After sufficient inspections, the travelers would select a *dahabieh,* have it submerged in the Nile for twenty-four hours in order to drown the fleas and rats that had taken up residence during its idle period at dock, and finally they would board the ship and make themselves at home. Nightingale and her friends rented a particularly elegant *dahabieh* for thirty pounds a month, a very high price for the time. "We shall have been on board a week tomorrow," Nightingale wrote to her mother, "and are now thoroughly settled in our house: all our gimlets up, our divans out, our Turkish slippers provided, and everything on its own hook, as befits such close quarters." Of his slightly more modest ship Flaubert wrote, "It is painted blue; its *rais* is called Ibrahim. There is a crew of nine. For quarters we have a room with two little divans facing each other, a large room with two beds, on one side of which there is a kind of alcove for our baggage and on the other an English-type head; and finally a third room where Sassetti [his Italian servant] will sleep and which will serve as a store-room as well."

Going by the popular contemporary handbooks for travelers in Egypt, the storerooms of those ships held saddles, bridles, umbrellas, telescopes, measuring tapes, flags, rifles, pistols, mosquito nets, charcoal, candles, mustard, easels, art supplies, twine, bedsheets, tents, thermometers, barometers, musical instruments for the crew, and a great deal of food and alcohol. Supplies recommended by one Baedeker's handbook included "1 doz tins condensed milk, 1 tin tapioca, 2 tins julienne soup, 13 lbs of bacon, 15 lbs of ham, 2 tins of ox tongue, 3 tins preserved meat, 1 bottle worcestire sauce, sardines, 60 bottles of medoc, 36 medoc superieur, 35 bottles of res voslauer, 25 bottles of white voslauer, 20 bottles of beer, 1 bottle of brandy and cognac each, 1 bottle of whiskey, one bottle vermouth, a little champagne for festivals and the reception of guests."

In addition, the early Nile tourists dragged a shockingly hefty supply of books with them. (Napoleon and his men had carried on their trip a library of five hundred volumes.) *Murray's Handbook* of 1858 recommended:

vols. ii and iii of Larcher's *Herodotys;* Champollion's *Phonetic Systems of Hieroglyphics, Letters, and Grammar;* Pococke; Denon; Hamilton's *Aegyptaica;* Savary's Letters; Clot Bey's *Apercu Generale de L'Egypte;* Gliddon on the Hieroglyphics; Mengin's *Egypte Sous Mohammed Aly;* Robinson's *Palestine and Mount Sinai;* Stanley's *Sinai;* Lane's *Modern* and Wilkinson's *Ancient Egyptians;* Hoskin's *Ethiopia;* Colonel Leake's, Lapie's, or Wilkinson's Map of Egypt; Captain Smyth's *Alexandria;* Wilkinson's *Survey of Thebes;* Costa's *Delta;* and Parke and Scoles's *Nubia;* to which may be added Burckhardt, Laborde's *Petra,* Ptolemy, Strabo, and Pliny.

A *dahabieh* provided great comfort for its passengers, but the crew—usually ten or twelve Egyptian sailors, the *rais* (captain), a cook, and dragoman—were generally expected to sleep outside on the lower deck with no pillows or mattresses and nothing for warmth but one rough blanket apiece. While the passengers enjoyed sumptuous dinners prepared by the cook, the crew ate little more than gruel or bread. It was written into the rental contract that the crew should be allowed to stop at certain towns along the way in order to use the ovens of the local bakers so they could store up a load of fresh bread for themselves.

Once the *dahabieh* was registered with the authorities in Cairo and fitted with an identifying pennant, the travelers were free to set sail out of Cairo and up the river.

It never surprised me that Gustave Flaubert might want to float down the Nile. He was a man who deeply disliked his own country, had a longtime love of things oriental, was interested in the baser aspects of humanity, and was capable of writing in a letter to a friend that women generally confused their cunts (his word) for their brains and thought the moon existed solely to light their boudoirs. Florence Nightingale, however, was another case.

As a child (and, I am embarrassed to say, well into my teen years), I thought Florence Nightingale was a fictional character—the "Lady with the Lamp" of idealized storybook illustrations, afloat on the same cumulonimbus of wonder that carried Snow White and Cinderella. She was a mythological emissary from heaven, pure and incorruptible, ageless, parentless, and glowingly good. Then I got a little older and Florence Nightingale got real, transmogrifying into a historical figure; yet still she was selfless and holy and good, and therefore my attention tended to shut down at the mention of her. I had the impression, founded on precious little, that Nightingale was unworldly and dull, circulating within her tiresome purview of bedsores, disinfectant, wound dressings, and germ theory. In adolescence I preferred Amelia Earhart in her flaming plane, or Harriet Tubman who had dug her way out of slavery with a soupspoon (not, of course, quite what Harriet Tubman had done, but such was the vague and slightly fantastical quality of

my perceptions), or the more modern Angela Davis who pick-
eted a TV station with a gun hidden in her huge hair, or Annie
Oakley who could shoot a bullet through the eye of a needle—I
preferred them all to the blameless Nightingale in her pale
green sickroom.

Naturally, then, I was stumped when, several days before I
left for Aswan, I found in a Cairo shop a book titled *Letters
from Egypt: A Journey on the Nile, 1849–1850* by Florence
Nightingale. It struck me as uniquely unlikely, like finding a
book called *Mother Teresa's Personal Guide to the Mississippi,*
or *Notes on the Volga* by Grandma Moses. I thought it had to be
some other Florence Nightingale. It wasn't. I opened the book
to its dead center and read:

> We saw the whole crew start up, fling down their oars, and
> begin to fight violently . . . howling and screaming and kick-
> ing, the boat of course drifting down upon the rocks mean-
> time . . . Out rushed Paolo with an ebony club,—which I had
> bought from the Berber savages coming up the cataract . . .
> [and] fell upon the mass of struggling heads, and began to
> belabour them with all his might, so that I thought he would
> have broken in their skulls. He was alone against the eleven,
> but he did not seem to think of it, though he was generally a
> great coward.

and then, of a group of Ethiopian slave women:

> They were sitting round their fire for the night; they came out
> to beg of us, and, in the dusk, looked like skulls, with their
> white teeth; they set up a horrid laugh when we gave them
> nothing: our guide poked one with his stick, when it was sit-
> ting down, as if it were a frog.

I bought the book, and as I read it a remarkable person
emerged from the traducing haze her legend had engulfed her

in. I was struck by the force of her writing, by its bristling intelligence. Nightingale's powers of description rivaled many of the known writers of her day, including Flaubert's. Written chiefly to family and friends in England, the letters revealed a curious, keenly observant mind and an enormous range of knowledge. Nightingale was already well traveled before she went to Egypt, spoke several languages, and was astonishingly well read. She was adventuresome and passionate. She had, above all, a wicked sense of humor, which surprised and delighted me. Her characterizations were sharp, subtle, often comical. Her interests were many and various: artistic, philosophical, spiritual, and temporal.

In Egypt, Nightingale disguised herself in an Egyptian woman's robes and veil and visited a mosque, where she was jeered at by Egyptian men, an event that prompted her to write, "I felt like the hypocrite in Dante's hell, with the leaden cap on." She went to the catacombs in Alexandria "which, after those of Rome, are rather a farce." She shot the rapids of the Aswan cataracts in her *dahabieh,* visited a harem with unabashed enthusiasm, examined nearly every tomb and temple in Egypt with the dedication and understanding of a true Egyptologist, dined with German counts and Belgian scholars, and rode a donkey across the desert. "The donkey is very small and you are very large . . . You sit upon his tail; and as he holds his head very high, you look like a balance to his head . . . You set off full gallop, running over every thing in your way, and the merry little thing runs and runs and runs like a velocipede."

Far from being an insufferable saint, Nightingale was a woman of deep opinions, discriminating, decisive, and sometimes unkind. Her observations could be harsh but were clear eyed and unsentimental. She was also democratic. If she was capable of writing this of the Arabs: "an intermediate race, they appeared to me, between the monkey and the man, the ugliest, most slavish countenances," or this of the Nubians in

Aswan: "Troops of South Sea Savages received us . . . not shiny as savages *ought* to be, but their black skins all dim and grimed with sand, like dusty tables, their dirty hair plaited in rats' tails, close to their heads, naked, all but a head veil. I heard some stones fall into the river, and hoped it was they, and that that debased life had finished," she was also capable of criticizing her own beloved Anglican Church, after having visited one in the Coptic quarter in Cairo: "One's feelings towards the Anglican Church are very different when she is hiding in corners, struggling with the devil . . . to when she is stretched out in fatness, with the millstone of the richest hierarchy in the world about her neck, and the lust of the world tempting people to make her a profession and not a vocation."

Florence Nightingale was so interesting, daring, and intelligent that reading her letters I had begun to feel, by comparison, frivolous, meek, and not terribly bright.

~~~~

MY SECOND NIGHT IN ASWAN, I sat on a pier in the dark, staring at a small rowboat docked between two huge feluccas, feeling anxious and foolish and depressed that I still had no boat. The river and the town seemed to vibrate with joyful shouts and laughter and winking yellow lights. Bats skittered around the shadowy trees. Herons muttered and screeched in the reeds. Cruise boats lumbered into Aswan like drifting carnival rides, with their thousand lights blazing, their horns bellowing, and their names—*Seti First, Papyrus, Nile Sovereign, Seti Two*—emblazoned on their chins. The ships docked six deep along the ghats of the east bank, while above them loud music blew out of the shorefront restaurants—the mannish voice of Oum Kalsoum throbbing in competition with Michael Jackson and Elton John. At night the Nile looked dense and black and slippery as motor oil; three feet from me, big silvery creatures that could only have been fish jumped spookily in the water with a lot of plump splashing. They jumped and disappeared so quickly it was hard to see exactly what they were.

As I stood on the pier fretting and musing and muttering to myself, a young man in a dark gallabiya came up behind me and said, "Something you need?"

I was tired and didn't want to answer him, didn't want to go through the list of questions, the ridicule and banter and haggling over money. It was wearing, like being poked in the face all day with a sharp stick. How many men had I spoken to about boats? Fifteen? Twenty? All of them had rebuffed me. And I was growing weary of having to be secretive and evasive, of telling people that I wanted the boat not for myself (wanting it for myself was too outlandish) but as a surprise for a nonexistent husband who was perpetually asleep in the hotel. It was ten o'clock but the sun's heat stored in the granite boulders along the riverbank still wafted up into the night air in suffocating gusts. My damp blouse clung to my back.

I explained to the man that the boat I was looking at was not unlike the boat I had at home, that I liked rowing and hoped to try rowing around Elephantine Island while I was here in Aswan. I stared at the stars, bracing myself for the verbal pokes and slaps, but the man remained silent. Without asking how old I was, where I was from, or whether I was married, he said softly, "This is my boat. You can using it any times. It is always in docked across in front of Oberoi Hotel. You don't need ask. Just take if it is there."

The pier was illuminated only by the dim lights of restaurants on the bank above it, and it was difficult to make out the man's features in the moonless night. His words carried trust and respect and were surprisingly devoid of the usual distancing banter, the jokes, the sexual innuendo, or mention of money. He spoke gently and slowly, and I sensed from the tone of his voice that it wasn't a ruse, that his offer was sincere. He was a felucca captain, he said, and didn't use the rowboat much. His name was Amr Khaled. He didn't ask me my name or whether I knew how to row. He expressed neither doubt nor prying curiosity. That made him an odd Egyptian, and interesting. I thanked him for his offer, said I would take him up on it. Excusing himself, he left me there. This was odd too. No Egyptian man had ever left me standing anywhere; usually they hung around as long as they could, waiting to see what would happen next with me. In Egypt I was forever in the position of having to bring the conversation to an end and make my retreat.

With my spirits buoyed, I went into one of the many riverside restaurants along the corniche to get something to eat, and realized too late that I had blundered through the back door of the restaurant and landed in the kitchen, where two elderly men in white turbans sat at a table dicing a pile of vegetables. A third man was bent over a stove beneath a mantilla of billowing steam, stirring two pots at once. The kitchen was low ceilinged and hot, and under the fluorescent lights I saw that it was in a state of great disorder. Boxes and sacks of produce lay willy-nilly across the cement floor: a glittering crate of small fish the size and color of pigs' ears; a wooden box that resembled a birdcage full of tiny strawberries; baskets of damp greens, sacks of onions; a papery pile of garlic; tubs of olives. Wilted lettuce leaves had been crushed and mashed underfoot, and the place smelled not unpleasantly of vinegar and boiling oil. A small black-and-white television parked atop a refrigerator showed a tiny soccer game going on in Morocco. An electric fan atop a crate of beer breathed slack gouts of damp air in the direction of the stove.

The two elderly chefs stood up at the sight of me. With the retrograde gallantry characteristic of Egyptians who had learned their English in the days of King Farouk, the taller one bowed and said, "Good evening, Miss Madame. Welcome in Aswan. Very it's pleasure. Where you are come from?"

I told him I was from the United States of America.

"Beel Cleelington!" he said.

With a paring knife in one hand and a muddy tomato in the other, the shorter man stepped forward and added wryly, "Monica!"

Neither of them looked anything like a chef. They looked like two dandy charlatans in a French farce. They wore billowing trousers that narrowed at the ankles, large headdresses, and silken vests. They had long, well-groomed mustaches. For want of anything better to say I said, "Do you like Monica?"

They let out a ripping shriek of laughter that plainly meant, *Are you nuts?*

"Monica *mumtaz!*" they cried. Monica is great!

The man at the stove, who seemed to understand little English, turned from his pots in recognition of the word *Monica* and grinned and nodded and raised his ladle in salacious assent. All three men were hot faced and cheerful. The short one asked, "Cleelington good president?"

I said not a bad president, not a great husband.

"Heelary," the tall one said darkly.

My face was blanketed with sweat and dirt after a day of wandering up and down the river, and having stumbled in out of the darkness I felt wan and naked under the bald lights. The shorter man signaled for my attention with an important wave of his knife. Speaking carefully and with authority he said, "Beel Cleelington is likes young girl. She is beautiful. Older man always is likes the young girl. Since ancient time. Cleelington don't not do nutting new."

Undeniable truths.

The taller man smoothed his great mustache and said, "Heelary got boyfriend too."

They all smiled with delight, their coconut-colored faces gleaming with perspiration. My sudden appearance had presented them with an excellent opportunity for laughter, jokes, and flirting, the favorite Egyptian preoccupations.

I said good-bye to the men and went around to the proper

end of the restaurant, which was actually a floating barge with a roof of palm fronds. From the restaurant deck, I could see cruise ship deckhands in blue sailor blouses, carrying heavy boxes and bundles of supplies on the napes of their necks, bounding barefoot up the gangplanks.

I sat at a table, and a fat, very tall waiter brought me a menu that included, among other items: *lamp meat, grilld pigeon, balady salad, stuffed pigeon, roast lamp, snaks. Every dinner no matter only six bound total.* The waiter stood at my side with his notebook poised, reading the menu over my shoulder, as though he had never seen it before. He wore a maroon dress shirt and a skinny black necktie fixed in a Windsor knot. Before I had a chance to order my meal, he informed me that he had been married and divorced twice. I offered my condolences. He giggled nervously. He had the merry eyes and plump, slightly rueful face of Jackie Gleason. As if to quell any doubts about his marital expertise he said quickly, "Both divorces was not because of a problem with me."

I ordered a beer, he went to get it, and on his return he explained, without solicitation from me, why his job was difficult. "The Koran says you cannot involve yourself with the alcohol. You cannot even serve it to other people. But I have to go to the money. The foreign people drink the alcohol and have the money, so I serve it to keep my job."

I asked him what he thought about people who drank alcohol. Diplomatically he said, "Madame, it is different for the foreigners." I told him that I had noticed a lot of Egyptian men in Aswan drinking beer. "They are not Egyptian," he corrected me. "They are Nubian." And he glanced behind him at a lone middle-aged man sitting at a table in the shadows, drinking beer and smoking. The man sat slightly slumped, his head hanging low, his watery eyes blinking and muddled, his cigarette a damp stump between his fingers. He looked miserable and distracted and swamped with worry.

"Nubians drink?" I said.

With neither disdain nor admiration the waiter answered, "Nubian peoples always like be happy and singing and drunk. I am not Nubian."

Later that night, I found it too hot to sleep, decided to wander around the Aswan *souq,* the crowded shopping district, and fell into a conversation with a young man working in a shop full of cheap wooden carvings, Nubian drums, hammered brass plates, glass perfume bottles, garishly painted papyrus, and Formstone imitations of pharaonic sculptures: Akhenaten, Anubis, Nefertiti, the owl, the cat, the ram, Toth, Seth, Mut, Nut, Tut, Ra, and the rest of them. The same dusty clutter being sold by the truckload to tourists all over Egypt.

The young man wore not a gallabiya but the shiny rayon trousers and polyester dress shirt that seemed to be the uniform of many young Egyptian shopkeepers, an approximate stab at modern Western style. We sat on the doorstep of the shop and watched a man selling perfectly spherical watermelons off the back of a wagon in the busy square. Predictably, the conversation turned to sex. The young man told me he had had an affair with an English woman whom he loved. He had had sex with her, though they were not married. "I was twenty-two the first time I made sex," he said. After a long pause he added, "Now I am twenty-eight."

Foreign women who dressed in scanty clothing he did not respect. "I would try to touch them and make sex with them," he said. "When I see foreign men and women friends greeting each other with huggings and kissings here in the market, I think they are like animals making sex in the street. Egyptian people would never do this."

I pointed out that when different cultures met, misunderstanding and suspicion were bound to arise.

He stared stonily at me, as if he had suddenly lost his hearing. Since he seemed to have set the parameters for a certain level of frankness in this conversation, I pressed on, explaining that some people in the West had similarly disdainful views of Arabs, believing that Arabs were backward, fanatical, and rapacious.

The shopkeeper's face went dead, and in a voice gone childlike with disbelief he demanded, "Because of why?!"

Knowing it was risky, I repeated for him something a disgusted Australian woman had said to me that morning: *They are pigs! They throw their garbage in the river! They brutalize their animals and defecate in the street! They treat their women like beasts. They won't eat pork because they think it unclean, and yet they will sit in the middle of a stinking rubbish pile with their children!*

The man looked shocked, as though I had reached over and slapped him square across his plump cheek. Confusion brewed behind his face. He seemed to be waiting for the voice of outrage to catch up with him. Presently it did. "But our way is the right way! It is in the Koran!"

And he began to speak at great length in a humorless, resentful, persecuted tone. He spoke of holiness, law, right actions, the Prophet, honor, and God. As he talked, I found myself tugging the sleeves of my blouse lower over my wrists. He told me that there was prostitution in Egypt but that if you visited a prostitute you would gain a bad reputation. If his sister had sex with a man before she was married, he said, he would kill her. I asked him if he was serious. He was completely serious; he would not hesitate to take his sister's life. I asked why. "Because she has no future and has shamed my family's name." When I ventured that this seemed extreme, illogical, and not terribly humane, he talked on, as though he hadn't heard me. "If your wife is not a virgin and you find out, you can kill her. For your pride."

"So you kill her, get arrested, go to jail, and then your life is over too."

"I don't care. No one would blame me."

"But you were willing to take such a risk with the English woman you loved and were not married to."

He gave me a look that said, *You fool!* "She was foreign!"

"She was a woman."

"It is not the same for her. Her family wouldn't care."

"If a woman's virtue is so important in your eyes, why would you not respect that same virtue in any woman you loved, no matter where she's from? Don't *you* care?"

I had begun to sound like an overearnest youth counselor futilely laboring in a reform school. I wanted very much to get out of this conversation.

The shopkeeper squirmed on the stoop, clucked at my stupidity, and looked around the market with impatience. He spat into the dust in front of the shop. He pouted and sulked. He had no answer. I had offended him. I looked into the square, wondering what to do next. Nearby a barefoot boy with huge hands, a brass pinkie ring, and red polish on his nails was wrestling with the puffy snout of a hobbled camel twice his height. The boy pried open the camel's jaws, and with the sweeping gesture of a man throwing water on a fire he sloshed a jug of water down its throat. The camel smacked its bewhiskered lips and did a little tap dance of protest on the broken pavement.

The young man turned toward me again, inspired with a new idea. "Some foreign women are evil!"

"Evil?"

He glared at me. "They show their flesh to tempt us on purpose, even during Ramadan."

I was preparing to tell him that some foreign women didn't understand the importance of covering their bodies while they were in Egypt, and then I thought, *Why explain?* It seemed hopeless in the face of this universal age-old contradiction: women were calculating temptresses whose sexuality needed to be stifled at any cost, and yet they were the object of constant speculation, interest, and discussion. They alone were to be blamed for the thoughts and desires and irresponsible behavior they provoked in men.

Encouraged by my silence, the shopkeeper posited some hypothetical questions: If my husband had sex with another woman and I found out, what would I do? If my husband had taken a drink and in a weak moment had sex with another woman, what would I do? If my husband had an affair with a woman, and I didn't know about it, but he confessed it to me, what would I do? If my husband had been seduced by a wicked woman whose fault it was, and I found out, what would I do? He had devised so many intricate and specific moral dilemmas that it was as if, after studying the subject in great depth, he was now about to prepare a Koranic treatise on it. On and on he hypothesized about infidelity and adultery, while I stared, beleaguered, at the camel's spindly legs.

Finally, when the shopkeeper ran out of depressing variations on marital transgression, I asked him why he was asking me these things. His answer was "Heelary Cleelington is a good wife." I asked him if he would question an Egyptian woman in this manner. He simply laughed in a way that meant, *Of course not!,* and it dawned on me that in the Islamic scheme of things, the breezy eagerness of so many Egyptian men to talk about sexual matters with me and other foreign women could have been interpreted as a supreme insult.

On my way back to my hotel that night I came upon a very old woman sitting barefoot on a street corner selling small cones of paper filled with peanuts. She was tiny in her black veil and gown. Her bare ankles against the concrete of the sidewalk were no thicker than the handle of a hockey stick. She moved slowly, arranging and rearranging the cones in her wicker basket with delicate care and attention. Her head looked heavy on her thin neck and slight shoulders. She wore a big pair of horn-rimmed, government-issue eyeglasses that in their weightiness resembled a chemist's protective goggles. The street was dark and dirty. I gave the woman two pounds for two cones of peanuts. Nearly blind, she lifted the paper money to within an inch of the enormous lenses of her eyeglasses and scanned it until an expression of guarded satisfaction appeared on her face, then she adjusted the glasses with both hands—money clutched in one of them—and nodded at me without a smile and went back to adjusting the cones.

In my hotel room, I ate the roasted peanuts and realized that the old woman had fashioned the paper cones from lined notepaper covered with a grandchild's penciled math homework—$3 \times 11 = 33$, $3 \times 12 = 36$—an act of recycling thrift that I found inexplicably moving.

The First Small Boat in Egypt

HE NEXT DAY was scorching hot, and when, with sweat trickling down my back, I said somewhat vapidly to my hotel manager, "It's hot," he replied in a correcting, foreboding way, "It is only the beginning of hot."

It was too hot to row Amr Khaled's boat in the middle of the day, too hot even to leave the hotel. All day I lay on my bed in my underwear with one forearm slung across my eyes, listening to a fly careering against the lamp shade, lifting the arm now and then to stare at a lizard on the ceiling or at the wall beside me that was dotted with little brown stars of dried blood: a constellation of violently mashed mosquitoes.

Unable to sleep, I read the books on Egypt that I had brought with me and learned numerous things about Aswan. It was rated among the hottest places in the world. Its population was about a million. It was one of the oldest towns in Egypt (evidence of predynastic culture seven or so thousand years ago; seriously old). The fruit of Aswan's date palms had a "high reputation." Once, twenty thousand Aswanians died of the plague. Most of Egypt's ancient monuments were made from granite quarried at Aswan. When poor old Juvenal was banished from Rome for his satirical writing, they sent him to molder in Aswan. Aswan's famous wells (summer solstice, high noon, sun fully reflected in bottom of well, no shadow, etc.) had inspired Eratosthenes' formula for determining the circumference of the earth. During the nineteenth century a group of people called the Howling Dervishes had a house in Aswan; they met there on Fridays. Also during the nineteenth century, the Egyptian taverns that sold *boozah* (said to be the origin of the English word *booze*) were run mainly by Nubians who concocted the drink themselves and served it to customers, both men and women, from a large wooden ladle that was passed, presumably with some hilarity, around the room. In 1838 Edward Lane described *boozah* as an intoxicating liquor made with crumbled barley bread mixed with water, then strained and allowed to ferment. "It is commonly drunk by the boatmen of the Nile," he wrote, "and by other persons of the lower orders." Finally, I learned that by the 1820s Aswanians were already considered "the shrewdest people in Egypt," famous for charging foreigners prices three times what their merchandise was worth.

When I got bored with the reading, I went to the window. My view was of a tall minaret, a colonial-looking boys' school, the public toilets, and the brand-new Hospital for Eyes, with paint splattered on its windows and cabbages growing in the dirt on either side of its entrance. Just beyond the boys' school was a little tailor's shop where a sad old blue-eyed tailor sat every evening waiting for customers. He spoke no English, but when I stopped and said hello to him one evening he slid the sleeve of his shirt up his arm and showed me the bluish tattoo of a cross on his inner wrist. Like most of the tailors in Aswan, he was Christian, and like most Egyptian Christians he wore this tattoo as proof of his faith.

That afternoon two Nubian women were selling live pigeons in the shade of the public toilets. Draped in black gowns and veils, squatting on their haunches, their fine black hands visoring their eyes, they had sat all day waiting for customers. Their skin was so black that from this distance of a hundred feet their only discernible facial features were their frost-white teeth and the whites of their eyes. The pigeons had been stuffed, one hard upon the other, into bamboo cages. From time to time one of the women would take a swig of water from a red plastic gasoline jug, yank a pigeon from the cage with a roughness that seemed to spell immediate destruction, fit the pigeon's beak between her own lips, transfer the water to the bird, then stuff him back in the cage, patting the others down to make room for him. They handled the birds like dirty washrags. When a potential customer came down the hot street, one of them would haul a dozen birds out of a cage, pinch their wings together, and display them six in each hand, like a fan of playing cards.

A woman came down the street pushing a baby stroller, and it struck me that the women in Aswan who could afford strollers—most women simply carried their babies astraddle one shoulder—were always dressed in the Islamic veil, the long cloth wrapped around their heads and under their chins. No hair showing, no neck, just the face revealed. The veil hung down to the backs of their thighs over a black gown that hung to their ankles. They had noble faces, full voices, and walked with straight backs.

At four o'clock I ventured out to look for Amr Khaled's boat. The city looked as though it had been baked senseless during the day. Nothing moved. Even the river seemed to have slurred to a halt. The simmering streets had surrendered their utility as streets; empty, the pavement threw up ripples of heat like beds of hot coals. Over time, thousands of bottle caps had been trampled into the molten surface of the corniche; at that hour they glinted dully like the profligate scatterings of some drunken millionaire. Every car in sight sat still, with an open-mouthed body stretched across the front seat. Semicomatose figures lay sprawled under trees and awnings or flopped over in doorways. I had the strange sense that if I turned on a radio in this heat, I'd find nothing but static on every station.

On the hotel ferry, I made the short trip across the river to Elephantine Island, and when I arrived at the dock in front of the Oberoi Hotel, eight felucca captains were standing by their boats, waiting for customers. They appeared to be the only up-right people in Aswan. In their long white gowns they were like idling priests. Though he had only ever seen me in the dark, Amr Khaled recognized me and came forward. In the daylight I realized he was a dark-skinned Nubian. I saw too how small his rowboat was—approximately seven feet long. Its name, *Happy,* was hand-painted on its prow in rough black letters that called to mind angry profanities scrawled on a highway underpass. In the cockpit, written on the cubbyhole door, were the oddly ominous words "Don't Worry," in the same intemperate handwriting. The oars, lashed to metal pegs with strips of what looked like floppy rubber cut from a bi-cycle inner tube, were a pair of termite-eaten two-by-fours. Wooden floorboards had been laid over the steel hull.

As if reading my mind Amr said sheepishly, "It is small boat."

I nodded.

"The first small boat in Egypt."

I looked at him. "The smallest boat in Egypt, you mean?"

He tilted his head and grinned, abashed. "I mean. Yes. Is smallest."

We sat down on the dock to talk. He was an unusually calm man and an attentive listener. He had large, gentle eyes, the whites of which were a muddy yellow, and long curling black lashes. His mustache was traced with veins of white. His skin was dark and his face had a toddler's pudginess. Everything about him looked pleasingly rounded: his small mouth was round and his cheeks were round, and his belly pushed roundly at the front of his gallabiya. He was stocky and thick shouldered, and though he was no taller than I, he looked fiercely powerful. His tongue was heavy and he spoke in a crowded way, with an almost imperceptible lisp. He had a habit of reducing the word *than* to nothing but its final *n*, so that "This is better than that" became "This is better 'n that." While most men in Aswan had brown spots on their teeth, Amr's teeth were impeccably white. His age was impossible to determine. His short hair was the complex gray of a squirrel's tail, but he had the smooth skin of a young man. In the center of his forehead he bore the raised and darkened callus that came of frequent prostration in prayer; the unofficial term for it was *zabib*, which meant "raisin." The callus was worn proudly as a sign of great piety and devotion. The more you prayed, the bigger the raisin. It was widely known that in an act of religious vanity some men rubbed the spot with a stone in secret, deliberately and falsely increasing its size. On some Muslim men this callus was so large and so dark it looked like a horrible hematoma. Amr's *zabib* was small and looked genuine.

Eventually Amr suggested that I take my row. I climbed into the boat, and while Amr untied the lead the other felucca captains twitched their gowns and looked on in uncharacteristic silence, taking their cue as much from the unexpectedness of the situation as from Amr's polite gravity. I told Amr that I would row around Elephantine Island and return in an hour or so.

"As you wish," he said, with no trace of mockery, worry, or doubt.

I pushed off from the dock and began to haul the boat upstream. The oars were immensely heavy, with thick wooden handles that had been coarsely fashioned with a machete, and one oar was longer than the other. Though I didn't know it at the time, it happened to be a Coptic holiday that day, doubling the river traffic, which usually came to life at this hour when the heat began to abate. Long, underpowered launches moved back and forth across the river, overloaded with singing, clapping, bongo-thumping revelers. On some boats, spontaneous dances had erupted: twenty dark heads bobbing up and down on the decks, while the boats teetered this way and that. The atmosphere was one of general hilarity. The water seemed to thrum.

Nervous under the watchful eyes of the seven felucca captains and unsure of the current, I rowed hard and began to make progress toward the top of Elephantine Island. Men in large feluccas sped by, slicing through the water just inches from my bow, grinning wildly and shouting, "Come here, madame! I help you!" or "Come in my boat!" Others simply stared, surprised into silence at the sight of me. I tried to ignore them, to concentrate on the oars and the water. Amr had placed such unusual confidence in me that I was determined not to disappoint him.

At a mile long, Elephantine Island forced the Nile to divide into two channels on either side of it. I rowed up the narrow eastern passage between the Old Cataract Hotel on the mainland and the enormous rounded clifflike boulders near the top of the island. One of the many theories for the derivation of the name Elephantine was that from a distance these boulders resembled elephants. Floating not two feet from the smooth rocks, I could see clearly the unfinished cartouches and hieroglyphs that had been chiseled into them millennia before. Just above these rocks was the Elephantine nilometer, built by the pharaohs to measure the river's annual inundation and rebuilt by the Romans.

The water was black, glassy, and, squeezed as it was through this narrow channel, very swift. I rowed hard until I rounded the top of the island and could rest a little. Because of the huge boulders that lurk just below the flat mirror of the water's surface, the currents here were tricky: shifting and twisting with turbid force. At the top of the island, I was dazzled by the sight of twenty white rowboats anchored in the shallows below the ruins of the Temple of Khnum, every boat freshly painted, and every one perfect for my purposes. I realized that among the boats a young man was bathing in the river stark naked. He saw me looking at him yet didn't seem to care. In fact, he waved his skinny arms and shouted at me to come and sit on a rock with him and drink tea. When I began to row off he screamed, by way of introduction, "I am in the army!" and jumped out of the water and bounded toward me across the rocks, desperate for my attention, his naked body glistening, bands of silvery water streaming from him. A big felucca passed behind me, and its captain shouted coyly at me, "Hey, Egyptian! Want to come in my boat?"

The distractions and confusion made the coordinated labor of rowing the boat nearly impossible. My linen trousers were transparent with sweat; the legs of them clung to my shins. The metal hull of my boat grazed a rock just below the surface of the water with a grinding squeal. Seconds later, coming through a narrow passage between two small islands, the prow of a felucca called *Smile* glanced off the stern of my boat and spun me around like a pinwheel. I had never seen so many sailboats moving so fast in such a small space, nor had I ever witnessed quite this daredevil brand of sailing. The sailors in Aswan operated their feluccas the way adolescent boys operate dirt bikes in a mud pit, with flashy flourishes and abrupt precision; their stunts were the nautical equivalent of fishtails, hairpin turns, and wheelies. A lifetime of sailing had given them a kind of rollicking freedom on the water. I envied them.

I was tired and realized that my hour was quickly passing. I didn't want Amr to worry about his boat. I rounded the southern tip of Elephantine Island and headed easily downriver on the western side of it, the current coaxing me swiftly along. The river was less crowded on this far side of the island, and there was some semblance of peace here. The sun, though far from setting, had sunk fully behind the high desert dunes on the west bank of the river, cloaking the water in purple shadow. A boat overloaded with young police officers raced by without noticing me.

Farther along, a boatful of gamesome Nubians moored in an island cove sat smoking marijuana. One of them shouted at me, "Whose boat is that?" Another said, "Please come in our boat and smoke!"

When I asked what they were smoking, they giggled and showed their dazzling white teeth.

"Lady, you know what we smoking. You have any we can buy?"

I said no.

"We would pay for it!"

"I don't have anything to give you," I said and thought of the sign I had seen in the Cairo airport the first time I arrived in Egypt, a sign informing visitors that should they be found carrying anything faintly resembling intoxicating drugs, their hands might be cut off, they might be executed, and either way they would certainly have to pay the Egyptian government something like a million-pound fine. Who would dare? But many of the sailors in Aswan smoked marijuana and hashish, and I had seen a small but unmistakable Rastafarian element among some of the young Nubian captains. Some wore their hair in dreadlocks, not a natural Nubian style, and boldly smoked their ganja in the open air. In Aswan I had seen an anomalous few feluccas with the names *Hash Family, Rasta Famely,* and *Jamaica Famely.* Chiefly Muslim, the sailors' interest in Rastafarianism seemed to have less to do with religious belief and a devotion to Haile Selassie than with Jamaican fashion and the ethnic identity that grew out of it. The pot smoking in this Muslim country struck me, but according to some of the earliest travelers in Egypt the use of the hemp plant as a narcotic was an old and common tradition here. Charles Sonnini, who traveled from France to Egypt in 1777, claimed that the consumption of hashish in Egypt was "very considerable" and that hashish was to be found in all the Egyptian markets. Sonnini wrote, "The Arabs and the Egyptians compose several preparations from this plant, with which they procure for themselves a sort of pleasing drunkenness, a state of reverie which inspires gaiety and produces agreeable dreams. This sort of annihilation of the faculty of thinking, this kind of slumber of the soul, has no resemblance to the intoxication produced by wine or strong liquors, and our language has no terms expressive of it."

Edward Lane in his 1836 *An Account of the Manners and Customs of the Modern Egyptians* noted that though the sale of hashish and *Cannabis indica* was then prohibited in Egypt, Egyptians still employed this "pernicious and degrading custom," and that hashish could be got at coffee shops and smaller private shops called *mahsheshehs,* which were exclusively for the sale of hashish "and other intoxicating preparations." Lane wrote, "It is sometimes amusing to observe the ridiculous conduct, and to listen to the conversation, of the persons who frequent these shops. They are all of the lower orders." He went on to explain that in Egypt the Arabic word *hashshasheen,* which meant "users of hemp," was often applied to "noisy and riotous people," and that during the Crusades the name *hashshasheen* (the origin of the word *assassin*) was given to Syrian warriors who used mind-altering drugs to confuse and disarm their enemies.

I waved good-bye to the pot smokers and moved on past

Kitchener Island, a small island wholly taken up with the most exotic botanical garden I had ever seen. It was filled with tropical trees and flowers, everything marked in Latin and Arabic. On another trip I had seen a horseradish tree there, a cape honeysuckle, a mountain ebony, a baobab, an ironwood, a rubber vine, a spotted gum, a silver trumpet tree, and an enormous mahogany. I had seen a *Strychnos nux-vomica,* a strychnine tree, and had put one of its spherical seedpods in my pocket, then later threw it away for fear it would poison me. Kitchener was cool and quiet and shady, and it was home to a curious cat that had one green eye and one blue.

Half an hour later I rounded the bottom of the island and pulled myself up to Amr's dock. He was still standing there with several other sailors, still waiting for work. As I climbed out of the boat he looked at my face, took the oars from me, and said nothing. When I moved to hand him some money for the use of the boat, he shook his head, showed me the palm of his hand in protest, and then pressed it to his chest, an indication that he could not possibly take money from me.

Such a refusal was unheard of in a man in his line of work. I offered the money again; again he protested. Clutching the knot of tattered Egyptian pounds, I asked Amr if I could come back and take the boat again the next day.

He smiled. "Any time you feel."

That evening the woman who tended the front desk in my hotel invited me to come to her house. In her late thirties, Christian, married with three children, Safaa was short, solid, intelligent, and spoke English very well. She was gap toothed and good natured, well educated, had a sense of humor and a sometimes comical manner, but was often bored and frustrated and glum about her life. She had the air of one whose ambitions had been thwarted at every turn. She spoke freely, as though she had known me for years. She was tired of being poor, disliked Egypt, and wanted to travel. She had nine-year-old twins, boy and girl, and a six-month-old infant whom she referred to as "the surprise." Every day Safaa's husband minded the baby until the twins came home from school in the afternoon, then he would go off to work and the twins would take over the babysitting until Safaa returned home at eight.

Safaa valued education and was depressed about her twins; they were smart but didn't study. They spent all their time watching television, and the husband never lifted a finger to prevent them, though she complained about it again and again. "When they with my husband, they watch TV all day," she told me. "Soon as I come home from work I turn that crap box off. And then my twins, they do nothing. They won't read a book. I have to put the book in their hands and point their heads at it and say, 'Now, you two little dogs, you read!'"

If the children refused to study, they would never pass their exams, and what sort of future would they have if they didn't pass their exams? They'd end up poor like everyone else in Aswan.

Safaa had learned the word *crap* from some Australian guests in the hotel and used it often and with relish. Like most Christian women she wore modest cotton dresses that covered her arms and knees and never wore a veil or a head covering of any kind. Because of their relative freedom of dress, their exposed shins and ankles, their uncovered necks and heads and fully visible hair, Christian women were easily identifiable on Egypt's streets. They always looked more modern, lighter, freer, less alien and mysterious than the Muslim women.

That evening we walked together to Safaa's apartment. Along the way I praised the dress she was wearing, a pleasant, long-sleeved, flowered gown with a black Peter Pan collar. She looked down at the dress and said, "I like this one too, but my manager in the hotel, he says, 'Safaa! That's a crap dress. It so old-fashioned; from the days of your old mother.' But I give no damn. I like it. He tells me don't wear it. I wear it anyway."

We walked through the older streets of Aswan, away from the river. The farther we got from the corniche and the markets, the darker the streets became, and eventually the pavement gave way to dust, and we were walking in a black maze of small pathlike alleys between run-down two-story houses that looked on the verge of toppling. The smell of cooking and coal smoke drifted through open doors; dim yellow lights shone in open windows. Dogs barked in the distance. Suddenly Aswan felt like a small village. Safaa pointed to a row of dark buildings in a narrow street and said, "I hope they rip those craps down! They are only empty and dangerous! And kids like to play in them and sometimes they get hurt. Aswan is a crap."

At the end of the street a group of older Muslim women stared as we approached, and one of them asked Safaa why she was walking with a foreigner. Safaa told the woman, "She's my American cousin, and it's none of your business anyway," then translated for me what she had said, tittered at her own impertinence, and added "Crap!" for good measure as we walked on.

Safaa's apartment was big, clean, and appointed in the Egyptian fashion with a lot of heavy and uncomfortable hand-hewn wooden furniture. An enormous television sat on a table in the middle of the room. The walls were covered with Christian symbols and decorations: a picture of Mar Girgis, or Saint George, slaying a pathetic-looking dragon who was rigid and twisted with agony; a picture of the Coptic Pope Shenouda with his big grizzly beard; a picture of an Egyptian-looking Blessed Virgin with big dark eyes, a long nose, and a wide mouth; and beside the Virgin a fuzzy reproduction of *The Last Supper*. The knob on the front door was embossed with a cross and the words "God is Love" in Arabic. And on the mantel stood a two-foot-tall statue of a Caucasian Jesus in a rose-colored robe cradling a slightly cross-eyed lamb in his arms. Dust had collected in the ceramic folds of Jesus's gown and turned the rose color to gray.

The modern Coptic Christians are the descendants of pharaonic Egyptians who had been converted to Christianity by Saint Mark in Alexandria. It is believed that the later pharaohs spoke the Coptic language, a modern form of Egyptian heavily influenced by Greek. Copts now make up only 15 percent of the Egyptian population. Safaa liked Hosni Mubarak because he defended and protected the beleaguered Egyptian Christians. Sometimes, she said, Muslims kidnapped Christian women and forced them to convert to Islam by threatening to rape them if they didn't convert. In Lower Egypt, north of Qena, there were constant fights, gun battles, even small riots between Christians and Muslims.

I asked Safaa why all the tailors in Egypt were Christian. She said disconsolately, "I ask myself that." Her view was that in the fifties and sixties there had been many more Christians in Egypt and that when Nasser came to power he stole the important jobs from the Christians and gave them to the Muslims. "So that's why the Muslims have all the good jobs. The professional jobs. Now the Christians that's left here can only be tailors and other crap jobs. Nasser took the Christians' money and their land."

This reminded me of Florence Nightingale writing in 1849, "Abbas Pacha is so furiously Mahometan that he has just dismissed all Christians from his service . . . besides 900 Coptic scribes who are fallen into the lowest poverty thereby."

At the sound of our voices, Safaa's children came out from a back bedroom. They were pale faced, dark haired, handsome, and small. The daughter Mary carried the six-month-old infant expertly on her hip. The boy, George, stood behind them. The infant, very tiny and naked from the waist down, was beaming and gnawing on the edge of a small saucer gripped in her hand; later I saw that the saucer was painted with an image of the Virgin and Child. The three little children had been home alone all afternoon minding each other. They stared at me with sweet, fascinated smiles.

Safaa brought me mango juice, a cup of hot karkady tea, and two pears. The twins turned on the television and, like children anywhere, began frantically flipping through the channels, past glimpses of Arab rappers with baseball caps worn sideways on their heads, past the BBC world news, past CNN, Yasser Arafat, Benjamin Netanyahu, Omar Sharif looking elderly with longish white hair, a nightclub singer wailing *"Habibi"* into a microphone, and multiple car advertisements from Saudi Arabia that showed sexy long-haired women purring, "Next Ramadan, buy a new Jaguar for your wife." The life depicted on the television bore no resemblance whatever to life in the streets of Aswan.

Safaa dandled the baby on her knee and sighed. "I spend all my extra money on the house, good furniture, new floor in the kitchen. And my husband? What he do? He spend all his money on the stupid TV. A hundred channels that crap TV has. And these kids they never stop watching it. Look at them, Rose."

The children stared at the television, openmouthed, dead eyed, deaf to the world. Like their mother, they had small blue crosses tattooed on their inner wrists. The baby began to cry. Safaa bounced her up and down on one knee, kissed her, then passed her over to Mary, who bounced her, kissed her, then passed her over to George, who walked her around the room and kissed her until the diaperless baby emitted a rude shower of diarrhea on his little arm. Calmly, as though he was entirely used to this, George took the baby into the bedroom, changed his shirt, washed the baby, and brought her back to the living room, again diaperless.

Safaa was annoyed with Mary because Mary had fed the baby nothing but juice all day. "She do that because it's easier than giving her real food," she said to me, then she turned to Mary and said hotly, *"Kula yom kida!* Every day it's like this! I tell you to feed her food but you give her juice! That's why she has diarrhea."

Pale-faced Mary stood up and protested loudly with a long string of angry-sounding Arabic. She slapped her own forehead like an elderly woman, then flopped down on the couch and sulked. I couldn't blame her—she was far too young to be held responsible for the diet and welfare of an infant.

Safaa lifted up the baby and studied her face. "The baby isn't beautiful," she said flatly. "I am not beautiful. I am look like Indian lady. I have big nose and dark skin." It was true. "And I got a big wide mouth. My daughter Mary is more beautiful than me. She is whiter. I hope the baby will be better looking later."

Safaa asked me how I liked the hotel I was staying in. I told her it was very good for such a cheap place—clean, safe, with a pleasant staff. My only complaint was that every time he saw me, the chef in the rooftop dining room—a fat, unshaven, toothless old man—invited me to go dancing with him. "It's a bit tiresome," I said.

Safaa howled with laughter so loud the startled baby began to cry. "Oh, that big crap!" she said. "He has had five wives and many children and he thinks he is a young man but he isn't and he has no teeth in his head and also bad breath on top of it. God, that old goat."

Safaa told me that last year the manager of the hotel had found pornographic magazines "for sex" in a cupboard in the hotel kitchen, and in a fury had burned them on the roof of the hotel and had shrieked at the chef that if he ever brought such filth into the hotel again he would fire him.

The children were now staring at a film on the Christian

Channel; a story about a Muslim man who wanted to convert to Christianity because the corrupt Muslim leaders were always telling him he had to kill people in the name of God, and how on earth could *that* be holy and right? The Muslim imam ranted incessantly at the man about how he should live and what he should do. The imam looked like a caricature of the devil, leering in a skullcap, with a long unkempt beard and hard little lightless eyes and two hands like menacing claws with which he pantomimed his rage and hatred for the Christian infidel. The would-be Christian convert was, of course, handsome, noble, and gentle. He admitted to the imam that he wanted to become Christian, whereupon the rabid imam flipped his lid and tried to strangle the traitor with the two claws.

I watched the scene in fascination, wondering how the Christian Channel could get away with a show like this. Christians were a tiny minority in Egypt, were persecuted and maligned, and yet they had managed to air on national television this incendiary polemic portraying Muslims as fanatical murderous maniacs.

That show ended and another began. From what I could glean from the imagery and from Safaa's occasional translations, this one concerned a smart Egyptian lawyer who goes to a party, is so upset—or perhaps just so depraved—that he has to drink straight out of the host's whiskey bottle, gets drunk, feels up a buxom young woman in a back room, then drives home, and accidentally kills people with his fancy car. The next morning he's hung over, unshaven, and disheveled but brilliant in court. He ends up redeemed mostly because he's handsome and smart and because he brings presents to a boy he has crippled in the accident. That show was followed by an advertisement for a talk show interview with a famous Egyptian movie star reputed to be very funny. In the ad, the movie star was crying sincerely and tamping her eyes with a hankie. I asked Safaa why she was crying.

"Ah, those silly craps!" Safaa howled. "They always pretend to cry! They have to! People like it!"

And finally we sat staring at a show in which women were discussing what you should do if your daughter has a baby before she's married.

Surprised, I said to Safaa, "That happens?"

"All the time, Rose! Just last month an infant was found abandoned in a basket two blocks from here."

Safaa grabbed the TV remote from Mary, clicked it off, told the kids to go and do their mathematics and take the baby with them, then she turned to me and began to speak with rueful envy. Outside Egypt things were different, better. She knew this because she worked in a hotel and met many foreigners. Men and women could sleep together before they were married, and the women didn't have to ask their parents before marriage if the husband was an acceptable prospect. Egyptians were too obsessed with sex and marriage and family. And women couldn't do anything on their own. For Egyptian women, marriage was the only way you could really get out of your father's house. Safaa hadn't married her husband for love. He was a nice man and a good husband, but she didn't love him. Sometimes she wanted to go to Kitchener Botanical Garden alone just to sit and relax and look at the pretty trees that she had heard so much about, but she never mustered the courage to go there because strangers—men—would incessantly ask her whether she was married, where was her husband, where were her children, and why wasn't she at home minding her family. She clucked her tongue in disgust. "Women here can't do anything alone."

When I told Safaa that I did many things alone she said, "And I know it! I see you. You go out in the world by yourself. You can go in Aswan by yourself. You go to Kitchener Island, Elephantine, Luxor, and Cairo by yourself and you can enjoy. And you wear trousers. I saw you run once. On the corniche you was running. You can talk to strangers and men and ride in the felucca with the captain. But Egyptian women? No! Egyptian women—doesn't matter Christian or Muslim—can't be like you."

Safaa stared at the blank television screen with utter disdain. "Rose, I tell you. I wish I could be free like you."

The Cataract Islands

ARLY THE NEXT MORNING I went back to the place where I had seen the twenty white rowboats at the top of Elephantine Island. As I walked among the boats, examining them, a tall, very thin young Nubian man came up behind me and said gloomily, "I will help you. What you need?"

I told him I needed a boat. He said, "I have a friend with felucca. We can take you sailing." I explained that I wanted a rowboat. He tried to persuade me that a rowboat was not the best means of seeing Aswan. I had had this conversation so many times here that I was numb with boredom. I said, no, I was looking for a rowboat not in order to see Aswan but in order to buy the boat.

The man went silent for a moment. And then we ran through the tedious, unvarying charade:

Why you want?

"Because."

Because why?

"Because I want to buy a boat."

For what?

"For a surprise for my husband."

Where your husband is?

"Asleep in the hotel. It is his birthday. I want to surprise him with the gift of a boat."

Where you are from?

"America."

How you will take the boat home to America?

"Well, we live in Cairo now. We'll use it there."

Why you don't buy boat in Cairo?

"The boats here in Aswan are better than the boats in Cairo." (This always flattered them.)

Yes. That is true. I know a boat you can buy. But! No one will sell you the boat.

"Why?"

It's difficult. It will cost you lot of money.

"How much money?"

Three thousand bounds!

"Who owns this boat that you have in mind?"

A man.

"Could you introduce me to him?"

Please sit over here with me.

This particular fellow was inviting me to sit on a fallen palm tree in the middle of what looked like the village dump. I declined. He asked why. I explained that I wasn't keen on sitting in the garbage. He looked at me hungrily and invited me to visit his family's house; the look on his face positively shrieked, *I want your money!* He was the most cheerless person I had met in Egypt. His name was Hashem.

We got up, and I followed him down a shady path through a

grove of trees until we came to a pumpkin-colored adobe house with an open courtyard in its center. "Hashem" was handwritten over the door in roman letters. As we came into the house a woman who had been feeding sticks and twigs into the mouth of a stove in the courtyard scurried out of sight, struggling to cover her hair with a veil, which had slipped back onto her shoulders as she worked. I caught a glimpse of her hair before she had a chance to hide it; it was black, surprisingly long and straight, and very soft looking, with distinct streaks of gray in it. It looked utterly different from the Nubian men's brittle Afros.

"That is my mother," Hashem said.

The mother went into the kitchen to make tea, while Hashem and I sat in the sitting room, a long, narrow, windowless vault crammed with furniture. At one end of the room a full-sized refrigerator stood, still housed in the cardboard box it had been shipped in. Because of the deep dovecote ceiling, a particularly Nubian architectural feature, the room was cool as a wine cellar. There were cotton rag rugs on the couches, and on the floor a rug made out of what looked like polypropylene rope.

As my eyes began to adjust to the darkness of the room, I saw that Hashem's face bore the turbulent expression of a man who is dying and knows it. He began to talk about many things, none of which had anything to do with rowboats. The house had been in his family for years, but he wanted his own house, off Elephantine Island. But there was the matter of money—he had none. He would never do felucca work, for it was immoral. It was not the right way. It was only about money and more money with those bad felucca captains. He was the oldest brother in his family and therefore was obliged to take care of everyone. He was angry because he wanted to do something solely for himself.

Hashem spoke in a droning, lowing way. He told me that his sister was soon to be married. He would have to come up with the money for the wedding. A lot of money. As if to prove the sister's existence, he opened a box, took out a Polaroid photograph of her, and handed it to me. She was pretty. When we were finished looking at the photo, he put it down on the couch beside him. A minute later, realizing in the middle of a sentence that the photo lay face up, he reached out and turned it over, to protect his sister's purity.

I asked Hashem if his brothers were married. The question made him indignant. "They are younger than I am!"

I asked why his name and not his father's was written on the front of the house.

"My father don't work anymore. He is not the one taking care of the family. He is not getting the money. He live next door."

I asked him about the garbage that seemed to be strewn all over Aswan's villages. He nodded knowingly and said that at one time the government had given the people of Aswan assistance with garbage removal, but for some reason they stopped helping and so now there was no way to get rid of it.

"I drink beer," he said suddenly and with the bored matter-of-factness with which one delivers one's date of birth. "One or two times per week, because sometimes I feel that I need it."

There was an air of calculation about Hashem. I sensed that he was fully aware that complaining and self-pity can bring sympathy, and sometimes gain, and though I wanted to trust him, I didn't. He expressed no interest in anything but his own woes, which admittedly were considerable and varied.

I listened to Hashem for what seemed like an eternity, while a plastic clock on the wall with "Big Ben" written on its face played "Camptown Races" every half hour. Hashem was indisputably boring. His laugh, when it came, was sepulchral. As he talked I noticed one of his sisters peeking through the doorway at me; the whites of her eyes glowed for a moment and she disappeared again.

I found it difficult to feel compassion for Hashem because of his sourness and lack of humor, but I tried to gather some perspective on his situation. Such destitution and unhappiness commanded sympathy, but what sympathy I could muster felt distant and abstract. He seemed plotting. He hadn't invited me here simply to be hospitable. He wanted something. But so did I.

"Hashem," I said. "What about the rowboat?"

"You can buy mine."

"Where is it?"

He waved an arm. "Down there."

"Can I see it?"

"We will go."

As we were leaving I noticed Hashem's sister and mother sitting on the floor in another small room. It seemed rude to have spent time in their house without saying a word to them. I told Hashem that I wanted to say good-bye to them. Without consulting them, he said, "They don't want come out."

On our way to the boat, Hashem showed me his family's fields. "This is my father's side," he said, waving at groves of trees. "And this is my mother's side," waving at fields. The groves on Elephantine Island were dark and eerie. The shade was dense and the ground was very dry. Enormous banana leaves crackled underfoot, crows bleated, doves hooted spookily. Ancient, the mud walls here sagged, and everything was blanketed in a veneer of brown dust the thickness of cupcake frosting. It seemed a miracle that the trees were able to photosynthesize under all that dust.

Hashem's family owned guava, mango, lemon, fig, date, orange, and eucalyptus trees, as well as grape bowers. Hashem explained that he sold his fruit by the tree: each tree had a price no matter how much fruit it yielded. "That tree is four hundred bounds," he said pointing at a mango. "That one is three hundred."

He didn't smile. He seemed to take no joy whatever in being alive. He looked intensely dissatisfied. When we came to the spot where his boat was anchored, I could see why he was willing to sell it. It was a rotting hulk, full of garbage, with both oarlocks missing and a broken bow. It was nothing like the boats at the top of the island. I declined the boat and knew that he wouldn't introduce me to anyone who would sell me a good one. This was a problem in Aswan: finding someone who would be truly helpful, who would not be jealous that you were giving business to someone else.

As we waited at the river's edge for the ferry back to the mainland, Hashem insisted on buying me a Coke. I thanked him, said it was very kind of him but not necessary, and that anyway I preferred water. He bought me a bottle of water, which I hadn't realized was far more expensive than Coke. In a desperate attempt at some sort of recompense for his expense, he asked me to give him the nearly empty bottle of water I had with me. His obvious depression made me soften slightly, and I handed him a twenty-pound note—six U.S. dollars or so—which he refused to accept until I couched the money in terms of gratitude for his hospitality. His face relaxed as he pocketed the twenty.

The level of appeasement a few pounds could generate in an Egyptian soul was chastening and edifying. Having seen again and again the salubrious effect of a small contribution, I found it impossible to be stingy here.

Three days in a row I used Amr's little boat, all the while debating whether I could take such a small boat on my trip down the river. So far, Amr seemed like the only truly approachable and serious man in Aswan. With each day of rowing I grew braver and went farther up the river, trying to explore the Cataract Islands. The High Dam was not visible from Aswan, and the knowledge of its majestic presence so nearby was tantalizing, like the pot of gold at the end of a rainbow. I was curious to see where the Egyptian Nile began.

The farther upriver I went, the more the islands seemed to multiply in the distance, each one more beautiful, isolated, and exotic than the last. But with every island I passed, the current grew stronger, the river rockier and more complicated, seeming to divide itself into a dozen separate creeks. As I approached the top of each island, I had to struggle mightily to surmount the surge of water that the head of the island had diverted. Going higher on this part of the river was a bit like climbing a mountain. (Florence Nightingale had referred to this place as "the staircase.") Every major step was a struggle, interspersed with moments of blessed rest. I picked my way, crablike, backward up the river. I rested by wedging my oar behind an island rock or tree trunk, and it was only then that I had time to look around and see where I was. The islands were uninhabited, supported no man-made structures, and offered a pristine glimpse of what the Nile was like thousands of years ago; the grasses and plants that were here had remained unchanged for aeons. Every so often I saw this government sign posted on an island shore: SALUGA AND GAZAL PROTECTED LANDS. SCIENTIFIC PROJECT. DO NOT GET OUT OF THE TRUCK. ANYONE DAMAGING THE PLANTS OR DISTURBING THE ANIMALS WILL BE PROSECUTED BY EGYPTIAN LAW.

Exotic birds—reed larks, olivaceous warblers, little green bee-eaters—perched on swaying reeds a mere foot from my face and stared boldly at me. They seemed unafraid. Minnows skittered through the duckweed that floated along the banks in billowing rafts, like blankets of worsted green gauze.

One day as I sat resting in the boat on the bank of an island, I realized there was a dark face just behind the bougainvillea bush I was hanging on to—a fisherman wrestling with a long strip of tin, which he was shaping into some kind of animal trap. Beyond him was a tiny shelter made of reeds and bamboo, a makeshift lean-to cluttered with fishing nets and cooking pots and glass bottles. The solitude I had found on this part of the river was so pleasant that at the sight of the man and his little dwelling I wanted to slink away, but he caught sight of me before I could leave, and with shocking speed he scuttled around the bush on his hands and knees to gape at me. He was so startled, he appeared to have stopped breathing. He was barefoot and small and movie-star handsome, and his mustache was black and full. His eyes had an almost feral brightness. The legs of his tattered cotton trousers were carefully rolled up, revealing hairless brown shins and knotty calf muscles. He studied my boat, the oars, my bare feet, my face. We stared mutely at each other for a weirdly long time. Finally he raised one hand and conveyed his incomprehension with a particularly Egyptian gesture: a brisk twist of the wrist that exactly mimics the tossing of dice, and in a near whisper he spoke one incredulous Arabic word: *Lay?* (Why?)

Not an unreasonable question. Why would a foreign woman do the work that rowing required when she could hire any Egyptian man to do it for her for a pittance? On the Nile, rowing was not a pastime. It was work that no one wanted to do if he didn't have to. It was tantamount to laying railroad tracks or digging graves or tarring highways.

The rushing water slewed and whirled beneath my boat, rocking me slightly. Limited by the few Arabic phrases I had learned, I gave the fisherman a typically Egyptian answer: *Mafeesh lay.* (There is no why.)

"Drink tea," he said abruptly. It sounded like a command. He pointed at a narrow path that led to the center of the island through a wild overgrowth of bushes and brambles and acacias and weeds. I thought of the government warning: *Don't get out of the truck.* I declined the tea, smiled politely, and began to row farther upriver. The fisherman followed me, stumbling along the shore, saying, *I can row for you.* Again, smiling,

I declined the offer and rowed on. The fisherman resigned himself and went back to twisting his piece of tin.

Twenty minutes later, as I neared the top of the island, I saw him again. He was studying me from behind a bush, his white teeth glowing like jewelry beneath his hanging mustache, his bright eyes pinched to slits in the sunlight. As I readied to round the top of the island, a task that I could see would be difficult, if not impossible, for the swiftness of the water, he sprang up and rushed at me through the bushes, smashing reeds and twigs under his bare feet and crashing into the river up to his knees. "No, no, no!" he said, pawing furiously at the air with one hand, the frantic motion of a dog digging a hole, another peculiarly Egyptian gesture, which means *Come here.*

I chose to ignore him and headed into what amounted to a minor rapid. After trying three times to beat the current, I gave up and allowed myself to be pulled downriver.

The fisherman gestured wildly at me with his piece of tin, indicating that I should come through a skinny inlet that led out to the top of the island, a shortcut that would thoroughly circumvent the most difficult part of the current. The inlet was narrow, passing between two rocks. With pure luck I managed to haul the boat through it, and the fisherman showed his approval by giving me a double thumbs-up.

"Now I will row for you," he said decisively.

I looked at him. "Why will you row for me?"

"You can't do it. Only I can do it."

"But I don't want you to do it," I said. "I want to try it."

He nodded and shrugged and watched as I tried to leave the island behind. The current now was too strong for me to beat. I rowed with all my strength but remained hovering in the same spot, flapping my wooden wings like an osprey fluttering above its prey. I tried and failed several times and eventually gave up, steering myself to the bank and grabbing hold of a purple bougainvillea frond to keep myself from careering downriver on the brisk current.

The fisherman was entertained and clearly interested that I had come this far upriver. He grinned and nodded and for lack of any other English phrases he said, "I am bolice."

He wasn't the first to make such a claim. It was beginning to seem that every fisherman and shop clerk and felucca captain in Aswan was a member of the police force. Even the man selling postcards and stamps in the Oberoi Hotel had declaimed in aid of nothing, "I am bolice," waving his identification card at me.

As for the on-duty police, when I completed my day's row and returned toward Aswan, I passed a teenage slew of them sitting in their black woolen uniforms in an inflatable boat on a dock. They were drinking black tea out of tiny glasses, and like all Egyptian men they held their glasses between thumb and forefinger in a strikingly light and delicate way. They watched me closely as I approached, but there were no hellos, no waves, no smiles, as if they had been told by their commander that it was unacceptable and unseemly for the tourist police to flirt with foreigners. Their silence and restraint was notable. They sat staring at me as I rowed by. All of them. Intently. They were young. They all wore black mustaches. There was something touching about their professionalism, and I couldn't help smiling. One of them bravely—or foolishly—smiled in response and, like a dark set of dominoes falling fatally one by one, the entire group collapsed into smiles, and then giggles, and before long they were waving and cheering at me and hoisting their glasses like spectators greeting an astronaut just back from the moon, and one of them tossed all caution to the wind and threw out a joke: *You go to Cairo in boat?* I smiled and nodded and said, *Yes, Cairo,* and all fifteen of us had a long, loud convivial laugh at that. To them I was silly and harmless. That fact gave me strength; they would never expect me to do the forbidden thing I planned to do.

The next day when I returned to Elephantine Island, Amr Khaled invited me to sail upriver with him. His felucca was called *Fantastic.* It was twenty-two feet long and eight feet wide, and like all of the feluccas in Aswan it was very clean and freshly painted and tidily kept, with everything stowed and lashed in its proper place. The entire ship looked as though it had been steeped in chlorine, and the extreme whiteness of it seemed to throb in the sunlight. When we boarded the boat in front of the Oberoi Hotel, Amr immediately removed his shoes, like a Japanese woman entering her home. Shoes, he said, made the boat dirty, and furthermore it was easier to sail without them. The soles of Amr's wide feet were thick as elephant hide and yellowish and full of cracks and gouges, like slabs of Spanish corkboard. Considering their density and durability, I saw no reason for Amr to wear shoes at all. The dark brown tops of his feet carried a fine whitish bloom, as if freshly dusted with baby powder.

He sailed me up the first cataract—far beyond where I had been able to row myself—where the river roared around large boulders, its eddies shoving the felucca from side to side. Most Nile travelers who had passed through the cataract in order to venture farther south into Nubia had been compelled to describe this place in their letters and travel accounts. I now understood why. It was not simply the danger of the passage but the stunning proliferation of bizarre rocks that made the place memorable. The rocks, rising eerily up out of the water, were strangely shaped, blackish, sometimes reddish, and seemed to be masked with a layer of lacquer that shone as acutely as buffed silver. Florence Nightingale had described the cataract as "an expanse of heaps of Syenite, with rapids between them; the rocks hollowed out into the most inconceivable shapes,—some like bowls, some like boilers, some like boot-jacks, some like etruscan vases." Major R. Raven-Hart, who went up the Nile in 1936, wrote of the cataract, "The rocks have that curious stove-polish coating, shiny black over the granite: Darwin says it occurs also on the cataracts of Congo and Orinoco." What Darwin actually said was:

> At the cataracts of the great rivers Orinoco, Nile, and Congo, the syenitic rocks are coated by a black substance, appearing as if they had been polished with plumbago. The layer is of extreme thinness . . . The origin, however, of these coatings of metallic oxides, which seem as if cemented to the rocks, is not understood.

In his characteristically terse and graphic fashion, Flaubert described the rocks as "dark chocolate-color, with long white streaks of bird-droppings that widen toward the bottom." And Amelia Edwards, with her habitual detail, wrote of the cataract:

> The Nile . . . here spreads itself over a rocky basin bounded by sand-slopes on the one side, and by granite cliffs on the other. Studded with numberless islets, divided into numberless channels, foaming over sunken rocks, eddying among water-worn boulders, now shallow, now deep, now loitering, now hurrying, here sleeping in the ribbed hollow of a tiny sand-drift, there circling above the vortex of a hidden whirlpool, the river, whether looked upon from the deck of the dahabeeyah or the heights along the shore is seen everywhere to be fighting its way through a labyrinth, the paths of which have never yet been mapped or sounded.

Many Ancient Egyptians believed that the cataract was the true source of the Nile, that its waters bubbled up from beneath this rocky ground, one half flowing north to the Mediterranean, the other half flowing south into the Sudan. The belief was hardly surprising; the place, with its chaos of boulders, tumbling water, and churning currents, felt nearly supernatural. The ancient Egyptian name for Aswan was *Sun,* which meant "opening" or "entrance," because the Nile entered Egypt through this treacherous and narrow cataract.

Sailing upriver here was a matter of waiting for a gust of wind strong enough to counterbalance the river's rushing pressure. It was a strange brand of sailing, one in which we spent long minutes parked in trembling stasis, while the water rushed past and beneath us, and the wind strained forward in the sail with equal force. It was a bit like being in the eye of a cyclone, terrific energy teeming around us while we sat still, gently bobbing and swaying, the cotton lines creaking in their blocks and pulleys. We were passing up a narrow corridor between two small islands on the west side of the river, with no room to tack or turn. When the wind failed momentarily, we had no choice but to slide slowly backward on the current, a deeply disquieting sensation in a place riddled with boulders, many of them invisible, just inches below the surface of the water. It was like sailing an obstacle course.

I could see from the way Amr leaned against it that the wooden tiller was incredibly heavy. Under these conditions, the slightest mistake or moment of inattention could mean rapid disaster, yet Amr appeared calm and controlled, reflexively clutching up his gown at just the right moment to keep from tripping on the hem, sometimes steering the boat with his outstretched foot, as hand over hand he trimmed the sail or raised the centerboard. From time to time he would point at some random-looking spot in the water and say, "Is a rock down there." When I asked him how he knew there was a rock, he just shrugged. He knew by heart the location of every eddy and every underwater hazard in the river at Aswan and how to avoid them in the nick of time, feinting and dodging

mere inches left or right with dazzling finesse. When the wind
lagged, he would tuck the boat behind some large boulders to
evade the press of the current, then dart out again at just the
right moment to catch a countervailing gust of wind that
would press us forward another fifteen feet. The whole operation looked about as easy as controlling an eighteen-wheeler
skidding down an icy hill. When I commented on his skill,
Amr only shrugged again and said that like most sailors in
Aswan he had been sailing since he was a small boy.

Watching Amr manage this passage so gracefully, it was
easy to picture the famed Shellalees, known also as the Cataract Arabs, the Egyptian sailors of years past whose sole occupation had been to navigate these rapids of the first cataract.
Because of the Shellalees, hundreds of large *dahabiehs* had
successfully surmounted the cataract in the nineteenth and
early twentieth centuries without mishap. Passing through the
cataract, Florence Nightingale had been struck with the acu-
men of these sailors, comparing their skill to that of the American Indian who by sheer inheritance of instinct could navigate
an uncharted forest with almost magical ease. "In America,"
Nightingale wrote, "the wild Indian tracks his way through a
trackless forest, by an instinct to us quite as miraculous as
clairvoyance, or anything we are pleased to call impossible;
and in Egypt the wild Nubian rides on the wave, and treads
upon the foam, quite as securely as the Indian in his forest."

In Nightingale's day some forty to fifty *dahabiehs* went up
the cataract each year during the tourist season—November to
March—but a hundred and fifty years later, there were few
travelers on this part of the river. That afternoon Amr and I appeared to be the only people heading upriver from Aswan. In
the span of an hour we saw no one until we came alongside the
steep flank of a mountainous camel-colored sand dune that
spilled down the cliffs of the west bank from the Libyan desert
and dipped its parched hem in a cove of the river. There, on the

powdery skirt of the dune, four Egyptian men sat huddled near the water's edge in the scant shade of a skinny acacia tree.

It was not merely the political climate and the threat of terrorism that kept tourists away from the cataract, but the fact that since 1902 the Aswan dam at the southern end of the cataract had completely blocked the passage of river craft. Now, a trip up the cataract could only be a few hours' excursion before, at the base of the dam, the boat would have to turn around and retrace its steps.

Sailing was Amr's profession. For a fee, he would take foreigners anywhere they wanted to go. Like most felucca captains in Luxor and Aswan, his specialty was three- or four-day trips down the river, camping on the boat at night. Most captains carried groups of six or eight people on these planned adventures, predominantly young northern Europeans and hardy Australians who seemed to take inordinate pleasure in traveling rough. Amr said he had not had one trip so far this winter. Diffidently he showed me his business brochure, a much-handled photocopy of a text detailing the various trips one could make, with a map of the river from Philae to Esna and a black-and-white photograph of himself. The brochure said:

WELCOME TO ASWAN!

Hello, my name is Amr Khaled and I am the captain of the Fantastic felucca. I have seventeen years experience in the felucca business. Anyone who has visited Aswan will tell you that a holiday here is not complete without a ride on our traditional sailing boats. I am not associated with any tour company, but offer an independent and personalized service to my customers. Whether you would like a few hours sailing around the islands of Aswan or a five-night journey to Luxor, the Fantastic felucca and my good self are at your disposal.

The cheery self-promotion and the mannered English of "my good self" didn't sound like Amr. I asked whether he had written it.

"I cannot write English," he said with a laugh. "A British friend wrote it for me."

I had a bottle of mineral water with me and offered him some. He declined it, saying, "I cannot drink that. It makes me sick."

I assured him that the water was pure, but he grimaced with mistrust, as if only a fool would drink bottled water. I asked him why.

"Minerals," he said. "I am not used to them." Presently he took a tin cup from beneath a thwart, dipped it into the river, and drank from it. I must have looked surprised, for he said quickly, "It is clean enough here to drink. And swim in. Even for foreigners."

Amr told me that when his parents were young, before the High Dam was built, the river water was extremely sandy because of its great volume and turbulence. When his parents scooped up a jug of water they had to wait half an hour for the sand to settle in it before they could drink. Flaubert, who marveled that the water of the Nile was very yellow because of the soil it carried with it, would probably have appreciated this detail and would most likely be disappointed to learn that now, since the construction of the High Dam, the sand and silt were gone.

I asked Amr what his parents had thought of the arrival of the High Dam. "They were happy," he said, "because the dam would mean they'd have more farmland."

The Aswan High Dam, built in 1964 just above the first dam, had radically changed the mood and pace of the Nile; it had brought the natural annual inundations to an end and had altered the style of Egyptian farming. Before the arrival of the dam, the Nile flooded once a year, allowing farmers only one opportunity to plant crops in the rich silt the receding river left behind. Though the onset of the Nile's flood always remained constant, occurring usually in mid-June, the size of the flood did not, and for millennia predicting the amount of water the flood would bring had been one of the most important preoccupations of Egyptian life. Too little water meant drought, famine, and death, yet too much could be equally devastating. Unable to control or predict the behavior of the river, Egyptians had been utterly at its mercy.

During the nineteenth century, with Muhammad Ali's campaign to modernize Egypt, the population began to grow for the first time in three thousand years, and at an astounding rate—in a mere hundred years it boomed from four million to ten million. It soon became obvious that Egypt would need a more efficient system of agriculture and a more constant and reliable supply of water to support its people. Many Egyptians were starving; the life expectancy in Egypt at that time was thirty-five. In 1960, financed by the Soviet Union, Abdel Nasser's revolutionary government began construction of the High Dam just above Aswan. On completion of the dam in 1970, the Nile flowing up the African continent backed up and spread into the red desert of Nubia, forming Lake Nasser, which now covers an area approximately eight miles wide and three hundred miles long and holds enough water to meet the needs of the Egyptian population for approximately three years.

With the flow of the river under human control, Egypt suffers no drought, as Nigeria, Sudan, and Libya do; Egyptian farmers have more cultivable land and are able to produce two or three crops a year instead of one; famine has been eradicated; electricity is cheap and widely available; and the once devastating Nile floods are controlled. But with these gains have also come heavy losses. One hundred and fifty thousand Nubian people who had lived for centuries in the desert of southern Egypt were displaced by the High Dam project; their villages—along with many important pharaonic structures—were submerged under the waters of the lake; and much of their ancient and unique culture was destroyed. With controlled flooding, the valuable silt once carried by the river to the floodplain of Egypt now sinks in the still waters of the lake and settles uselessly there. Deprived of the soil that essentially created a garden in one of the world's harshest deserts, Egyptian farmers are now forced to use toxic synthetic fertilizers, and though their crops are more frequent, the quality and yield of these crops have been reduced. In addition, the present constant irrigation of the soil has caused the underground water table to rise, oversaturating crops. And without the flushing action of the natural flood, the soil has grown increasingly salty, a threat to both crops and the ancient stone monuments.

Amr told me he remembered the rise of the river before the High Dam was completed; the water used to rise right up to the edge of his village. He pointed to a dark level line that ran across the smooth boulders four or five feet above the water. "That is how high the river comes now in summer when they open the dam," he said. Then he pointed to a scrawny shrub growing out of the side of a dune some fifteen feet above the dark line and said, "And that is where it used to rise before the High Dam."

If that was true, then many of the islands we were looking at would have been completely submerged when the river was in full flood.

As we entered a wider part of the river and prepared to turn around and go back to the city, Amr spotted a large dead fish floating on the surface of the water twenty feet upstream. "Rose," he said, "I will bring the boat near so you can catch the fish."

"Catch the fish?" I said, somewhat alarmed. "With *what?*"
"Hands."

Amr was such a serious person and so apparently confident and in command in his milieu that against my own inclinations I found it impossible not to go along with his strange wish. I leaned over the gunwale, and as the fish rounded the bow of the boat I made a grab for its tail. Hard and cold and so slippery it felt coated in olive oil, the fish simply slithered through my grasp. When I turned around to tell Amr that I had missed it, he was steering the boat with one hand and nimbly hauling the fish out of the water with the other. He held the glistening greenish log up for examination in the afternoon sunlight. Then, taking the fish in both hands, he put his nose into its open mouth and sniffed. He stared vacantly at the deck, his lips pursed in thought, then sniffed again. "Well, half and half," he said, looking at me as though I had asked him a question. "Still good to eat now, but already when we get home it will be bad." He frowned in disappointment and tossed the stiffening fish back into the river. "Look," he said. "Another one."

Sure enough, another large glittering fish floated belly-up past the stern of the boat. I asked what had killed the fish.

Amr swung the boat northward. "The white powder."

I looked at him. "What white powder, Amr?" I said.

"You know, the powder that is white. The fishermen put that powder in the water near High Dam to kill many fish together. Then they catch them with the net and sell in the market."

I tried not to look shocked. "This white powder," I said, thinking *strychnine, cyanide, arsenic*, "does it have a name?"

"I can't think what its name."

I had read somewhere that in Tanzania, on Lake Nyasa, crocodiles had been poisoned regularly with cyanide because they interfered with fishermen's nets. Tanzania wasn't so far away in the greater scheme of things. "Well, if it kills the fish, wouldn't it also kill the person who eats the fish?"

Amr shrugged. "No. No problem."

It was all I could do to keep myself from saying, *Fat chance you'd catch me eating these fish!*

Amr called out to a very old man rowing upriver in a skiff that there were dead fish here that he might want, but the old man couldn't hear him and rowed obliviously by, and Amr clicked his tongue at the thought of all that good poisoned fish going to waste.

As we neared Elephantine Island, I saw a woman in a small cove walking into the river in a full black gown and veil. Standing neck deep in water, she began splashing her face. I asked Amr what she was doing. "She is making a shower for washing herself," he said, as though this should be obvious.

I had seen plenty of men bathing in the Nile, some of them fully naked, but never a woman. When I told Amr this he said, "Lot of women wash like this, but they has to be very secret. They can't be doing free like a man. That why you don't see so much."

"How can she really wash herself when she's wearing all her clothes?"

Amr smiled wearily at my naïveté. "She can."

Amr brought my attention to a boat that had sunk the day before between Elephantine and Kitchener islands. The boat was nothing but a jacket-sized scrap of sail clinging to the top of a mast poking straight up out of the water. Like the tip of an iceberg in the middle of an ocean, there was something spooky about the sight — so much hidden mass lying still and silent and possibly sundered below it.

Amr seemed not just unsettled but bewildered by the sight. "This could not happen to Nubian captain," he said, shaking his head. "Egyptians in Aswan sometimes try to be felucca captain to get money, but they has not enough experiences and sometimes is not clever. They don't watching the wind." He waved his arm at the steep dunes on the west bank. "Wind can be changing and changing all the time. Sometime it can come"—he snapped his fingers—"very fast from the desert, and is full of sand and if you don't seeing it, it can put the boat over in three seconds."

At Elephantine

N EARLY A WEEK had passed, and still I had no boat of my own. The chances of finding one seemed to grow slimmer the more I searched. I had been to the street of the wooden boat makers on the edge of Aswan and watched the men there working. Their boats were beautiful and simple, made mostly of wood imported from Russia. They sold for a mere nine hundred Egyptian pounds: approximately three hundred U.S. dollars. But it would be two weeks before the boat makers had finished their next boat, and that one had been commissioned by someone else. I left there feeling deeply disheartened. This project had become a bit wearing. I was tired of having to hedge and pretend with every man in Aswan and frustrated that none but Amr seemed to take me seriously. Amr's tiny boat was rowable but impractical for the trip I had in mind. Finally I went to Elephantine Island to see Amr, and I told him what I hadn't told anyone here: I wanted to buy a rowboat and row it down the river.

Sitting cross-legged on the dock in front of the Oberoi Hotel, Amr listened with one round fist pressed gently to his lips. He was, I had already determined, an admirably discreet person. He kept his own counsel. He was polite, straightforward, reserved, and disliked small talk. I never saw him engage in the juvenile jocularities Aswan's felucca captains were always tossing back and forth among themselves and their foreign customers. His intelligent face was peaceful and difficult to read. He was imperturbable. When I said, "I want to row down the river alone," it was not Amr's face that betrayed his apprehension but his muddy eyes. He blinked several times, rapidly, as if a sudden sliver of hot wind had lodged beneath both eyelids, then his eyes fixed on mine for a long moment as his thoughts gathered.

Slowly he stood, and, glancing furtively at the other felucca captains sitting not far from us, he said gravely, "Rose, please come in my house for tea."

I followed Amr up a dirt path behind the Oberoi Hotel; I had been on the path before and knew that it led to Elephantine's three Nubian villages. We walked for five minutes without talking. Amr's body was dense and muscular, yet he moved with economy and grace, his short arms gently swinging in a manner reminiscent of a sumo wrestler. I could not imagine what he was thinking, couldn't imagine what he would say or do when we got to his house. Tea he had said. Was he angry? Would he chastise me for even proposing my harebrained idea? I had no fear that he would harm me in any way, or even speak harshly to me, but I wondered if I had somehow insulted his Nubian sensibility.

Elephantine Island was thick with date palms and gnarled sycamores, and the mango groves were dark and spooky. All

around us doves cooed and roosters crowed and sparrows and
finches clicked and buzzed, eerily re-creating the sounds of a
video arcade. Goats locked horns in the woods. Mud-brick
walls divided the island into little fiefdoms, and narrow canals
irrigated the small green fields. There were no cars on the island, and the footpaths were narrow as horse stalls. The Elephantine houses had an almost European feel, like Tuscan
cottages painted in vibrant colors—ochre and cadmium yellow and olive green, the colors of Van Gogh's palette. Through
open doorways the houses looked dark inside, and cool. I heard
laughter and voices coming from a few houses, but for the most
part the villages were remarkably quiet. Here was an abun-
dance of what I later came to think of as the second-story syn-
drome, a phenomenon ubiquitous in Egypt: fully inhabited
houses with the uncompleted skeleton of a second floor clapped
onto the roof. These second floors were always hastily constructed brick walls with rusted rebar bristling out of them
like unkempt hair. A second floor was a sign of status; everyone had to have one.

There were many small outbuildings for animals here and a
network of low mud walls to corral them. Elderly women sat
on stoops in black gowns and veils. I never heard shouting
here, and in the time I was here no one had ever said hello to
me or asked me where I was going or tried to sell me anything
or pleaded with me to hire them or beseeched me to give them
a pound or a pen. Everyone looked sleepy in the midday heat;
everything moved slowly. We came upon an old woman in a
black veil and gown sitting peacefully at the edge of the footpath on a pile of dirt. A fly scribbled at her ebony cheek. She
looked at us as we went by, said nothing, looked down at her
hands in boredom. Another woman came toward us carrying
a small electric washing machine on her head. Only her eyes
were visible behind a black veil. She walked with gliding
ease, straight-backed as a caryatid. When a goat approached
her, she drew a stone from the pocket of her gown and threw it

at him. The goat reared up and clicked his heels, and the granite-spined woman glided on. A pride of kittens caked in mud came skittering out from behind a wall, crossed our path, and disappeared. Like most of the cats in Egypt, they looked as though they had slid down a dirty chimney and hadn't eaten in months.

As we walked on I noticed bloody dripping handprints on the doors and fronts of shops and houses. I had seen this same thing elsewhere in Egypt—it always looked like the remnant of some horrible massacre. It called to mind Mansonesque symbols of evil and destruction. Not knowing what was going through Amr's mind, what mood he was in, I had been hesitant to speak. While it seemed it would be nearly impossible to say anything truly inappropriate to the other felucca captains in Aswan, with Amr I constantly feared being indelicate. But my curiosity about the handprints overwhelmed my apprehension. I had to ask him about them.

"It is *khamsa*," he said. "For eyes."

Trailing behind him with my head down, I tried to make sense of that. *Khamsa* was the Arabic word for "five." Five fingers, I supposed. "But what does it mean?"

Amr glanced over his shoulder at me. "Mean it keeps away the other people's jealous. When they build maybe new house, they take the goat blood and put the hand on the house. For keep away evil eyes."

I knew it was an Egyptian belief that other people's envy could bring a person down. Admiring another person's infant was considered bad manners, for it represented a threat and a bad omen, and some Egyptians deliberately left their children dirty in order to ward off the evil eye. The belief must have been strong here, for every other structure on Elephantine Island seemed to be branded with a bloody handprint.

Amr's house was big and painted a pleasing ochre yellow. We went through the door into a small dark room where an elderly woman lay on a couch, her face turned toward a tiny black-and-white television. On the television, throngs of pilgrims dressed in white were circling the mastaba at Mecca, a scene that appeared with surprising frequency on Egyptian television. The woman glanced up vaguely as we came in, gave us no greeting, and went back to staring at the television. She had the sagging reddish eyes of a hound, and one long front tooth that jutted between her lips like a little ivory latchkey. Amr muttered something to her. She moaned in response, feebly lifted her hand into the air and dropped it again onto her thigh. Frailty and sadness seemed to be holding the woman captive, and it made me uneasy to be standing there looking at her this way. It was as though we had walked in on her lying naked in a bathtub, though she was fully clothed in the way only a Muslim woman can be *fully* clothed—in wraps so thorough she looked mummified.

As he led me out of the room and through the kitchen, Amr said, "That my mother." At the door of another room he said shyly, "And this my sister," pointing his thumb at a young woman who was sitting on a bed watching Egyptian cartoons on another small television. Introducing his family, Amr seemed, for the first time, uncertain and slightly apologetic.

Like the mother, the sister was dressed in a long black gown. She was fat and pretty, with a round shining humorous face, a short neck, very white teeth, and an inquisitive smile. When I stepped into the room to shake her hand, she giggled and covered her mouth with her plump fingers. I could hardly blame her. Sunburned, greasy with sweat, wearing dirty trousers, dusty boots, and a brimmed hat, I must have looked absurd to her.

Amr led me up some cement stairs to the second floor and into a small room.

"This my bedroom," he said, motioning for me to sit down on the only chair, while he sat on the bed. Amr's bedroom seemed like a very intimate place for me to be sitting alone with him, and I couldn't help wondering what his mother and sister might be thinking below. If I were an Egyptian woman, I would certainly not have been sitting here. What did it say to them that I was? Amr had spent years dealing with foreigners. It was his job, and certainly his family had grown accustomed to visitors like me. Still, it intrigued me that what would never be acceptable for an Egyptian woman was wholly acceptable for me.

The room was small and its walls were crowded with photographs that had been clipped from magazines and calendars, mostly pictures of the main tourist sites in Egypt—temples and pyramids and tombs. Over the door hung several framed passages from the Koran written in elegant Arabic lettering, a feature as ubiquitous in Egyptian homes as pictures of the Sacred Heart were in Irish ones. There were several photographs of Amr posing with foreign visitors, and a large poster of what looked like Vermont in autumn. Amr's possessions were few: two gallabiyas hanging on hooks on the wall, a small red television, a copy of the Koran with a bookmark in its middle, and a mirror. Beneath the bed I could see an enormous metal cooking pot and a latched wooden trunk. Draped over the bed was a blue and white hand-sewn canopy. Like his boat, Amr's bedroom betrayed a deep fastidiousness.

Amr went to the door and shouted something down the stairs, then came back into the room and said, "My mother will make tea."

I thought, She *will?* She didn't look as though she could stand up. As if reading my mind Amr explained that his mother, who was sixty-five, had had rheumatoid arthritis for twenty years, that she took several pills every day for the pain, and that she never went out of the house.

"She should do more," he said. "Maybe the garden. Something to make her feel better. But only she lie down and do nothing. She don't go out. She just looking at the TV."

I asked about his father. He looked at his hands. "My father been died for eight years."

Amr had been in northern Egypt at the time, in the army, and one day a telephone call came that his father was dead. I asked him what his father died of. He said, "I don't know why he died." The father was only sixty years old. Amr returned home for the funeral, and when he and his brothers cleaned out his father's room they found more than five hundred empty liquor bottles there. "He drink too much. Maybe that why he die. Egyptian liquor is very bad."

Looking out the window at the burning sky, Amr said his father was a nice man who had at one time in his life been very rich. He had owned six feluccas and this big house. He had worked for a hotel for many years and then suddenly had lost his job. After that he began drinking and that was the end of him.

"He never hit me, how some father do. When I am little boy, if I am sad, my father feel sad too."

Amr said that his mother, on the other hand, was "too strange." If you were sitting in the house with her and you put an ashtray down on the left side of you, she would tell you to put it on your right side instead, and if you didn't put it where she wanted it, she would become very angry. Amr spoke about his mother in a rueful, resigned way, but not without affection.

Amr sneezed, wiped his nose with a Kleenex, and said, "Half of village has a cold because the weather. The wind by coming from in east. It was cool before. Now today is very hot. That why everyone sick."

I had heard this belief before—in hot climates the shifting direction of the wind was responsible for general ill health. It always sounded like pure superstition to me.

Amr's eyes had grown watery and red. He dabbed gingerly at them with the Kleenex. It struck me that he was wearing a dress and I was wearing trousers and a man's hat.

"Half of village," Amr said, then threw the Kleenex out the open window. His easy littering surprised me, and then I was amused at my own surprise. Amr's world and its concerns were very different from mine. Pollution, conservation, an aesthetically pleasing environment, these were hardly issues foremost in the consciousness of a people preoccupied with merely surviving. I remembered that years ago in China, I had once asked a man why Chinese people never had cut flowers in their houses. The man said, "They have no time to think about these trivial things. They are busy just trying to get their next meal." Poisoning fish seemed to me to be a case in point—it wasn't sporting, and it was environmentally objectionable. Yet when one is starving, who cares about sportingness or long-term consequences?

I crossed my legs and folded my hands in my lap and looked around the room, nervously waiting for Amr to raise the subject of my rowing proposal, but he said nothing. He simply stared out the window. The window overlooked the village footpath below and an enormous tangled sycamore that Amr said was nearly two hundred years old. Beneath the tree a pair of glossy baby goats pranced and skittered. I could see women in black sitting on a nearby stoop and two young women stepping out of a dark doorway and into the street with large cans of water on their heads. They walked slowly in a swaying, wide-hipped way, their long skirts trailing dramatically behind them like the costumes on a Greek chorus. The village, pretty as it was, was smattered with trash.

For want of anything else to say I said, "You're lucky to live here, Amr."

Amr gave me a tepid smile and said nothing. He was an admirably still person, untroubled by social silences. He had none of the forced and calculated friendliness of his peers. Beside him I felt like an anxious, chattering jack-in-the-box. The silence stretched. After a while I said, "You don't think you're lucky?"

He wagged his head noncommittally and said with resignation, "I have lived here all my life." He told me he was building a house on the other side of the river, at the top of the hill above the Cataract Hotel. "My new house will be better 'n this," he said, "because there you could see everything and feel free."

Though Elephantine Island was perhaps my favorite place in Egypt, I understood what Amr meant. I had spent several days combing every inch of this island for a boat, and despite its beauty and tranquillity, the place did also have a hermetic, claustrophobic feel. It was one of the oldest continually habitated spots in Egypt and one of the least changed by the passage of time, which lent it an exhausted, haunted air. On the high barren hill of the southern tip of the island lay an amazing jumble of the architectural remains of various settlements — predynastic, dynastic, Jewish, Greek, Roman, Christian, and Fatimid — all the eras tossed in together in ruins, one built upon the other, many uncovered from beneath forty feet of soil that over the years had been shoveled onto the island by the flooding river. In this one small place there were the ruins of Abu, which had been settled by ancient Egyptians; the old-kingdom Temple of Khnum; a Greco-Roman necropolis; a gateway from the time of Alexander the Great; and Queen Hatshepsut's ruined Temple of Satet. The ground there was positively littered with ancient potsherds and human bones, like a dusty museum of history set up under the open sky. I had stepped on a human jawbone there, found pieces of ancient turquoise faience and gorgeous fragments of hand-painted pharaonic pots, and had been startled by the sight of a mummy's linen-wrapped skull and shoulders poking out from the side of a mound of dirt. Florence Nightingale had been horrified by this particular spot, calling it "one mountain of broken pottery, fragments of red granite, sand, and mounds . . . Such a world as might have been turned out of the Caldron of *Macbeth*'s Weird Sisters," a description still dead-accurate a hundred and fifty years later.

Yet accurate too were the observations of Amelia Edwards

and Edmé-François Jomard, a member of Napoleon's 1798 expedition, both of whom had ventured beyond the southern tip of the island and had been as delighted as I by its gentle beauty. The northwest shore, studded with palm trees, green fields, and sandy coves, was idyllic enough that Amelia Edwards claimed she half expected to meet Robinson Crusoe there, "with his goat-skin umbrella, or man Friday bending under a load of faggots." Jomard had written, "The verdure and freshness of this region contrast so agreeably with the arid land that it has been named the blooming island and 'the tropical garden.'"

Nevertheless, Elephantine was Amr's home. He had lived there all his life and was acquainted in one way or another with most of the island's six thousand inhabitants. Though to me the three small villages on the island felt essentially like one, to Amr they were as distinct and discrete as if they lay miles apart.

Looking at the street below, Amr said that every inch of earth under these houses held rare antiquities from the pharaonic periods. The deeper you dug, the older the find. Though it was illegal, some local men made good money selling these antiquities.

Amr's sister's round face suddenly appeared in the doorway. She was carrying a tray with tea glasses on it, and as she came into the room I saw that she walked with a marked limp. Her right foot was twisted at an unnatural angle, which gave her gait the awkward, jerking rhythm of a seal laboring back to the sea across a sandy beach. She was short but heavy; her large rear end and big thighs filled her billowing black gown. The rubber flip-flops on her feet were twisted and crushed with overuse. When I thanked her for the tea, she cocked her head at me in curiosity, visibly fascinated by the sound of my words. She had the big round eyes of a startled infant.

"She don't speak English good," Amr said. "Her name is Hoda."

Hearing her name Hoda smiled appreciatively, self-consciously. Her head was bare, her black hair pulled into a small bun at the back of her head. Like most Nubian women she wore dangling gold earrings. I asked her how old she was. She thought a long time, translating, her eyes vacantly darting in thought, then gamely she said, "Twenty-two."

I thanked her again for the tea. Comprehending, she *tsk*ed loudly, almost defiantly in response, and rolled her eyes at me in a way that meant, *It's nothing!* She limped out of the room, glancing over her shoulder at me with a triumphal grin.

As soon as Hoda was gone, Amr said, "My sister she got problem with foot. Since she a baby." He explained that over the years he and his three brothers had paid for three separate operations to try to correct the twisted foot, but each one had been a failure and the foot was no better now than it had been before.

When I asked him if his sister worked, he said, "She takes care of the house and cooking and cleaning and washing. Because my mother too sick." I asked if he had any other sisters; he had had one other who, like his father, had died when he was in the army. She was cooking something at the stove, and her dress caught on fire, and the fire spread throughout the kitchen and she died. She was twelve years old at the time of her death.

Amr showed no emotion discussing these events in his family history, and when I ventured that they were sad, he shrugged in his unquestioning way, a shrug that meant that although they were indeed sad, one should not dwell on things one could do nothing about.

We sipped at our tea. The tea glasses had once been jam jars, and the saucers beneath them had been lifted from an Aswan hotel.

Amr mopped his brow with the back of his hand. "This room always too hot in summer," he said softly, tapping his fingertips against the side of his tea glass, "and too cold in winter." His fingernails were a delicate seashell pink. The glass looked tiny in his big hands.

We sat silently then. I had run out of polite things to say and was distracted by the business I wanted to discuss. As if reading my mind, Amr said, "Rose, the boat."

"Yes," I said. "Do you think it's a bad idea?"

"No, Rose," he said. "It is good idea. You likes do something different from usual. I also likes do something different. And I know you can do it. I see you row. And other felucca captains see you row. They say, 'She looks like captain.'"

"Do they think I shouldn't row a boat?"

"No. They happy. It's something new. They cannot understand it why you know how to do this."

I told him that in America it wasn't strange for a woman to row a boat. I told him that I didn't plan to go very far down the river. Just from here to Qena, enough to feel that I had traveled, enough to see the river up close.

"I know why you likes go alone. But, Rose, there is problems. You hast get past police." At the bottom of every city along the river, he explained, there were police who monitored river traffic, both coming and going. No boat would be allowed to leave Aswan without permission. "They will not let you go."

"I'll leave at night," I said. "It's a small boat. They'll never see me."

Amr nodded indulgently at me. "But maybe other problem. Maybe you can tip over in the river. Maybe a fisherman can find you and get crazy if he see a foreign woman alone. I would worry all the time."

Amr did look genuinely worried at that moment, his placid face flexed in strain. *Maybe you can tip over in the river* was a sentence I had heard a dozen times now, and every time I heard it, it vexed me and made me impatient. Tipping over in a rowboat was not something that ever happened spontaneously or even easily. It took effort to tip a rowboat. Of course, the crazy-fisherman scenario that everyone was so fond of was always a possibility. There was no denying that. It was a possibility anywhere in the world for a woman alone. Yet it seemed to me it would have to be an awfully reckless Egyptian man who would dare attack a foreign woman, for if he was caught the consequences would be grave.

I knew that I would never persuade Amr to accept my line of thinking. I asked him if he thought I should ask permission from the police. "Better maybe not to ask," he said. "Our police are money police. And it will take a long time to get permission. And they will only give permission if someone man go with you. What man they send you don't know good or bad."

We sat there for a long time, thinking and staring at our tea. My skin was damp with sweat. Finally Amr wagged his head and offered to let me take his rowboat down the river. "And I can follow behind you in the felucca. For safeness."

I thanked Amr for his generous offer and pointed out that as much as I liked his little boat, it wasn't big enough to sleep in.

"You can sleep on my boat at night."

I liked Amr and trusted him as well as one could trust a person she's known for a week, and I knew he understood why I wanted to make this trip. I knew that he didn't think I was silly or strange. But I didn't want to take him with me. I didn't want protection. I didn't want a nanny. I wanted to go alone. One point of my trip was to make it without anyone guarding me. But I knew that I had come to an impasse. If I was going to leave Aswan in a rowboat, I would probably have to do it Amr's way.

I looked out the window at the ancient tree and tried to feel fortunate that of all the men I had met in Egypt, this pleasant, reserved, capable, and diffident man was the one I would most like to have trailing after me. I decided I had no choice but to take a positive approach, to take what I could get. "OK," I said, "come with me. We'll go as far as Edfu."

In his quiet fashion Amr was exultant. I saw it in the way he raised his hands and clasped them, as if in prayer, and in his gentle eyes. He had had no overnight trips so far that season and was restless to get out of Aswan. But for me it was a small defeat, and I was already planning that when we got to Edfu, I would finally find my own boat and make the rest of the trip alone.

Amr looked suddenly worried again. He explained that he would not be allowed to leave Aswan with me alone. By law, no commercial felucca was allowed to travel below the Aswan police station without at least three foreigners on board. Photocopies of passports needed to be handed over. Regulations needed to be met.

I looked at him, then stared out the window at the tired, dusty village without really seeing anything. I was utterly deflated. A trip to Edfu would take three or four days; I'd be making it with Amr and a couple of foreign strangers? It didn't seem worth it. In fact, the whole prospect seemed awful. I was about to decline Amr's offer when he told me that it might be possible to get past the Aswan police with only one other passenger on board, for he was in possession of a photocopy of an English friend's passport, which he could use as representation of the third person.

I frowned at him. "But won't they look for the third person in the boat?"

"Sometimes they don't count."

Now it seemed like Amr's turn to be overoptimistic. "But what if this time they *do* count?" I said.

He smiled and said in a quoting way, "We will cross that bridge when we come to it."

His sudden insouciance was encouraging. I had a good friend who lived in Cairo, an adventuresome American woman who just might fill in as the second passenger if I begged her to. Inspired by his eagerness, I told Amr that I would call my friend and see if she would join us. What choice did I have?

When I left Amr's house, Hoda was still sitting on the bed in her room watching cartoons, and his mother was still lying on the couch, still staring at her television, which now showed a bearded imam in an impressive white turban speaking fiercely into a microphone. In Arabic I thanked the mother for the tea. She turned her sallow face slightly toward me and muttered something unintelligible in response. On the wall above her were two oil paintings of feluccas on the Nile, one with the pyramids in the background. The paintings were dated 1964. I asked Amr who had painted them.

"My uncle," he said.

When I said, "Did your uncle go to the pyramids?" he laughed loudly, as though I had asked whether his uncle had been to the moon. "No," he said, "he never go out of Aswan. He only use the imagination."

I asked whether he had ever been to the pyramids.

"No. I never."

"Have you been to Karnak?"

"I been to Luxor. But I never saw the temple in Karnak."

That was unbelievable. Seeing the look on my face Amr shrugged. "Rose, we don't have a mind for this kind of thing. The pharaoh and the ancient temple. We don't have a mind for it. It not so important to us."

Hoda and the Women

THE FOLLOWING AFTERNOON I returned to Amr's house to tell him that my friend Madeleine had agreed to fill in as the third passenger on his boat, and when I arrived at the house I found Hoda dragging a burlap sack out the front door. She was dressed in a worn old housedress and had a flowered rag wrapped around her head in a style that called Aunt Jemima to mind; the rough knot that held the rag in place sent two rabbit ears of cloth sprouting into the air above her forehead. When Hoda saw me, her fat face ignited with interest. *"Ya saalam!"* she cried, which, though it literally meant "Oh, peace," was figuratively the Arabic equivalent of "Holy smoke!"

Hoda dropped the sack on the front stoop, spanked her hands clean, and limped eagerly toward me, her right hand raised to shake mine. I asked her where she was going with the burlap sack. She pointed to a little shed at the side of the house. I pushed the door of the shed open and found three goats, two chickens, and four pigeons staring up at me. Frightened, the chickens mewled like kittens. Hoda had been on her way to feed the animals, but now that I was here she happily canceled the task with a dismissive flap of her hand and waved me into the house.

Inside, the house was warm and dark but for the golden bar of late afternoon sunlight that fell through the front door. The front room was empty, and from the kitchen came the smell of fried fish. Seeing my surprise that her mother was not in the living room, Hoda indicated that she was upstairs sleeping. At Hoda's invitation I sat in the mother's place on the couch. The couch was hard as a church pew and so high that my feet didn't touch the floor.

When I asked if Amr was at home, Hoda put her face close to mine and cocked her head in that keen and slightly canine way, listening to my words. Her eyes were dark and luminous; her big body blocked the light streaming through the doorway; she blinked at me. No, Amr was not here but, God willing, he would be here soon. I should wait. And in the meantime did I want tea?

The Egyptian mania for tea is matched only by the Irish mania for it, and if you refused an offer of tea, the Egyptian host would react with disappointment and disbelief. I did not want tea, but in order to be polite I said that I did.

Hoda knocked the front door nearly shut, blocking out the light. She switched on a fluorescent overhead lamp and limped off into the kitchen.

By the sickly milk-white light, I saw that there was another couch opposite me and a large glassed-in bookshelf to my right. The bookshelf held an array of dusty trinkets—a pink plush Easter bunny, Frosty the Snowman in a black top hat, a vase of dust-encrusted plastic roses, some framed photographs, lace doilies—the sort of things that seem clever and significant when new but then quickly fade into useless clutter. The room was painted a pale mint green. Its only window was tightly shuttered on this hot day, and a metal wind chime hung listlessly in front of it. An indolent ceiling fan pushed the warm air and smell of fried fish around the room. Ajar, the front door inched back and forth in the evening breeze, creaking as it moved.

Through the kitchen door I could see Hoda waddling heavily in and out of view with cups and pots in her hands. Eventually she came back into the room, set a banana and a glass of steaming tea on the low table in front of me, put her hands on her hips, and with stern authority directed me to eat and drink.

Though she was twenty-two and endowed with a prodigious bosom, Hoda looked like a sixteen-year-old. She had an adolescent's air of both innocence and boldness. I could see that she was delighted to have me here alone. Despite her nearly nonexistent English, she was an excellent communicator, speaking with her hands and her expressive face. Without a trace of shyness she sat close to me on the couch and asked was I married, did I have children, where was I from, how much money did I make. She questioned my shoes, my earrings, my watch. Between her thumb and forefinger, she assessed the material of my blouse. She approved of the cotton scarf around my neck. With no self-consciousness whatever, she leaned closer and examined my face in the slow, frowning manner of an art critic appraising a mediocre oil painting in a gallery. How old was I anyway? When I told her I was thirty-eight she told me I was not. Thirty-eight? Not possible, for I was not fat enough to be that old. I showed her the gray hair behind my ears. Triumphantly, instructively, she showed me hers. Gray hair proved nothing.

I asked Hoda if she was married. She grimaced and flapped her hands at me. She was not married nor did she care to be. Marriage was nothing but a burden and a greased chute to nowhere. A woman was better off alone. Why was I not drinking my tea? And what about the banana?

As I reached obediently for the banana, the front door swung open with a bang, and three substantial young women clutching patent-leather purses burst into the house in a chattering rush. They stopped in their tracks at the sight of me, their mouths hanging open in astonishment. They were elegantly dressed in gauzy black gowns and colorful flowing veils that tightly framed their dark faces, fitted close around their necks, and trailed over their shoulders and down their backs. They were fat-fingered, wore golden rings on every finger, and their mouths were glossed with a lot of rich red lipstick. They were on their way across the river to Aswan for an evening's excursion and had stopped in to say hello to Hoda.

With visible pride at the presence of a foreigner in her home, Hoda slung her heavy arm around my shoulders, introduced me to the women, and invited them all to sit down. They flopped heavily onto the couches and blinked expectantly at me, hands on their knees. Their fingernails had been recently painted. One of them could speak a little English, and through her the other two asked me the same questions Hoda had just asked, and, like Hoda, they insisted that I was too thin to be thirty-eight. When I admired their colorful veils, they were delighted and flattered and eagerly informed me that a dear friend of theirs had brought them all the way from Saudi Arabia. They asked whether we had veils like this in America and whether New York was very nice, for they had seen many pictures of New York on the television and, oh, the wide streets and the impossibly tall buildings! Praise God! Too tall. And yellow cars too. Ho-ho! A gift for the eyes! They all wanted to see New York one day. It was their greatest dream.

I asked whether they had been to Cairo.

No!

Had they been to Luxor?

No!

What about the impossibly beautiful botanical garden of Kitchener Island right here next door to Elephantine?

No!

Had they ever swum in the river?

No! They did not know how to swim.

That struck me as very sad. When I asked them where exactly they were going now in their finery, they said, "To the Aswan Moon," then howled with inexplicable laughter and covered their mouths with their hands.

The Aswan Moon was a pleasant riverfront café on the east bank in Aswan. I said innocently, "That's nice," and they hooted louder and raised their eyebrows and smirked knowingly at each other in a scandalized way and said but *of course* they were not going to the Aswan Moon. *Never!*

The women were not married, but one of them, Wafaa, who was sitting between Hoda and me, was to be married within the month, and each time she mentioned it (she mentioned it often) the others snickered with salacious delight and reminded each other that within twelve months Wafaa would have, God willing, a darling baby. Preferably a boy.

Hoda opined that while Wafaa was quite pretty, her fiancé was, regrettably, not handsome.

Wafaa slapped Hoda's fat upper arm in injured protest; her fiancé was *very* handsome and she loved him *dearly.*

Hoda straightened her slovenly head rag and smoothed her soiled housedress across her big thighs and giggled at her lap. I could see that Hoda, the only one of the young women not primped and groomed, had become self-conscious; she examined the others' outfits with a touching mix of envy, criticism, sadness, and awe. She looked absorbed, a little wounded, and wary. When I asked Hoda if she would accompany the other girls to Aswan that evening she made a sour face to indicate that such a pursuit was boring and beneath her.

Mouna, twenty-four, and Samira, twenty-one, both hoped to be married soon. Mouna announced that for her own part, she was smitten with Amr and could see herself quite happily married to him. Samira, a histrionic, rough-voiced woman with a mannish face and a raucous laugh, pressed her hand to her heart to show that she too was taken with Amr and was certain that they had a future together.

When I pointed out that the two could not both marry Amr at the same time, they screamed with laughter, fell back in their seats, grasped each other's forearms as if steadying themselves on the deck of a tossing ocean liner, and indicated in vigorous pantomime what a thoroughgoing card I was.

Then the front door slapped open again, and two more young women dressed to the chins burst into the room. They all greeted each other in a flurry of kisses, exclamations, and entreaties to God. The newcomers, too, collapsed dramatically onto the couches. Hoda switched on a radio, and the chanting, wailing sounds of Nubian music filled the room. She offered us cookies, which at first the women politely declined, but when Hoda presented the cookies a requisite second time, they all took two or three apiece and devoured them, laughing and chewing, the crumbs tumbling down their pretty veils and into their laps.

We sat that way for fifteen minutes, giggling, speculating about boys and fashions and Amr to the beat of bongo drums, while other dolled-up young women in flowing robes passed by on the dirt footpath in front of the house, pausing just long enough to fling their waves and hellos through the open door. The sun had just set, the call to prayer had begun, and the village seemed to be coming to life.

Through the door I could see the sky glowing blood red, and in their evening frenzy swifts and bats had begun to fill it. Songbirds thrummed in the palms across the way.

Wafaa, who was newly up on the Islamic rules of marriage, reminded us all that Amr *could* technically marry both Samira and Mouna if he first properly divorced one of them. Affronted, Samira declared that she would prove such an ideal wife that Amr would never have any reason or desire to divorce her. Decisively, dismissively, Hoda announced that she wanted someone very pretty for Amr and that Basma, for example, a girl who moments ago had passed by the front door in a pink head scarf, was not—no, certainly not—pretty enough.

The women's voices were excited and so loud they drowned out the Nubian music. The room was hot, the ceiling fan struggled overhead, the women tamped their perspiring brows with hankies, and suddenly, Amr himself stepped through the door. At the sight of him all the women struggled to their feet and fled to the street in a frantic rush, as if in response to an urgent alarm. Over their shoulders they flung hasty good-byes at Hoda and were gone, veils fluttering behind them.

Hoda immediately switched off the tape player, and without saying a word she quickly retreated to the kitchen to finish her cooking.

The hilarity had ended so abruptly and unexpectedly that even I jumped to my feet with the vague feeling of having been caught at something unseemly.

Alone in the middle of the empty room, Amr looked bemused. He carefully closed the front door and greeted me in his formal way, with a handshake and questions about my health, and he invited me to stay for dinner. Though I hadn't come for dinner and wasn't hungry, I felt it would be rude to decline his offer.

Amr said, "First, I must pray, then we eat. Please sit here a few minutes."

I sat again on the couch and watched through the kitchen door as Amr prepared for prayer by washing his face, neck, hands, and feet at the kitchen sink. He washed with the fastidiousness of a preoperative surgeon. Then he went into the

far bedroom, still within my line of vision, and without clos-
ing the door he faced the eastern wall and raised his hands
to either side of his face, thumbs touching his earlobes, and
began the elaborate physical ritual of Muslim prayer. He lowered his hands briefly to his waist, right hand holding the
left, then put them on his knees and stared at the floor. It
seemed to make no difference to him that Hoda was clanking
pots and dishes in the kitchen or that I could see him clearly
as he knelt down and pressed his forehead to the carpet, a
posture that struck me as so intimate and personal that I had
to look away.

When his prayers were finished, Amr called me into the
kitchen and urged me to sit at a very small table that Hoda had
laid with Nubian dishes—roast pigeon, fried fishes the size of
minnows, a savory dish of brown rice and soft bread, maca-
roni with gravy, potatoes, stewed tomatoes, a salad of minced
vegetables, and goat cheese. In the Nubian tradition we began
the meal with sweet dates soaked in water, and as we ate the
delicious dates I realized that for a tablecloth Hoda had used
several broadsheets pulled from an Arabic newspaper. In one
corner of the table was a small feature written partially in English. It contained some complicated physics problems. To the
right of my plate I read: *Problem: A gardener works on the
grass with a rake. If the angle between the arm of the rake and
the plane of the surface is 60 degrees, and the gardener exerts
a force of 10 N, find the work done when he moves through a
distance of 2 m.*

In the Nubian custom we had no napkins and nothing but
soupspoons for utensils. Amr ate most of his food with his
hands, scooping at the various dishes with a flat piece of wheat
bread. Hoda was in her room watching an Egyptian soap opera,
and when it became clear that she wouldn't be joining us at the
table, I asked Amr why.

"She will eat after us," he said. I knew it was not uncommon

for Egyptians to invite a guest to dinner and then seat the
guest alone at the dinner table while they sat separately in another room, a form of etiquette that felt exceedingly uncomfortable to me. Hoda had prepared the food; I felt rude eating it
without her. I wanted to ask Amr where his mother was but
sensed that the mother was a subject better left undiscussed.

I explained to Amr that I had come to tell him that my
friend Madeleine in Cairo had agreed to join us in order to
make our trip to Edfu possible. She would arrive by train the
day after next. Amr looked delighted and raised his water
glass at me in a toast. "So we can celebrate," he said.

We clinked our glasses and decided that we would leave Aswan in three days. Amr would make all the arrangements and
purchase all the necessary supplies. He would provide sleeping bags and pillows and everything else we would need for
our trip. I would pay him what seemed to me a less than nomi-
nal fee. All three of us would leave Aswan together, towing the
rowboat behind us, and once we passed the Aswan river police, I could take the rowboat off on my own. Amr told me I
wouldn't be sorry that I had agreed to take my trip this way.

We ate silently then for a few minutes, with the sound of
Hoda's television drifting into the room. I tasted one of the little fried fish and was disturbed to find that it had a slightly
chemical flavor, not unlike chloroform. Reminded unpleasantly of the mysterious powder that the Aswan fishermen were
in the habit of using to murder the local fish, I shoved the rest
of the minnow under my stewed tomatoes.

"The food is very good," I said, because except for the little
fish the food was indeed delicious.

Amr nodded. "Hoda is good at the kitchen."

The kitchen was a small windowless space at the bottom
of the main staircase. The staircase had been painted the
bright silver of an iron steam radiator. The walls were pale
green. Lit by a long fluorescent bulb on one wall, the room

had the impersonal, utilitarian feel of a rural bus depot. It held a refrigerator, a small sink, a mirror, and a Nubian water cooler—an unbaked clay vase with a conical bottom that was suspended in a wire holder; water seeped through the pores of the vase and through the process of evaporation the water within was kept cool. I saw no counter and no stove in this kitchen. When I asked where exactly Hoda had done the cooking, Amr pointed to a room the size of a coat closet at the back of the kitchen. In it were a gas stove and a small second sink. The doorway to this closet was so narrow that I wondered how Hoda fit her considerable hips through it.

Hoping to make cheerful conversation I said, "It's interesting how those girls who were here earlier all say they love you and want to marry you."

Amr's spoon, piled high with stewed tomatoes, stopped still in the air beneath his chin. He blinked at me, mute with surprise. "Who said it?"

"All those girls who were here earlier," I said. "Hoda's friends who ran off when you came in. They all said they wanted to marry you."

Amr put down his spoon. I saw instantly that he was annoyed by the very thought of these village girls. "They love me?" he said. "Why they don't talk to me, if they love me? Why they run away when I am here? Rose, it is only foolish talk. The women in our village have many faces. They play lot of games. When they see me in the street, they cover their face and don't looking at me when I go by. If they like me, why they don't say, 'Hello, Amr' when I am here? Why they run away like little children?" He imitated their laughter by slitting his eyes coyly and covering the lower half of his face with the wide sleeve of his gallabiya. He dropped his hands to his lap and snorted derisively. "I *hate* this way!"

My offhand mention of Hoda's friends had struck a nerve and provoked an unprecedented flood of words and emotions from Amr. He told me the village girls were stupid and sly and caused a great deal of trouble. They talked behind one's back and said things that weren't true. They cared only about their looks and their clothes and their jewelry. They were untrustworthy, dishonest, shallow. They called him on the telephone, and as soon as he picked up the receiver and said hello, they hung up. "Ten times a day they do this!" Their tricks and schemes made him incredibly nervous, and he could become so distressed by their games that he couldn't think. Even his sister talked too much and told other people his business, though he tried to teach her not to. These were the reasons he didn't like living in the village and was eager to finish building his house across the river so that he could move away. "Sometimes if I am too unhappy here I go and sleep in the new house to get peace."

I asked him why the young women had laughed so much at the mention of the Aswan Moon restaurant.

"They laugh?"

"They told me they were going to the Aswan Moon and laughed about it."

Amr shook his head in disgust. "Because they should not go to the Aswan Moon. They know this. But they go anyway and think nobody know this. But everybody know what they do."

"But what's so terrible about the Aswan Moon?" I said.

Amr extended his hands palms upward over the table to show me that the answer was obvious. "First of all, they is Muslim girls. They should not go to a place like that without they have a husband. There is foreigners and men there, and alcohol and smoking. It is not right they go there alone."

I told Amr that I had been alone to the Aswan Moon, had quite enjoyed it, and had survived the experience uncorrupted.

He twisted his mouth impatiently at me and showed me the palms of his hands. "Yah, Rose. OK. But you is not *Nubian* woman. It doesn't matter for you."

Not Nubian, not Muslim, not Egyptian—these facts conspired to disqualify me entirely from the female category. What mattered for a Muslim woman could never really matter for me. In Egypt, a Western woman would never truly be a woman, nor did she quite approach the status of a man; instead, her identity was more like that of a pleasant but irrelevant animal like, say, a peahen or a manatee. It was like moving through a strange kind of limbo, yet Amr seemed to take me more seriously than he did the local women. I felt no disrespect from him.

He said, "This is Nubian way from long time ago. Nubian women should not smoke, not drink the alcohol, not be going to public places alone. I know there is Nubian women in Cairo smokes. But they should not smoke. Nubian woman should not be doing nothing. Nothing. They should only be staying home and minding the house."

The sound of laughter came bubbling out from the television in Hoda's bedroom, and Amr's mind veered toward Hoda again. "My sister, she talk too much to other people outside the family. She tell people my business. She don't know how to keep the family business inside the family only, the way that is Nubian tradition. Because my mother always sick and don't teach her right."

I tried gently to defend the Nubian girls by suggesting that if they truly were childish and silly, as Amr maintained, then perhaps that was precisely because they were not allowed to have any experiences outside the home, because their world was too small and too unstimulating. Maybe if they had more freedom and more experience they'd be a bit more interesting, a bit more reasonable and judicious. But I knew that was probably too progressive an idea for Amr to absorb. The women had to be isolated, contained, and controlled; it was a long-standing matter of pride and power among the men. Florence Nightingale had been horrified by the state and status of the Egyptian woman: "She is nothing but the servant of a man . . . the female elephant, the female eagle, has a higher idea of what she was put into the world to do, than the human female has here." In a letter to Louise Colet, Flaubert wrote of the dullness of the Egyptian women: "The oriental woman is no more than a machine: she makes no distinction between one man and another man. Smoking, going to the baths, painting her eyelids and drinking coffee—such is the circle of occupations within which her existence is confined."

Respectfully but firmly, Amr shrugged off my notions. "No, Rose. They is just silly."

Amr was old-fashioned and intensely private. I sensed that he mistrusted his neighbors, whether male or female. Though he was traditional and proud to be Nubian, he seemed to dislike his own people.

I struggled for something useful to say. As if reading my mind Amr said, "I cannot marry any woman like these girls in Elephantine." He disliked the Nubian practice of a woman offering a dowry in exchange for marriage. "I can never marry a woman who has to give me money for it. I can never do this." He was traditional, yet some of those traditions were unacceptable to his sensitive heart.

I asked Amr why Hoda didn't want to get married. He looked at me a long time, his round cheeks and gray hair shining hotly in the fluorescent light. "Hoda say this?"

"Yes. She did."

Amr studied the many dishes on the table. He shook his head in thought. "Hoda say this because she know no one will marry her," he said. "With her foot like this. That why she say like that. Of course she want to be married and be like other girls."

A long silence followed. An electric clock on the kitchen wall hummed noisily. I stared at the newspaper tablecloth, at the weird little physics test written in English. *Problem: A body of mass 1 kg is moving with a velocity 2 m/s toward a body of unknown mass. After collision, they move together as one body as shown in fig. 1. If their velocity after collision was 2 m/s, find the mass of the second body.*

Hoda's television now offered the call to prayer, and then I heard a small squawking sound from behind the refrigerator, like a tiny chicken clucking. I looked at Amr. "What's that noise?" I said.

He smiled. "Is small animal."

The thing squawked again, a distinct little cry of protest, persistent, repetitive. I couldn't imagine what it was. "What *kind* of small animal?"

Amr indicated six inches with his fingers. "Is look like crocodile. Same face. Is green kind of color. Got a long tail. He is eating a fly; that why he make that noise."

A lizard or a chameleon. I had never heard a lizard make a noise before, but I believed Amr. I looked up to examine the ceiling and was startled to realize that we were sitting under the open sky. The kitchen sat at the bottom of an open well around which the house was built; it was essentially a courtyard but gave no sense at all of being out of doors. The well we were sitting in was so deep that without looking upward I would never have noticed that the room was roofless, and indeed hadn't noticed it the day before as Amr and I had climbed the stairs. This little square of sky above us, purple now, was dotted with three yellow stars feebly competing with the fading sunlight.

I asked Amr what happened in the kitchen when it rained. He scooped up some rice with a piece of flat bread and said, "It don't rains."

"But maybe once in a while it rains."

He would not be coaxed. "No. Never. It don't rains here."

"OK. But what about birds?" I felt certain there should be some peculiar consequence to setting up one's kitchen under the open sky—a puddle in the middle of the floor when you came down for breakfast in the morning, a pair of bats dangling from the edge of the sink, a pigeon snoozing on the staircase. "Don't birds fly in?"

Amr was amused by my curiosity and wonder. He smiled and showed his teeth. "No. They too afraid, Rose."

"Or bats maybe," I said hopefully. "They'll fly anywhere."

Amr didn't know what a bat was. I explained by pointing to the cloud of them flying far above our heads, faintly visible as caped little shadows skittering through the evening sky. He laughed. "No."

It seemed a delightful thing to be sitting in a kitchen at the dead center of a house with nothing but bats and stars for a ceiling and a lizard shrieking and chattering behind the refrigerator.

Eventually Hoda came limping out of her room and put a kettle on the stove in the little closet. I told her the food was excellent, but she dismissed my praise with the same grimaces and flapping gestures she had used to dismiss the idea of marriage and the excursion to the Aswan Moon.

Before I left Amr's house that evening to return to Aswan, I removed the cotton scarf from my neck and gave it to Hoda. Her big, pretty face beamed with surprise and pleasure as she held the scarf in her hands. She thanked me many times, wound the scarf around her neck, and asked me whether it made her look very beautiful.

It did indeed make her look beautiful. I told her so. And as I went out the front door I looked back and saw her appraising herself in the cracked mirror above the kitchen sink, her mouth curled into a smile of speculation and pleasure, her small black hands adjusting the scarf just so.

Not Floating but Flying

THREE DAYS LATER, when Amr, Madeleine, and I arrived at the police dock at the southern edge of Aswan, the presiding officer was standing barefoot in the bushes at the edge of the dock, chewing on a roasted chicken leg. Plump and mustachioed, shirt untucked, hair hanging in his eyes, he looked like a plumber relaxing at a Saturday barbecue. Egyptian officialdom, in theory so forbidding, religious, and stern, often materialized in such lax and unbuckled guises as this.

We had arrived in Amr's felucca, towing his little rowboat behind us, hoping to pass inspection and begin our trip to Edfu. It was the twenty-third of April. Amr showed the officer the necessary papers: photocopies of Madeleine's and my passports and of his absent British friend's passport, which Amr had used many times to create the feeble illusion of a third passenger.

The officer lovingly licked his greasy fingers one by one, wiped them on his shirtfront, ruffled Amr's papers, and made a wisecrack about the tiny rowboat we were pulling behind us. He radiated jolly irresponsibility. He could see clearly that there were only two foreign passengers on this boat, and yet he returned the documents to Amr and gave us a prompting wave off with his chicken leg, saying, *No problem!*

Only blindness in both eyes could have made this officer more amenable. This was a very auspicious start.

We moved away from the police dock, while our officer munched and grinned and tamped at his mustache with a look on his face that seemed to say, *God knows if we'll ever see them again!*

As the felucca glided heavily along the riverbank, I asked Amr why so many Egyptian men wore mustaches. He said, "Because they can. It proves they are a man," and as soon as he said it he seemed to see how silly it was, and his shoulders shook with nervous laughter as he raised the mainsail.

Amr told us that no felucca in recent times had ever left Aswan towing a rowboat behind it. In fact, word had already got out among the Aswan felucca captains about this unorthodox thing Amr was doing, and the docks were mildly aflutter about it. "Already we are famous," Amr said. Despite his unwaveringly calm and quiet manner, I could see that he was not only excited but very happy. He had told the officer he was bringing the rowboat to Edfu to have it repaired, but as soon as we were out of sight of the police dock he lowered the sails, and I climbed into the rowboat and began to row downriver.

I was nervous and dizzy with excitement that morning as I waved good-bye to Amr and Madeleine. Wa'il, the eighteen-year-old Nubian boy Amr had brought with him to assist with the sailing, stood on the deck watching me with teenage skepticism. I had given Amr money to buy us all enough food and water for four days, and he had stowed the food in the cabin of the boat, along with our luggage. We would cook and sleep on the boat. It wasn't the trip I had envisioned, not the conditions I had hoped for, but I consoled myself with the thought that although I'd be trailed by this trio of chaperones, I was still going to row a boat down the Nile. This was only the beginning. It would have to do for now. Downriver I would find my own boat; I was certain.

The early morning sun was gathering strength, already simmering in the pale blue sky. I had put some fruit and several bottles of water under the deck boards of the rowboat. Though I would have preferred to row all day alone, I agreed to meet Amr several hours later for lunch. Amr was nervous saying good-bye to me; I could see that he felt responsible. He stood on the deck of his boat with his hands on his hips and a faint frown on his face, as if he expected me and the boat to founder and sink before his eyes.

I began to row, and in my nervousness I rowed too hard, and within minutes I saw that I was already half a mile ahead of the felucca. There was no wind that day, and while I sped forward on my two lumpy oars, the felucca languished, moving no faster than the river's gentle current. I slowed my pace so that Amr could keep me in sight, although what I wanted was to forge ahead and be alone. I had the strange sense that I was towing the felucca behind me, that it was weighing me down.

The short buildings of Aswan had all but disappeared, and the cliffs and dunes of the west bank were transformed into open farmland—banana fields and shady palm groves and long flat vegetable patches of a brilliant green. The banana trees were short, not much higher than beach umbrellas, with cabbagey leaves that glinted like glass in the sunlight. Skinny, bare-chested farmers hacking at the earth beyond the shore saw me passing, and, dropping their hoes in astonishment, they ran to the edge of the river and shouted desperately, "Halloo. Come here!" I rowed on.

The river had a grass-green hue at this hour and felt supple and comfortable beneath me, like a down mattress. On the track that ran along the rubbly east bank at the foot of some sandy reddish cliffs, the train to Cairo clattered and whistled, stirring up a twister of dust behind it. Herons gargled in the bushes overhanging the river. Near noon the call to prayer began to emanate from beyond great stands of banana trees all along the banks; from this distance it was a melancholy lowing sound, warped occasionally by the idle wind. I stayed close to the west bank and rowed steadily while the sun crept higher in the sky. The current seemed to move faster the farther I got from Aswan. I was breathless with expectation, happiness, and anxiety.

A felucca with the 7UP logo on its sail headed upriver along the west bank. No one aboard seemed to notice me. A pump station appeared, and as I passed by it two ragged men lying on its dock sat up and stared at me, and then at each other, and then back at me. They were motionless with surprise. Their turbans were enormous, like stark white pumpkins, and their bony brown knees were like twisted knots of wood. I waved, which seemed to startle them. They both disappeared into the pump house.

A few other boats appeared on the far shore, most of them feluccas. I could see Amr's sail tacking endlessly back and forth from one side of the river to the other, still at a distance of perhaps half a mile, laboring vainly against the lame breeze. The white of his sail altered slightly each time he tacked, the sun brushing its canvas from a fresh angle. No matter how slowly I rowed, Amr's zigzagging sail grew smaller and smaller in the distance, and finally I gave up trying to let him protect me with his presence and began rowing at my own natural pace.

Down the middle of the river I rowed, feeling that I was not floating but flying. No one shouted at me because there was no one there to see me. The river was delightfully empty. This

was not like any other body of water I had rowed on. I knew
how far this water had traveled through time and space, and
what in the world it had inspired. Because the Nile idly, mind-
lessly slid down the incline of the African continent, human
beings had been able to develop civilization; sitting on top of
this water was like being reunited with my origins. Finally
alone on the river, I felt I had come face to face with a famous
ghost. I half expected the water to speak or a naked arm to
reach up out of the water to grab my oar. I was so nervous that
first morning of rowing that I noticed very little of what was
around me. Every few minutes I looked over my shoulder to
see what I was approaching downriver. Occasionally a small
island of phragmites grass appeared, a slight bend in the river,
the minaret of a mosque. Behind me, Amr's sail had disappeared entirely. I rowed this way, in an overexcited trance, for
approximately an hour before I began to feel guilty about stray-
ing out of Amr's sight.

Soon I veered toward the west bank and stopped, pulled the
rowboat up onto the sandy riverbank, and sat down under a
stand of palm trees in a deeply shaded spot that seemed safely
secluded. I was hyperconscious of the possibility that my solitary presence on this beach so far beyond the outskirts of Aswan might be considered—for reasons I might not even be
aware of—an affront or a spectacle or an annoyance to any
farmer passing by. I tried to make myself as inconspicuous as
possible by sitting slightly behind a stand of phragmites grass,
with my back against the trunk of a palm tree. I sat in the heat
in a kind of daze of wonder, staring at the shimmering surface
of the river.

Not a minute passed before my solitude was interrupted by
a tall, gaunt, spectacularly grinning young man who suddenly
appeared beside me on the beach—where he had come from
is impossible to say. He seemed to have materialized out of the
bushes, as Egyptian men often seemed to do. Just when you

think you might finally be alone in Egypt, a lurking gallabiya appears amid the phragmites, a white flash of teeth, a blinking golden brown eye. The man stared curiously at me, swaying in his stark white gown, crushing an aloe plant under his bare feet. His grin was enormous. In his hand was a pair of rubber flip-flops. *"Bititkallim Araby?"* he said.

I said, *"Shwaya,"* though in truth my Arabic was far less than a little.

He asked my name, where I was from. When I asked him if he spoke English, he gasped, wrung his hands, slapped his forehead, hopped on the aloe plant, shook his shaggy head, and giggled—an imaginative, energetic demonstration that English was wholly impossible for him.

I had enough Arabic phrases to last me about three minutes of vacuous small talk. We staggered along this way, bleating at each other, for ten, repeating much of what we said three or four times and making extreme gestures with our hands. His name, he said, was Hussein. His speech was so slow and his grin so credulous and inane that I began to wonder if perhaps he was a touch simpleminded. He inspected my boat as if he had never seen a boat before, nodding and gasping in surprised curiosity and rubbing his hands together. He asked me where I had come from, and when I said, "Aswan," he didn't believe me, though at this point it could not have been even four miles away. He wanted to know was I alone. I said I was not. My friends were behind me and would soon be arriving. He pointed at the binoculars in my boat. I got up and handed them to him. He raised them to his face and peered through the wrong end of them. I turned them the right way around. When he saw what an amazing thing the binoculars could do he nearly dropped them, as though they had suddenly burst into flames. Crouching on his haunches with his rubber sandals in his lap, he turned the binoculars over and over in his hands, saying, *"Ya saalam!"* and making a great show of his wonder at this magical instrument. He lifted the binoculars gingerly to his face again and slowly, carefully, fixed his sights on a felucca that was just rounding a bend upriver. His mouth hung open in wonder as he stared, his damp lips and enormous white teeth gleaming beneath the huge eyes of the binoculars. His bushy Afro, a hairstyle rare in Egypt, had a bowl-like dent in it at the back of his head and was studded with bits of dried leaves and straw, as though he had pitched backward into a field.

This wasn't the first time I had met an Egyptian who had never seen binoculars before. In Luxor, at the peak of the hill above the Temple of Hatshepsut and the Valley of the Kings, I had one day come upon a lone elderly man resting on his haunches in the shadow of a rock. He put my binoculars to his eyes and, on spotting a friend who stood magnified at the bottom of the hill, he said in conversational voice, "Ya, Ragab!" and stretched his arm out and groped at the air in an attempt to touch the friend who appeared so miraculously close.

I looked at Hussein, trying to determine who or what he was and thinking that he seemed gormless enough to be harmless as well, when all at once he announced in shockingly perfect English, "Well, well. Lookie here. Here comes my boat."

The English he had spoken was not only excellent but colored with an intentionally comical southern slant, the menacing drawl of a bandit. "You do speak English," I said.

"Of course," he said. His grin was slippery and sly.

"And you've looked through binoculars many times," I said.

"Of course." He handed the binoculars back to me with a dismissive toss, then threw one of his flip-flops up behind his back and caught it as it came down in front of him, a jazzy, vaudevillian gesture that he had obviously practiced many times. His laugh was self-congratulatory and aggressive. In an instant his entire affect had been transformed. The gawking, dim-witted rustic I had thought I was looking at had suddenly

been replaced by a sardonic, sophisticated wise guy. "I'm a felucca captain," he said. "That's my boat coming to get me."

"So, you tricked me, Hussein."

"Ha-ha!" he said, relishing the trick.

"Why did you trick me?"

"For a joke!"

"Egyptian men like to joke."

"You don't like it?"

I shrugged. "Some joking is fun, and some joking can be a
little hostile."

"Jimi Hendrix," he said.

"Yes, you look like him." He did, remarkably; he had the big
teeth and the big mouth, the colubrine eyes and lanky legs,
and his rumpled Afro had popped straight out of the 1960s. He
launched into "Voodoo Child," again in perfect English, swaying his hips and hitching his shoulders with excellent rhythm,
his long hands fanning the air in an elegant and humorous hula
motion. "Well I stand up next to a mountain . . ." As he sang,
stark scraps of morning sunlight sifted through the palm fronds
above us and danced across his gown like light projected
through the ragged ends of a film reel. His voice was beautiful,
and I thought of the fat waiter in the floating restaurant saying,
"Nubian love to sing!"

Hussein was an actor, worldly and ironic, and he had a chip
on his shoulder. He had tricked me, I knew, as much in bitterness as in fun. More than one felucca captain in Egypt resented the foreigners they served. It was understandable: they
earned a marginal living facilitating the leisure of privileged
people who came to delight in the exotic scenery and mysterious history of Aswan; people who stayed in five-star hotels
that the languishing locals in their dusty flip-flops were not
allowed to enter; people, pale and plump, who had enough
money to bask in a false superiority yet haggled ferociously
over pennies with their malnourished hosts; people whose

opinions and desires meant more to the local authorities than those of any tax-paying Egyptian citizen. Fear of the unfamiliar made the foreigner wary and—when hounded and harassed for money, as too often in Egypt they were—rude. Their rudeness in turn made the captains defensive. The foreign tourist (and there was, really, almost no other kind of foreigner here now) was a crucial economic engine but for some local captains a source of irritation. Until 1952 and the victory of General Nasser's revolution, Egypt had for two thousand years been ruled by foreigners. Foreign rule was finished, but the foreigner still enjoyed the benefits of a sort of economic colonialism. Flaubert's "It is unbelievable how well we are treated here—it's as though we were princes" was simply another way of saying, *We can get away with anything here!* The condescension Hussein showed me was likely an echo of the condescension he received.

Hussein's felucca approached the shore carrying another Nubian captain and four white passengers. Not far behind them I saw Amr's sail rounding the bend. I climbed into the rowboat and began to row downriver.

"Hey, wait a minute, lady," Hussein said. "You can meet my pals."

I wasn't enticed. "Maybe another time."

Hussein *tsk*ed theatrically. "Not friendly."

"Maybe we're well met," I said.

He grinned fatuously, his chestnut-brown chin glistening with perspiration, and after a blinking pause he said in that stagey panhandle accent, "Varmint."

The word and the way he pronounced it surprised and impressed me. It wasn't clear whether he meant it as an epithet or as a random demonstration of the breadth of his English vocabulary. It struck me suddenly as funny, this big-haired barefoot Nubian in a long dress standing at the edge of the Nile and speaking like Billy the Kid. I stopped my oars, unable to resist the challenge. "Critter," I said.

Hussein smiled. "Vermin."

That was a good one too, and I laughed at the stupidity of the exchange. Hussein laughed too.

"How do you know those words, Hussein?"

"Passengers from Arkansas. I studied hard." He climbed onto the deck of the felucca and began to sing and dance again, and this time the dance really was a silly taunt. I rowed away feeling duped and foolish for having been drawn into Hussein's game. He had played the guileless hayseed so cleverly and well that I fell for it. I had to admire his intelligence and his verve. No one executed pranks and jokes better than the Egyptian men.

At midday the brilliant sun gave the blue sky a smoky yellowish tint. When I seemed once again to be out of range of people, I changed my shirt for a lighter one, momentarily bobbing down the middle of the river in my bra. In the minutes that I lost sight of other human beings, I felt particularly elated, my whole body fluttering. As the hours passed and no disaster had reared its head at me, I began to relax, and in relaxing I seemed to regain my senses. I noticed the surface of the water, how it spun and gently swirled. I noticed the increasing heat of the sun roasting my ankles and the backs of my hands, the weight of the oars and the bubbling flop of the water as I pulled the oars through it. I saw long-legged, big-eyed birds picking their way along the shore and more birds soaring in slow, heavy flocks from one side of the river to the other. The river had narrowed slightly below Aswan. I approached a large island. From my feeble attempts to surmount the Cataract Islands, I knew that at the head of any island the river becomes flat and glassy, a faintly perceptible backwash of repelled current roiling up on itself. I knew that as you begin to head downriver past the top of the island, the current picks up speed, squeezed as it is between the mass of the island and the bank of the river. I steered myself into the rushing current, shipped the oars, and sat back for the ride. I loved the feeling of being carried so swiftly past the tall Nile grasses and short banana trees on the back of all this twisting green water that for so long had cut through Egypt's griddle of a desert. It was breathtaking, like the sensation of jumping naked into ice-cold water.

At two o'clock I stopped, reluctantly, and waited for Amr. When the felucca finally lumbered up, drifting on the current, its slack sail sadly hanging like a bedsheet on a clothesline, Amr greeted me with a mix of anxiety, relief, and amusement. He stood on the deck and looked me up and down, searchingly, as if checking to make sure I had incurred no wounds or bruises or psychic trauma. "You has any problems, Rose?" he said, lifting me out of the rowboat and onto the felucca by the hand.

I told him I had had no problems whatever, that so far the rowing had been easy, and we laughed about how slowly the felucca moved on a windless day. After anchoring the boat, Amr and Madeleine swam off of its stern. Madeleine, a professor at the American University in Cairo, was brave; warnings of snail-borne schistosomiasis and other dreaded Nile diseases worried her not a bit. She had been in Egypt for three years, long enough to imagine that she had developed Egyptian immunities, and imagination alone seemed to have been sufficient to keep her free from exotic ailments during her years here. I had known Madeleine for nearly fifteen years. I admired her for myriad reasons, not least of which was that she was adventurous and fearless. She had bought a car in Egypt and thought nothing of driving it across the Libyan desert all the way to the Siwa Oasis, or across the Sinai Peninsula, or, perhaps most dangerous of all, through the demented, traffic-crazed streets of her own neighborhood in Cairo.

I watched with fascination and dread and a little bit of envy as Madeleine and Amr splashed around the boat. Like most Egyptians, Amr swam in a hectic, slapping way, not fussily cupping his hands the way Madeleine did, but kicking and thrashing, as if sheer motion would keep him afloat. I was reminded of Florence Nightingale's description of the Nubian swimmer: "They do not swim as we do, but with their shoulders and arms out of the water, beating the water with their arms."

Amr cooked eggs and potatoes on a kerosene stove in the well of the boat, and we huddled in the shade of a canvas awning strung up over the deck and silently ate our lunch from tin plates. At this hour of the day, the heat was so intense it seemed to stop time. The bland yellow sky was like a smothering mask descending over the face of the desert. The big leaves of the banana trees glared and dangled. The long-legged birds cooled their shins in the shade. The banks of the river had become rotisseries of broiling vines and vegetation. Even the water, reflecting the sun, looked hot.

As soon as I finished my lunch, I climbed back into the rowboat and headed down the river. Amr had planned for us to spend the night at Barlooly Island, just north of Kom Ombo, and we agreed to meet there at around six o'clock. I tried to assure Amr that if he lost sight of me temporarily, he shouldn't worry; I would never be far ahead of him. He smiled in resignation, wished me luck, and began gathering up the lunch plates. I headed off again, thinking how curious it was that while Nubian women were expected to stay in their houses, Amr seemed to see no real moral problem with my casting off down the river in a boat. If a Nubian woman took it upon herself to do the same, she would face unbearable opprobrium.

The farther I rowed from Aswan, the fewer people I saw. All day I had seen not a single woman. The river was the men's domain but for the necessary washing of pots and clothing, which the women attended to crouched in the sandy shallows in their long black robes and veils, scrubbing furiously, chins between their knees. In all my time in Egypt, I had only once seen a woman swimming in the river. And never had I seen a woman operating a boat, large or small. But that was nothing so new, for it's generally true that just about anywhere in the world watercraft are operated chiefly by men. On an average Saturday in any average New England harbor, it's just as rare to see a woman proceeding alone in a boat. Why that is, I'm not sure. Perhaps it's because women don't know that it's fun. Perhaps it's because they don't know that they *can*.

I rowed steadily for four hours. There is something deeply soothing about rowing, the sense of freedom and isolation it creates, especially when the water is calm, as the Nile was. Any body of water is a kind of no-man's-land. On water there is really no such thing as trespassing, and in a rowboat there are no traffic laws to speak of. Your boat is your nation; whatever happens while you're in it is between you and the water that carries you.

Small flocks of pelicans and terns flew low over the water, up the middle of the river, racing toward me in curiosity, then up directly over my head against the backdrop of blue. The sight of these speeding birds made the world seem open and huge. I liked the fact that in a rowboat I was constantly facing backward, surveying the landscape I was leaving behind, watching it recede, like the melancholy view from the rear door of a caboose. The landscape changed little: banana trees on the right, the pale brown hump of the desert in the distance beyond the greenery, high desert hills on the left, tattered date palms slanting over the river, tall yellow grass, yellow patches of sandy beach. And the silvery avenue of water gently twisting and turning through it. Occasionally the palm trees that had walled the river disappeared, and then I could see east and west for miles, across low farmland, all the way to the horizon. Two camels slumped along across an open plain, gliding and bobbing like sea horses straining forward

underwater; a walking camel always appears to be enduring
great pain and hardship with noble resignation. Smoke from
sugar factories lifted gauzily into the sky. Here, approaching
Kom Ombo, Egypt was nearly as flat as Holland.

And then the Ptolemaic temple at Kom Ombo appeared in
the crook of a wide bend in the river, and I stopped rowing
and let myself drift, watching the temple grow slowly larger as
I approached it on the current. Massed and crumbling close to
the edge of the river on the east bank, the pretty sandstone
temple (Florence Nightingale, expert on ancient Egyptian architecture and far more discriminating than I, had slapped
Kom Ombo with the label "stupid temple" and moved on to
the next), with its columns and porticoes, stood gold against
the hard blue of the afternoon sky. The sight of an ancient
Egyptian monument from a distance is always at first slightly
surreal, like a mirage or a photographic image that has strayed
out of a book and superimposed itself onto real life. On seeing
it, you feel at first a little flustered and confused and think not
so much of the object itself but of the reproductions you've
seen of it and of the thoughts and emotions those reproductions once inspired in your imagination, then gradually you
grasp that what you're looking at is real, an object before you
that you can walk up to and touch. When Napoleon's soldiers,
who had never seen a photograph of any kind, rounded a bend
and caught sight of the Temple of Karnak for the first time,
they were so moved by the marvelous sight that they burst
into spontaneous applause.

A year before, I had walked alone through Kom Ombo temple. The temple is devoted to Sobek, the crocodile god, and to
Horus, the god with a hawk's head. It is full of crypts and passages and gateways, shrines and the usual huge columns.
While I was always impressed with the size, the age, the work-
manship, and the beauty of the ancient Egyptian monuments,
I was never entirely drawn in by them, never lingered over

the hieroglyphic texts or the depictions of one fine-featured god fitting an ankh into some other fine-featured god's mouth—perhaps because the history of Egypt was too vast and sweeping and epic. No matter how hard I tried to arrange the dynasties and the succession of pharaohs and gods in my head, I found it impossible to keep them straight. I never knew who was historical and who was mythological. The endless facts I read in guidebooks, the recitations I heard from guides, tended to sit in a tangled muddle in my head. More than the monuments and the kings and the gods, I was interested in the history of the simple Egyptian people, how they had lived their days. I didn't care much about Sobek and Horus, but I liked knowing that wealthy women in ancient Egypt had been obsessed with beautifying their hair and had regularly rubbed it with all manner of curious potions—hippopotamus fat, powdered donkey's teeth mixed with honey, the juice of juniper berries—and they decorated it with fine combs and flower blossoms. Sometimes they shaved their heads completely and wore wigs. I liked knowing that the prophet Muhammad was fond of cats and that he preferred to cut off the flowing sleeve of his robe rather than wake a cat that had fallen asleep on it. I liked knowing that when an Egyptian house cat died, the entire household shaved their eyebrows in mourning; when a dog died they shaved their entire bodies; and when an important man died, his female relatives smeared their heads and faces with mud and marched around the town beating their bared breasts. I was delighted to know that in the embalming process, the ancient Egyptians pulled the dead man's brains through his nose with an iron hook, and that at the end of a nice dinner party it was the custom for a man to wander around the room carrying a small coffin containing the image of a corpse, showing it to each guest and exhorting, "Look on this body as you drink and enjoy yourself; for you will be just like it when you are dead."

Like many of the ancient monuments in Egypt, the temple at Kom Ombo had been protected for centuries by sand that had blown in from the desert and covered the place nearly to its roof. To me, the most memorable thing in the temple was the vivid depictions of medical instruments carved into the walls. There were scalpels and forceps, pincers and pliers, and sharp-looking items so intricate and modern in appearance they were almost frightening.

I had gone to Kom Ombo temple alone, but as I walked through its dark rooms I had met a South American couple who had hired Leila, a nineteen-year-old Egyptian woman from Cairo, to be their guide. I walked along with them as Leila explained the temple's various architectural features. Leila was tall and hefty in jeans and running shoes and a long denim smock that hung down to her thighs. She wore heavy makeup and a mauve cotton scarf draped over her head like a veil. She was amiable but had a habit of repeating herself in a way that was almost Tourettic: "At one time the temple was used by Coptic Christians, so when it was used by the Coptic Christians the Coptic Christians made graffitis," and, "This is the room where the pharaoh kept the oils. Why the pharaoh kept the oils here? The pharaoh kept the oils here because this is the room where the oils were kept by the pharaoh," and, "This picture is two thousand years old, you see. So, two thousand years old. Imagine. Two thousand."

When I asked Leila when exactly the Coptic Christians had defaced the images on the temple walls, she looked at me in puzzlement and said, "Um . . . When exactly the Christians did the defacings of the images? The Christians did the defacings of the images eighty years before Christ."

I told Leila, gently, that that was not possible.

"Um . . . So, then the Christians did the defacings of the images eight years after Christ?"

Also quite impossible.

"Well," Leila said with a sporting shrug, "I think it was eight hundred years after Christ that they did the defacings of the images, because I know they was here and they did this damages of the defacings of the images."

I hadn't had the heart to tell Leila that eight hundred years after Christ was also not possible, since by that time the Christians had all but been driven out of Egypt. Leila carried on. "Madame, can I ask you one question? Where I can buy American clothes? *Real* American clothes?"

I suggested she try some shops in Zamalek, a fashionable neighborhood in Cairo. She flapped her hand at me. "Pah! Those clothes is only fakes made in Turkey!"

How could I explain that most American clothes are not made in America, that they're made in China and Venezuela and Cambodia and a host of other countries that would in no way appeal to Leila as sources of high fashion.

Leila stood in front of the wall of ancient surgical implements and said with passion, "I want American jeans and real American T-shirts!"

When I told her that I thought the best cotton in the world was Egyptian and that I liked Egyptian bedsheets, the look in her big black eyes said, *Christ, what a bumpkin!* "You got any American clothes you don't want, madame? Maybe I can buy them off you."

I asked Leila what size she wore. She turned slightly, lifted her smock to show me her considerable rear end, then looking me up and down she snorted and said, "Nahp! You got no clothes that fit me!"

Now, a year later, I was rowing past the temple in the smallest boat in Egypt, moving along the Kom Ombo curve, a nearly ninety-degree turn to the west. The river was very wide here, and off to my right the Libyan desert looked enormous and empty, its sandstone ridges and cliffs the color of rust. I rowed and watched the temple shrink as it receded, and remembered a comment that Flaubert had made about the temples and stones of Egypt: "Stones that so many people have thought about, that so many men have come to see, are a joy to look at. Think of the number of bourgeois stares they have received! Each person has made his little remark and gone his way."

I worked my oars steadily in that picking, crablike motion and was happier than I had been in a long time.

Maritime Etiquette

WHEN I ARRIVED at Barlooly Island (Amr had described it perfectly: "A sand place island on left side of Nile"), a string of six feluccas full of European travelers had already anchored there for the night, moored along the beach, each boat a mere broom's length from the next. With their idle sails wrapped tight around them, the masts resembled the spindly limbs of mummies swathed in winding-sheets.

I nudged the sandy shore and sat in my boat, waiting for Amr. I put my hand to the ground and found that the sand here was soft as velour. The sun had dropped behind the banana trees, and the slowly abating afternoon light gave the sky a gentle lavender hue. The desert that had made up the east bank of the river for most of the day had now given way to palms and farmland of varied shades of green, an exact mirror of the west bank. There were no houses visible here, no villages, no minarets, nothing indicative of human community. Several felucca captains were busy lighting campfires in the sand, while their passengers milled about on the small treeless island, smoking pot and drinking beer, snapping photos, checking their cell phones, and looking for private places in which to relieve themselves. Three dreadlocked Nubians tripped past me on the beach brandishing a bottle of raka wine. A few others sang and played bongo drums around a feeble yellow fire. The various parties of foreign travelers kept to themselves. I couldn't help thinking of the formality and civility with which nineteenth-century travelers in their grand *dahabiehs* had greeted each other. They were always dressing up in their best evening wear, inviting each other to twelve-course candlelit dinners in the great dining rooms of their ships, to piano concerts on the decks, to champagne parties and teas. Amelia Edwards wrote, "Other dahabeeyahs, their flags and occupants, are a constant source of interest. Meeting at mooring-places for the night, we now and then exchange visits. Passing each other by day, we dip ensigns, fire salutes, and punctiliously observe the laws of maritime etiquette." Howard Hopley, Edwards's contemporary, observed that "if you do not fire off a barrel or two in passing a compatriot on the stream, you are voted mean." Edwards noted, too, that most of the travelers on the Nile at that time were English and American: "In every twenty-five boats, one may fairly calculate upon an average of twelve English, nine American, two German, one Belgian, and one French. Of all these, our American cousins, ever helpful, ever cordial, are pleasantest to meet."

But all that was finished now. There were very few Americans here, and the novelty of the foreigner on the Nile, the excitement of spotting one of your own kind in such a far-flung place, had long since worn off. Foreign travelers on the Nile didn't salute each other, were not cordial, hardly even said hello, indeed seemed a bit embarrassed by the sight of each other. They slopped about in cutoffs and flip-flops, unshaven and unwashed, and drank cheap Egyptian beer out of tin cans.

When Amr and Wa'il and Madeleine arrived shortly after I did, Madeleine agreed with me that this seemed too chaotic a place in which to spend the night, but we could not persuade Amr to find a more secluded area. He was afraid to go elsewhere. "Don't know some people in another place," he said. "I can't trust. It not safe. Here is better than another place." The company of other Aswanian felucca captains was a form of protection. As he spoke, an enormous Sheraton Hotel cruise ship plugged past us, stirring up a rolling wake that caused the entire beachfront of feluccas to rock and teeter.

We didn't argue with Amr. We didn't want to upset him. He was too experienced and, now that dark was approaching, clearly too fearful to leave the people he knew. Having agreed that we would stay at Barlooly, Amr and Wa'il moored the boat to the riverbank with a big metal spike the size of a billy club. They furled the sails, tethered the rowboat to the stern of the felucca, then took off their gallabiyas, and, modestly dressed in shorts, waded into the river to bathe. They bathed with remarkable vigor, soaping their entire bodies in a lather so thick they looked whitewashed. They rinsed themselves thoroughly, over and over, with an almost ritualistic repetitiveness. Their fastidiousness was fascinating. To wash his hair, Amr applied a bar of Camay soap to his head like a rasp to a ball of wood, rubbing with such force that his head bounced and bobbed and jerked above his neck. He rinsed his hair so carefully and with such great dousings I thought he might drown. There was something satisfying about watching these two wash. I, on the other hand, had given no thought to how I would bathe. I had been warned so many times not to immerse my person in the Nile that I was reluctant even to wade in it.

Madeleine and I had brought beer with us, which we shared

with Amr and Wa'il, and when Madeleine mentioned that we had a little whiskey as well, Amr looked very pleased and asked, "What kind?"—a surprising question from a man whose religion forbade alcohol.

Madeleine said, "Johnnie Walker."

"Scotch whiskey," he said expertly and approvingly. "Very good. I can drink anything except Egyptian alcohol."

When I poured some whiskey into little glasses I had bought in Abu Simbel, Amr looked delighted. "Whiskey can make me talk more," he said. Wa'il declined the whiskey and sipped at his beer with dedication but no apparent relish. He was tall and lanky, with fine ankles and a handsome, boyish face. He rarely wore shoes, and the soles of his feet, like Amr's, were full of large cracks and faults and splits. Though he had brought a gallabiya with him, he seemed to prefer Western clothes, particularly those approximating a Californian surfing style, bright flowery patterns and loose-fitting cottons. He wore wraparound sunglasses, and when he pushed them back on his head he looked like a teenager sitting in a ski lodge in Vail, Colorado. He was shy and literally spoke only when spoken to. Whenever I looked at him, he ducked his head, blinked amiably, suppressed a smile, looked away.

Amr began to cook our dinner on his kerosene stove, which resembled an old tin can. He was efficient and skilled at this deck-top cooking. He cleared a place for a cutting board, and he and Wa'il chopped and minced and stirred, occasionally saying a word or two to each other. When Madeleine and I tried to help them with the cooking, Amr said, "We will cook. Please, rest." It was dark now, and their brown faces caught an orange glow from the fire as they worked. Wa'il lit several tallow candles and set them up inside empty water bottles to protect them from the wind. His fingers were long and fine, and he handled everything with delicacy and care and seeming reverence, always using just his fingertips when he carried any object.

Amr spread out our dinner on the deck: an egg-and-potato omelette, bread, salty white goat cheese, tahini, and balady salad—a mélange of minced vegetables popular in Egyptian villages. He urged us to eat.

All around us, felucca captains and their passengers were growing slightly drunk. Loud shouts and shrieks of laughter drifted through the soft black air, and little fires glowed orange on the decks, illuminating animated faces, gesticulating hands, mouths releasing spooky twists of cigarette smoke.

I commented on the general intemperance among the felucca captains. Amr said, "It a hard job for felucca captain. Too much responsibility. And they don't get much money. They hast drink."

As we ate, Madeleine and I couldn't keep ourselves from drilling Amr with questions. I was exhausted and still overexcited. Every so often a Nubian man passed by and made a comment about the rowboat, and Amr nodded mildly and continued eating. He was not one to fraternize and even seemed slightly wary of the other captains.

Amr had never been out of Egypt. He wanted to travel but never had the chance to; money, time, opportunity, permission—they were all too scarce here. He fantasized about going to Sudan to buy animals and then walking them all the way back to Egypt in a caravan to sell them for a profit.

"That's an awfully long walk, Amr," I said.

"It not long. You go slow. Take the time. Animals is much cheap there 'n here. And you can sell them at Daraw . . ." He waved his arm up the river in the direction of Daraw, a small town not far away that was famous for its camel market. I had seen the market once, a motley gathering of hobbled camels sitting forlornly on their skinny legs. Dark, turbaned men crouched amid them, drinking tea and smoking and spitting through their brown teeth. Some of the men indeed looked as though they had walked all the way from Sudan. They had desiccated, leathery faces, and the way they sat, with their knees up to their chins and their arms around their knees, suggested they would never walk again. A few men huddled around smutty little fires, warming their hands, though the sun had raised the temperature above one hundred degrees that day. Dogs with dangling, swollen teats sniffed at the mounds of camel dung. I saw a man with the anxious face of Richard Pryor shaving a donkey entirely bald with an enormous straight razor. The camels chewed their lips, batted their eyelashes, shifted their great weight, and stared into the dust in the most dejected way. They were skinny and moth-eaten, brutally branded and sweating with fear. Many had deep nicks and wounds on their flanks. Their thighs were no thicker than a human's. Feverish flies walked boldly across their faces and into their eyes. Every now and then, some camel or other would let out a haunting moan. Flaubert had been so struck by the sound a camel makes that he claimed to have worn himself out trying to imitate it. He described it as "a rattle with a kind of tremulous gargle as an accompaniment." To me, it was the sound of one of those farcically long plastic trumpets that drunken fans are always arbitrarily blowing into at football games. I never saw any transactions taking place at this market. No one was doing business, no money changed hands, and no one seemed the least bit interested in the camels, although now and then a man would get up and for no obvious reason begin mercilessly beating one of the beasts with a large stick.

Amr told us that he had been invited by one of his passengers to go to England for a month but he had chosen not to go, because, he explained, when people from Aswan went away for a month to another country, they always returned to find their lives more steeped in sadness and longing than they had been before they left. "A month is not enough time," he said.

I asked him where he would most like to go. He said, "If I had a restaurant in New York, I would be rich man in one year. It is my dream."

The faith in his eyes was heartbreaking.

"What kind of restaurant," Madeleine asked.

"Nubian."

While a Nubian restaurant in Manhattan would no doubt be one of a kind, Amr could not by any stretch of the imagination be called a good cook. Though his food was edible, it left a great deal to be desired. He used a staggering amount of salt and oil; after eating his meals, our tongues felt pickled and parched.

With the effect of the beer and whiskey, Amr became marginally more voluble than he had been all day. He smiled and sipped from his glass and proposed a riddle. "You have forty glasses. One is broken. How many glasses is left?"

Obligingly, we pondered the question, and knowing that we had to be wrong, we both said, "Thirty-nine?"

"No," Amr said gleefully. "Three! Because it was four *tea* glasses, I said." He chuckled, tipped back his whiskey, and chuckled some more. "I like that game."

Amr laughed when we asked him if captains ever brought their wives with them on these trips. "Of course no. There would be jealous and argument." He laughed some more, and Wa'il, who understood very little English, began to laugh too, caught up on Amr's rare wave of merriment. Wa'il's teeth were long and beautifully white, and the way his lips always rested slightly parted over them made him look startled and vulnerable.

Amr made us instant coffee, and a few other felucca men came over to our boat, perched on the gunwales, and, using a pair of Nubian drums I had bought in Aswan, began accompanying themselves in song. These men were all slender and barefoot. They sang loudly, but the cheer and camaraderie they worked to generate felt slightly forced. They wanted too much for the trip to be fun, to make it live up to that prototypical felucca party that captains in Aswan were always mythologizing, the perfect beach party that had happened perhaps once and was never matched again. No one seemed to have a desire to sing, least of all Madeleine and me. Everyone was ready for sleep. One by one, the fires faded and the travelers began to flop down on the decks for the night. The captains sitting on our boat looked crestfallen and began having difficulty completing any one song; each song they struck up simply died out, and they searched their memories for a better one. Glumly surveying the numerous horizontal bodies enveloped in sleeping bags on the decks up and down the shore, one of the men muttered, "It like hospital here. Everyone lying down. And no talking."

We were an unsatisfactory cargo of boring tourists, nothing like those ideal hard-partying passengers he'd had in the past.

Madeleine and Wa'il prepared for bed. As Madeleine brushed her teeth, leaning over the edge of the boat, Amr and Wa'il watched her as intently as I had watched them bathing. They were fascinated with the entire operation. They were careful not to do what they called their "bathroom" near where farmers lived, and they never urinated over the side of the boat. When Madeleine and I proposed setting up a makeshift toilet with a bucket on the deck, Amr politely protested.

Madeleine and Wa'il spread their sleeping bags on the deck and climbed into them. The clutch of visiting captains, muttering darkly, straggled off in search of something, anything, to entertain themselves. I wanted to go to sleep too, but I saw that Amr, fueled with whiskey, wanted to talk. I wrapped a blanket around my shoulders and listened to him. He sat cross-legged on the deck with a guttering candle near each foot. His yellowish toenails were torn and cracked and warped.

In the candlelight his dilated pupils were deep black and his white gallabiya glowed amber. He seemed suddenly very sad. He confessed to me that he had a problem asking for money.

One day the previous winter, he had taken a group of French tourists around Aswan on his boat. An hour, he had told them, would cost fifty pounds, approximately eight U.S. dollars, but the trip ended up taking four hours, because the wind was low and the people wanted to see just one more thing, and just one more thing. When they returned to the dock, the passengers made no move to compensate Amr with more than the agreed-on fifty pounds, and he couldn't bring himself to ask them for more. Another time, he agreed to take a group of tourists to Edfu—a three-day trip. They told him what food they wanted him to bring, and he went out and spent one hundred and fifty pounds on their provisions. The next day the group came to him and announced that they had found a captain who would take them to Edfu for less money, and therefore they had decided to go with that captain instead. Not only had Amr lost his fare, he was stuck with the bill for the food he had bought for them. Though he said he never liked to argue, he had been so angry that he threatened to take the entire group of foreigners to the tourist police. With much parsimonious protest, they finally produced a mere fifty pounds for his trouble.

From what I had seen, every felucca captain in Aswan was in desperate need of money. The job was difficult, a constant battle to win cash from wary, slightly frightened foreigners. And yet when I had offered to pay him for using his rowboat, Amr had refused to accept my money. He told me he was not good at drumming up business, that he didn't know how to chase and charm the foreign customers the way the other captains did—didn't know how and didn't want to know how. The oily sales pitch was an odious aspect of the captain's job.

Amr told me that black Americans sometimes came to

Aswan to visit a very old wise man who was well read and knew all of Nubian history. "When these American black people, they see the singing and the nice way of life here, when they hear there was Nubian kings and Nubian pharaohs, they want be Nubian." Some black Americans came and insistently claimed Nubia as their heritage, though they rarely had any evidence of Nubian forebears. A few years before, a wealthy black businessman from New York came to Elephantine Island, got very drunk one night, and stood in the middle of the village shouting at the top of his voice, "I am Nubian! I am Nubian!"

Amr stared into the tiny glass in his hands. His lips glistened pink in the candlelight. "That man could not make himself known," he said, and the empathy in his voice suggested a personal intimacy with the haunting sensation of being lost and misunderstood. He turned the little glass around and around in his fingers; the handblown vessel was blue and flawed and full of air bubbles, a coarse, lopsided, hastily fabricated device found in every corner shop in Egypt, and beautiful—to me at least—precisely for its roughness.

Amr told me that of the one million people who lived in Aswan, only twenty thousand were Nubian. Though he was born on Elephantine Island and was therefore Egyptian, he confessed that he often felt sad about the loss of Nubia in Egypt. In the 1970s, Nubia, which was once a string of small villages stretching up the narrow banks of the Nile from the first cataract in Aswan to Dongola in the Sudan, was buried forever under Lake Nasser, its displaced people scattered throughout Egypt and the Sudan. For centuries Nubia had been a source of slaves for the Arab world. In 1777, Charles Sonnini wrote that two Nubian caravans per year arrived in Cairo and that "the number of negroes annually exhibited in the market of Cairo may be estimated at fifteen hundred, or two thousand." Because of that association with slavery and domestic servitude, Egyptians tended to perceive the Nubian race as ignorant and inferior. Dark-skinned, culturally more African than Egyptian, Nubians had once been the object of considerable prejudice and disrespect in Egypt, and vestiges of that still lingered. Nubians, said by many to be the true pharaonic people, were Muslim, were Egyptian citizens, and yet they would never feel that they were truly Egyptian. Amr was proud of his Nubian identity, yet it cast him as an outsider.

Amr was religious, said he would never drink during Ramadan, and that he believed wholeheartedly in God. "God can make you feel very great if you talk to him enough and you keep Ramadan sacred." He said some Muslims pretended to keep Ramadan sacred but broke the rules of the fast—no eating, no drinking, no smoking, no sexual contact, nothing that would affect one's body from sunrise to sunset—when no one was watching them. "But it not important what other people think about you. It is only between you and God. If I go swimming in the river in Ramadan, and I dive down under and I take a drink of the water because I am thirsty, no one will know about it, but God will know. That why I don't do." During Ramadan Amr always read the Koran from start to finish. The Koran, he said, contained everything a person needed to know about life.

Amr stood up, scooped a bucket of water from the river, and made tea with it in a tin can on his kerosene stove. He told me a felucca like his cost eight thousand Egyptian pounds without any of the equipment or rigging. In all, a man would need ten thousand pounds to set himself up as a felucca captain. When I asked him what the sail cost, he said, "Nothing. I made it."

"You have a special sewing machine, I guess."

He stitched at the air with his fingertips. "No machine; only with my fingers and one needle. And all the time the needle is breaking."

The canvas of the sail was the thickness of shoe leather, and yet its seams looked factory tight and precise. It was a stunning piece of handiwork. Amr had also made the removable canvas canopy that shaded the deck at midday—a seven-by-ten-foot sheet.

"That looks like a lot of work, Amr," I said.

He pursed his lips and dipped his chin, and said dejectedly, "I have too much free time," and he began to roll a joint, an enormous cigarette full of seeds. He offered it to me, and though I loathe marijuana I took a puff to be polite. Amr smoked a bit and his mouth grew dry and his eyes grew heavy. He showed me a brass oil lamp someone had given him and said, "He gave it to me for a president." I didn't correct him. Like most Egyptians Amr pronounced the word *next* as "neckist" and *sixty* as "sickisty," and if a person was not on time he said, "You are lating." He said "oping" for *open* and when things went wrong he said, "What it's the problem?" He introduced me to people as a "writer woman," referred to Elvis Presley as a "singer man," and when I mentioned Hashem, the gloomy young man I had met on Elephantine Island, Amr scowled and said, "Hashem a liar man."

He fished his license out of the pocket of his gallabiya and proudly showed it to me. Egyptian men seemed inordinately attached to the official documents they carried. In the photo, Amr's hair was completely dark. When I commented on how different his hair was now, he said ruefully, "The white hair is new."

"I'm getting gray hair too," I said in a feeble attempt to cheer him up.

"I do not see them, Rose."

The conversation was running out of steam.

"Rose," Amr said, "how come you know to row a boat?"

"I row at home every day."

"Why?"

"For fun."

"Fun." I could see him sincerely wondering how such a useless expenditure of energy could be fun. "Where you row?"

"Narragansett Bay, near my house."

"It's water there is salt water or Nile water?"

"It's the ocean, so it's salt water." I asked him what *Nile* meant.

"*Nile* mean soft."

"Fresh?"

"What it's mean 'fresh'?"

I explained what freshwater was, and he repeated the word a few times. I asked him if he had ever been to the ocean. He said, "One time I been in Red Sea. I was very hot. I saw so much water. I think oh, good, so big, so nice. I want to wash. I jump in with soap, and"—he made a vigorous scrubbing motion, which in any other person would have been comical and exaggerated, but which in Amr I knew was a literal demonstration of his bathing technique—"oh, terrible. I cannot wash. The water is heavy. It hang on me. Soap can do nothing. Like a stone." He laughed, shook his head, drew a finger-sized twig from the pocket of his gallabiya, and began to chew on it.

"What's that," I said.

"Toothbrush."

He got up and began to wash our dishes in the river.

What was it about Amr that so impressed me? He was straightforward, unself-conscious, and unhurried. He was good-natured and gentle. He knew how to listen. He was not preoccupied with making people like him. And he was patient, a great gift that had not been bestowed on me.

I said good night to him and headed for my sleeping bag, alongside Madeleine's. Amr and Wa'il had laid planks across the deck of the boat to create enough room for all of us to lie down comfortably, and on the planks they laid cotton-batting cushions, like small futons. Wa'il lay flat on his back with his arms folded across his chest like a mummy, his nose pointed at the sky.

The moment I crawled into my sleeping bag, my ankles and wrists began to prickle with sunburn, a needling sting that was not unpleasant. When I shut my eyes, the day that had just passed loomed in front of me, the flashing green water, the palms, the broiling sun, the constantly changing color of the sky, the flapping oars and slightly rocking little boat passing down the wide flat corridor of the Nile. The images were so vivid I opened my eyes. Above me the stars were so bright and so numerous that the sky seemed to tremble with the ice-blue weight of them.

Dogs quibbled in the dark distance. Donkeys screeched in hysterical fits that sometimes lasted a full minute. Herons squawked and muttered along the riverbank. Fish—or perhaps some other, more sinister creatures—splashed and gurgled around the hull of the boat. At 4:45 a.m. the call to prayer began in the many mosques of nearby Kom Ombo, an insistent din, like the throbbing discord of a bees' nest. Many voices vibrated from the same general vicinity, no two in step with each other. Technically, believers were required to rise and begin praying now, but not a soul in the camp stirred. Amr and Wa'il and all the other felucca men snored on. I was always a little disappointed that the call to prayer never seemed to evoke any immediate response from anyone I had acquainted myself with in Egypt. I, however, was highly conscious of it, even enamored of it, and had fallen into the habit of humming its pleasant tune, probably blasphemously, under my breath wherever I went.

It was delightful to be sleeping on the Nile under the open sky, yet still I was nagged with dissatisfaction, with a feeling of incompleteness. I wanted to be here alone. I lay on the deck plotting what I would do when I left Amr in Edfu, determined that I would find my own boat, and soon I fell asleep with that Islamic tune running through my head.

When I woke the next morning, Amr was sitting propped against the mast in the withering sunlight with a doleful look on his face.

"Rose," he said.

"What is it, Amr?"

A long torpid silence followed. "You has any aspring tablets?"

I looked at him—the squirrel's hair, the chipmunk cheeks. He had drunk three cans of beer and two glasses of whiskey, and his hangover had taken the form of a headache so large it was, from where I sat, nearly audible. The whites of his eyes, always a bit yellowish, this morning were the color of mustard and were laced through with scarlet fractures. His eyes looked scorched. His mouth looked bruised. White hairs had begun to sprout on his dark chin. It was another utterly windless day, and I knew that Amr had long, hot, tedious hours of drifting and fruitless tacking ahead of him.

I rummaged in my bag for aspirin. My rear end was sore from so many hours spent on the hard seat of the rowboat the day before, and my neck was stiff. I gave Amr two aspirin and took two myself.

As I walked up the beach past the line of feluccas to find a place where I could wash with a bottle of water, I heard a voice behind me say, "You don't say good morning to me, Miss Rose?" I looked over my shoulder and saw that it was Hussein, the man who looked like Jimi Hendrix, unreeving his mooring line and grinning insolently at me.

"I didn't see you," I said.

"Unfriendly lady."

It was too early in the morning for this silly nonsense. "Well, Hussein," I said, "since you didn't say good morning to me either, I think it might be fair for me to say 'unfriendly man.'"

"Well met," he said tartly, parroting what I had said to him the day before, and again we both laughed at the stupidity, and at the strange intimacy, of our exchange.

I went off up the beach thinking, *So much for maritime*

etiquette, and within half an hour I was back in the rowboat
pulling myself down the river once more.

~~~~

IN 1878 Baedeker's *Guide to Lower Egypt* offered this bit of
advice to the prospective visitor to Egypt:

> The traveller can hardly be recommended to start alone for a
> tour in a country whose customs and language are so entirely
> different from his own; but if he has been unable to make up a
> suitable party at home, he will probably have an opportunity of
> doing so at Alexandria or Cairo, or possibly at Suez or port
> Said. Travelling as a member of a party is, moreover, consider-
> ably less expensive than travelling alone, many of the items
> being the same for a single traveller as for several together.
> Apart, however, from the pecuniary advantage, a party is more
> likely to succeed in making satisfactory arrangements with the
> natives with whom they have to deal.

Most nineteenth-century travelers followed that advice, traveling in parties of anywhere from five to twenty, and because
the Nile was navigable only four months of the year, most
flocked to Egypt during one season. Lucie Duff Gordon, a British writer who went up the Nile in 1862, remarked in her letters, "See what strange combinations of people float on old Nile.
Two Englishwomen, one French, one Frenchman, Turks, Arabs,
Negroes, Circassians, and men from Darfour, all in one party,"
and, further, "Thebes has become an English watering place.
There are now nine boats lying here." Edward Lear, the British
painter and writer of nonsense verse who first went up the Nile
in 1849, wrote to one friend, "You cannot imagine the extent of
the American element in travel here! They are as 25 to one English. They go about in dozens & scores—one dragoman to so

many—& are a fearful race mostly," and to another friend he wrote, "Every day brings heaps of people here . . . As far as English company goes, there is no lack of it." Florence Nightingale lamented the great number of travelers on the river. Arriving at Aswan on her return trip to Cairo, she noted, "There was such a 'ruck' of English boats there—all the N___ party and a thousand others—and nothing to eat, for they had devoured everything like locusts, even all the rice and milk of Syene [Aswan], that we turned savage and sailed before sunrise."

Newly rediscovered, Egypt drew all manner of adventurers and artists, botanists and scientists, academics, entrepreneurs, and oddballs. Some came in the hope of making money in the antiquities trade, some because they had come into a sum of money and needed a way to spend it. With a female companion, Lucie Duff Gordon went to Egypt in 1862 in the hope that the Egyptian climate would ameliorate the symptoms of tuberculosis; she stayed seven years and eventually died in Luxor, where she had established herself as a kind of medicine woman and savant. She had begun smoking cigars to ease her coughing, found she quite liked the taste of them, began smoking them regularly, and was not the least perturbed by the shocked reactions she received at this habit. The English traveler Howard Hopley, who stated his own purpose in Egypt as merely "health and relaxation of mind," described the first of his two *dahabieh* companions as a middle-aged Englishman "bent in the journey on catching rare birds, and stuffing them, on collecting insects, reptiles, and eggs, on the study of hieroglyphics in general, and particularly on cramming-up in the Theban dynasties," and the second as a "stout and enterprising American, bent on getting thin by exercize." Hunters came for the great number of birds to be had along the banks of the river. Hopley wrote with disgust of one Englishman in particular who seems to have run amok with his gun:

He had brought from England a little mahogany boat fitted with a swivel-gun, wherewith he waged flagitious warfare with whole commonwealths of unsuspecting geese and spoonbills—birds whose peaceful manner is to assemble by myriads on the shoals and sand banks left high and dry in mid stream . . . Hidden in the hollow of his boat, which looked like a waif on the waters, he would quietly float down until the current had borne him within murderous range, then let fly a pound or two of buck shot slap into the midst of the astonished assembly. The effect was prodigious; not so much in the matter of killed and wounded—though he is said to have bagged a hundred at one blow—as in the noise and whirr of the discomfited legions taking flight in a general *sauve qui peut* . . . He also fell foul of flamingoes and storks and other harmless birds of singular grace and beauty. The published account of his prowess while on the sacred river is as follows, all within two months be it understood:—Total, 5576 head; namely, 9 pelicans; 1514 geese; 328 wild ducks; 47 widgeon; 5 teal; 66 pintails; 47 flamingoes (!); 38 curlews; 112 herons; 2 quails; 9 partridges; 3283 pigeons; and 117 miscellaneous.

Others went to Egypt in pursuit of larger prey, particularly the crocodile. Much as Hopley was horrified with the slaughter of birds, Amelia Edwards was horrified by the slaughter of crocodiles: "That a sportsman should wish for a single trophy is not unreasonable," she wrote, "but that scores of crack shots should go up every winter, killing and wounding these wretched brutes at an average rate of from twelve to eighteen per gun, is mere butchery, and cannot be too strongly reprehended; year by year, the creatures become shyer and fewer."

The effect of so many enthusiastic tourists took its toll not only on the wildlife of Egypt but on Egyptian art and architecture as well. Every traveler who wrote of his experience in Egypt complained that others before him had carved their names into the stones of the temples and tombs. "The scribbling of names is quite infamous," Duff Gordon wrote. "Beautiful paintings are defaced by Tomkins and Hobson, but worst of all Prince Puckler Muskau has engraved his and his Ordenskreuz in huge letters on the naked breast of that august and pathetic giant who sits at Abou Simbel. I wish someone would kick him for his profanity." Flaubert was likewise irritated by the graffiti. "In the temples," he wrote, "we read travelers' names; they strike us as petty and futile. We never write ours; there are some that must have taken three days to carve, so deeply are they cut in the stone. There are some that you keep meeting everywhere—sublime persistence of stupidity."

Fifteen decades later those names are still there. At Philae you will find, as Flaubert likely did, "GODFREY LEVINGE 1833," at Abu Simbel you'll see "LECAROS 1879" carved deep into the right shin of one of the seated colossi, and at the Ramesseum there's the particularly large and beautifully carved "DEGOUTAN THEDENAT 1820." Graffiti has been appearing forever in Egypt in hieroglyphic, hieratic, demotic, Greek, Latin, Arabic, French, and English. After a long enough lapse of time, a name carved into a stone becomes less offensive, becomes simply part of the history, another archaeological detail. At the Temple of Khnum on Elephantine Island, I was fascinated to see these ancient Greek words carved into a block of the nilometer: ΔΙΜΙΤΡΙΟΥ ΚΑΙ [ΕΡ]ΜΙΟΥ ΚΑΙ ΤΟΝ ΑΔΕΛΦΟΙ—"of Dimitris and Hermes and the brothers." Long before Godfrey Levinge and Degoutan Thedenat, Dimitris—whoever he was, in his tunic and sandals—had had that universal human impulse to commemorate his presence, and thereby elevate his status, at the phenomenal sites of Egypt.

Edward Lear chose to commemorate his journey in Egypt in pictures and words. In 1885 he wrote a letter to Amelia Edwards in the hope that she, who had published an immensely

successful account of her Nile journey, could help him pub-
lish his Egyptian journals.* He told Edwards that he had kept
a "detailed diary daily from almost hour to hour," called the
diary "photographically minute & truthful," and noted in exasperated self-defense, "It is hardly worthwhile adverting to
the remarks of silly=narrow folk, who say 'Oh! The Nile!' as if
anything new could be written about that river!!—"

By the time the nineteenth century rolled toward its end, it
would indeed have seemed that nothing new could be written
about the Nile, for nearly every foreigner who traveled in Egypt
wrote a book's worth of letters and notes about the experience.
Amelia Edwards, Lucie Duff Gordon, Gustave Flaubert, Florence Nightingale, Wallis Budge, Edward Lane, William Thackeray, Howard Hopley, and innumerable others—they all
boarded a *dahabieh,* set off upriver from Cairo, and wrote it
down. They all commented on the hectic streets of Cairo, the
beggars, the slave markets, the Mosque of Sultan Hassan. They
all wrote about the difficulty of passing through the turbulent
first cataract at Aswan and all admired the skill of the Shellalees who steered the boats through it. They all wrote about
climbing to the top of the Great Pyramid at Giza. They all wrote
in rapturous detail about Karnak and the Valley of the Kings
and commented with dismay on the huge number of one-eyed,
nine-fingered Egyptian men. Nightingale wrote, "The number
of one-eyed men you see is frightful." Edwards reported that in
a crowd of ten thousand Egyptians at the marketplace at El
Minya, "at least every twentieth person, down to little toddling
children of three and four years of age, was blind of an eye."
Howard Hopley noted that three of the crew on his boat were
missing a forefinger and two were missing an eye. "Sooner than
serve as a soldier," Hopley explained, "a man will cut off his
finger or pluck out his eye. For the latter mutilation, though, he

* The journals were never published and have since been lost.

is mostly indebted to his mother; she squeezes, as they say, some herb-juice into the orbit, and the eye withers up. As to the former, it is an old custom—old as the palmy days of Rome, when men were wont to cut off their thumbs from the same motive." Of the crew he shared with Flaubert, Maxime du Camp remarked that all but three of them were missing a forefinger; two were also one eyed. All the foreign travelers wrote about the Coptic monks who lived in caves in the cliffs above the river and how they would rush down naked when they saw a boat approaching and swim out to collect alms from the travelers. (Flaubert was delighted by these swimming begging monks; Nightingale, with her pride and concern for Christianity, was disgusted, not by their nakedness [she was, after all, a nurse] but by their begging and by their reputation as thieves.) They all brought trunks of books with them, and all seemed to be able to read several languages, including Hebrew and ancient Greek. They all raved about the beauty of the Temple of Philae—many of them even set up bedrooms within it and lounged about there as if in a London hotel. Lear's party hauled "luggage, beds, cookery things" up to Philae and "swept out rooms in the great temple, & have been quite comfortable in them during our stay. 3 or 4 English boats have generally been on the island, so we have had dinner parties, & music every evening nearly." They all wrote about the rapacious tomb robbers of Qurna who lived like ghouls among skulls and bones in the dusty tombs of western Thebes and made their living selling mummies and looted antiquities. They all said the moonlight on sand looked like snow. Flaubert: "so bright on the sand that it looks like snow." Nightingale: "it is exactly like snow." Lucie Duff Gordon: "snow."

Every one of them wrote about, and reserved their greatest outrage for, other travelers who left Egypt with filched mummies and antiquities stuffed into their luggage, and then all of them eventually, inevitably, came up with excuses for why

they too were justified in making off with one little antiquity
or two. Writing to her husband, Lucie Duff Gordon confessed
unabashedly that an ancient stone lion she had shipped off to
him from Egypt was stolen. "I stole him for you from a temple,
where he served as a footstool for people to mount their donkeys. A man has stolen a very nice silver antique ring for me
out of the last excavations—don't tell Mariette* . . . My fellah
friend said, 'Better thou have it than Mariette sell it to the
French and pocket the money; if I didn't steal it, he would'—so
I received the stolen property calmly." Nightingale reported
ruefully on the state of the private tombs, "They are vexation
of spirit, for they have been cruelly mauled," yet in the next
paragraph she added with innocence and no self-reflection, "I
bring home some little figures found in the tombs." As early as
1818, Edouard de Montulé wrote of the looted tombs with despair, "If any perfect ones still exist, I sincerely wish they may
escape the research of the curious antiquary . . . for the sar-
cophaguses and mummies which they contained would inevitably take the road to London or Paris." Before long De Montulé
himself took off for France carrying a beautiful double sarcoph-
agus within which lay the well-preserved mummy of an ancient woman. At Luxor, Amelia Edwards pondered this strange
contradiction:

> The whole plateau is thickly strewn with scraps of broken pot-
> tery, limestone, marble, and alabaster; flakes of green and blue
> glaze; bleached bones, shreds of yellow linen; and lumps of
> some odd-looking dark brown substance like dried-up sponge.
> Presently someone picks up a little noseless head of one of the
> common blue ware funereal statuettes, and immediately we all
> fall to work grubbing for treasure . . . And then, with a shock
> which the present writer, at all events, will not soon forget, we

* French Egyptologist Auguste Mariette.

suddenly discover that these scattered bones are human—that those linen shreds are shreds of cerement cloths—that yonder odd-looking brown lumps are rent fragments of what was once living flesh! . . . We soon . . . learned to rummage among dusty sepulchres with no more compunction than would have befitted a gang of professional body-snatchers . . . One looks back afterwards with wonder, and something like remorse . . . but so infectious is the universal callousness, and so overmastering is the passion for relic-hunting, that I do not doubt we should again do the same things under the same circumstances. Most Egyptian travellers, if questioned, would have to make a similar confession. Shocked at first, they denounce with horror the whole system of sepulchral excavation, legal as well as predatory; acquiring, however, a taste for scarabs and funerary statuettes, they soon begin to buy with eagerness the spoils of the dead; finally they forget all their former scruples, and ask no better fortune than to discover and confiscate a tomb for themselves.

Most of these nineteenth-century diversions and concerns are essentially nonexistent for the modern foreign visitor in Egypt. Hunting is now forbidden; there are no crocodiles remaining in the Nile; there are so many guards about that you couldn't possibly carve your name into a temple wall or even quickly spray paint it; the streets of Cairo are still hectic and filled with beggars, but the donkeys and camels have been replaced with French and Japanese cars; the first cataract has been shut down by the High Dam and so the Shellalees have gone out of business; there are no slaves for sale and nothing you could really call a harem; camping at the temples and climbing up the Great Pyramid are strictly forbidden; it is rare to see a one-eyed, nine-fingered Egyptian (though a notable number of Egyptians suffer unfortunate eye diseases); the tomb robbers at Qurna have been effectively shut down (though occasionally on the mountaintop above the Valley of the Kings, you'll meet one of their skinny barefoot bandy-legged descendants limping along, usually drunk, in a tattered gown and dusty turban with a little faience torso in his pocket that is unquestionably a fake); there are no antiquities left to steal, and besides you'd go to jail forever if you tried to take one out of Egypt. Across the span of a hundred and fifty years, only one thing has truly remained the same: moonlight still makes the Egyptian sand look like snow.

A Night at Silwa

O
N THAT SECOND MORNING of rowing, I passed a mosque
with a tall yellow minaret towering above the palm trees.
Now and then I saw feluccas on their return trip to Aswan,
empty of passengers and making haste along the far edges of
the river, riding the reverse currents with their sails on a
broad reach. Occasionally two feluccas sailed side by side and
lashed together, on a run with their sails extended on either
side of them, like the wings of a great bird, doubling their sail
power. They moved quickly, and I was relieved when I realized that Amr's return to Aswan, though it would be against
the current, would be faster and easier than the trip down to
Edfu. At the moment he was laboring far behind me, just as he
had done the day before, his sail a bright speck forlornly zigzagging in the glittering distance.

I rowed on and lost Amr completely. The day was still and hazy, and by eleven o'clock the heat was immobilizing as a straitjacket, and the sky was a sickly swimming-pool blue. Farmers along the banks of the river forced their horses into the water to cool them off. Dogs wandered into the river and sat down up to their necks, blinking grimly in the terrible sunlight. I saw an old man sitting naked at the edge of the river, idly toying with his penis before plunging into the water to bathe, and near him a younger man standing in the water with a fishing pole. Women in black walked slowly along the riverbanks with jugs on their heads, disappearing in and out of stands of eucalyptus trees, and all along the banks I saw children tending fires in fields, burning the stubble of crops—a diabolical job to have to perform in such heat. The fields were rectangular and evenly divided by irrigation canals and mounds of black earth. Beyond the fields were the caramel-colored hills and the huge expanses of roasting desert rubble. There were mud-brick villages here, with houses painted yellow and blue, and men riding donkeys, and crumbling mud-brick walls, and brown sheep trotting through the dust beneath stands of date palms. I saw a white camel lying near the riverbank with his nose lifted high in the air and a man in nothing but an enormous white turban and white underwear standing scarecrow-still in the middle of a flooded field. I saw mud-brick graves in the distance—rectangular mounds of earth with palm fronds stuck into them as markers—and boys carrying hoes on their shoulders and girls carrying brittle cornstalks on theirs. These were exactly the scenes of ancient Egyptian life depicted over and over on the walls of ruined temples. A gunshot rang out in a banana grove, and a hundred white birds flew up out of the greenery with sharp cries of alarm.

Wherever you were on the Nile, whatever you saw along the banks, the ever-present ridge of the desert loomed beyond the greenery, walling the floodplain on either side, a long chain of

hills both east and west, often with pale chutes of sand spilling down them, blown in from the desert beyond. The burned
desert cliffs were a constant reminder of how tenuous was the
strip of green at the water's edge, how dependent it was on the
constant flow of the river.

There were more people along the banks than there had
been the day before—still I was surprised that I had seen so
few. Egypt occupies an area of one million square miles, only 5
percent of which is habitable, which means that these narrow
banks of the Nile should have been among the most densely
populated places in the world. Where were they all? They must
be beyond the trees, I decided, sitting in their houses or quietly
doing their farming, just as they'd been doing for thousands of
years. Now and then when I saw spirals of smoke rising from
small villages beyond the banana trees, I wanted to stop, beach
the boat, and go have a look. But it was illegal for foreigners to
venture alone into this part of the country, and, worse, as a foreign woman alone I knew I would arouse such curiosity and
chaos that stopping would bring me nothing but trouble. Occasionally a man on the riverbank noticed my face and in pure
curiosity and wonder howled for me to stop, and sometimes
the man would even run along the riverbank following me and
waving. But I kept moving.

At midday I stopped to rest on a small barren island in the
middle of the river. I sat in the hot sand. The sun bounced off
the water and into my face. I could feel the heat on my tongue,
in my ears. The world was a furnace. Everything smelled
toasted and dry. When I took off my head covering, I could
smell the sun baking my clothes. My hands were blistered and
raw; the calluses that had formed on my palms at home in my
regular life of rowing had not been nearly enough protection
from so much constant friction.

I sat on this tiny island in a kind of stupor, smelling the
smoke from the brush fires across the river. The biggest bee I

had ever set eyes on landed on my thigh, seemed to doze drunkenly there for a moment, then picked its way toward my knee, stumbled, dozed a bit, and eventually rolled off and fell to the sand with a tiny thump, where it lay shocked to stillness by the heat and the glare. The river was completely flat—no ripples, no eddies—and looked as heavy and gray as mercury; it seemed miraculous that the water wasn't boiling and steaming in the heat. Green bee-eaters flew low over the water. Doves hooted sadly in a withered thorn tree. I saw a crested lark and a tiny Nile Valley sunbird, bright blue and shimmering like a hummingbird, with a long forked tail and yellow stomach, and another tiny brown bird with a slender, upward-pointing tail like a twig. A brilliant green lizard with a brown stripe down his back skittered over my foot near the edge of the water. Lapwings chipped anxiously in the grassy shallows on the east bank of the river. There was no shade on this island. The heat worried me; my rear end burned from the hot sand beneath me. (In 1799 members of Napoleon Bonaparte's company recorded the effect of the heat in this part of Egypt: "If, at midday, one remains for a minute in the same place, or walks slowly, a burning sensation is experienced in the soles of the feet that is stinging and insupportable—relief cannot be obtained by marching quickly.")

I got up and walked the two hundred feet to the other end of the island, which had its own little sculpted dunes and wind-scoured hollows and a few stunted starving shrubs. I saw snake tracks purled into the sand and huge ants skidding single file along a sand dune; the ants were so light they left no tracks at all. The only sign of human industry on this island was a small stone wall crumbling on itself and enclosing nothing. It could have been a year old; it could have been four thousand years old. It was impossible to tell here. A rickety white-muzzled dog on the eastern bank wandered over and began barking hysterically at me across the water, curling his lips and baring a row of pumpkin-colored teeth. The force of his barking caused his paws to slide backward in the wet sand. Eventually the dog exhausted himself and wandered away to a lonely part of the beach and began yipping half-heartedly at nothing.

Two men in a fishing boat farther down the river banged on an oil drum to frighten fish into their nets; the sound vibrated in the heat. I drank a lot of water and took a photograph of my-self, holding my camera at arm's length—evidence for a later time when this episode would surely seem like a dream. Look-ing at that photo now, I see a solitary, roasted, unbalanced-looking person standing between two dunes, scowling into the camera, a flat blue strip of river beyond, above that a dark low line of green, and above that a blue sky of tremendous depth. My face is greasy with sweat, my hair matted flat by my hat, my lips burned and chapped, my eyes fried and blood-shot. I look hollow cheeked, wary, and obsessive.

Soon, Amr's felucca appeared in the far distance, and I climbed back into my boat and moved on.

That evening as the sun began to set, we were nowhere near the next appointed camping place and had to stop at a place called Silwa, near Silsileh, at the base of an enormous sand dune. This made Amr unhappy. The day had been long and suffocatingly still. Because his boat had moved so slowly, I had lost him for hours and had even turned my boat around and rowed back up-river again to find him. I, for one, was delighted to be stopping in this lonely, beautiful place at the foot of a tall, white sand dune. The sand here was the softest I had ever walked on, like powdered sugar, and it slid straight into the river with no inter-mediate berm of earth or beach grass. The slope reflected the setting sun in a brilliant gold, the sky was nearly mauve, and the fronds of the palm trees looked blue on the west bank of the river. But Amr was disappointed with the place and kept look-

ing upriver to see if any other Aswanian feluccas might come
straggling down to provide familiar company for the night. We
were very alone in this place, there was no protective cove, and
Amr felt we were too exposed to the wind should it come up in
the night. A small village lay nearby; that, too, made Amr uneasy. He didn't know the people there. "Cannot trust" was what
he said, and when Madeleine, cramped and restless from two
days sitting cross-legged on the sailboat, disappeared into the
banana groves for a walk, Amr anxiously watched her go, fearing she'd meet a robber or a mountebank or some other misfor-
tune. I tried to assuage his fears, reminded him that Madeleine's
Arabic was excellent, and that she was strong and had been all
over Egypt on her own.

The sun was falling low in the sky, touching the tops of the
palms now, enormous and flaming. As we prepared the boat
for the night, a pathetic metal felucca, all rust and dents and
shredded patchwork sails, crossed the river from the west bank
and bobbed up alongside us. Its captain was a ragged, whis-
kery, middle-aged man wearing an enormous pair of eyeglasses,
like an aviator's goggles. He muttered a few words to Amr from
his seat in the stern of the boat. The lenses of his glasses were
so thick they were almost opaque; they refracted the sunlight
in a distracting, prismatic way. Many older Egyptians wore
these government-issue glasses, and their clunkiness, their
utilitarian crudeness, always made the wearer look vulnerable
and weak and a little bit wounded.

Amr answered the man, and the captain, emitting a constant flow of soft utterings and moans, climbed up onto Amr's
deck with a cotton bag slung over his shoulder. He moved
slowly and carefully, as if to keep from stubbing his toe or
stumbling in his blindness. Amr knew the man; they shook
hands. He was here to sell us some marijuana, which, though
illegal, was beginning to seem ubiquitous in Upper Egypt.
This man was a kind of floating, boat-to-boat drug dealer. He

fished in his canvas bag for his paper pouches full of weed and pulled out a purse, a screwdriver, a bottle of water, a newspaper, and a length of rope, all the while grimacing and muttering beneath the bulwark of his goggles.

His boat was full of junk: tin cans, old newspapers, coils of what looked like telephone wire, a cooking pot black with soot, a wooden stool with only one leg, rumpled clothing, and cardboard boxes. Rust had reduced the steel deck top to a fine brown lace. Amr took two pouches from the man in exchange for two ten-pound notes. The drug dealer, still muttering and moaning to himself like a roosting dove, gathered up his personalties, returned to his boat, and without a word of good-bye drifted slowly away. His boat sailed in a limping way. Long shreds of torn cloth hung like wet stockings from his slack sails. The sails had been patched in a hundred places, and his mast was battered and shaky.

Amr and Wa'il dipped tin cups into the river and drank. This practice had always fascinated me and given me pause, and yet this day, desperate to wash, I thought that if Amr and Wa'il could drink from the Nile, I could certainly bathe in it. The water at the edge of this pretty dune was tempting and warm, very clear and surprisingly soft. Standing beneath the prow of the boat, I took off my clothes and with a bar of soap I waded into the warm river in my underwear. Amr and Wa'il stayed politely behind the stern of the boat while I washed. I stood up to my neck in the water. It was thrilling to stand in the Nile, and as I washed I tried to frighten myself with images of a ravening crocodile's needle-nosed snout rearing up out of the water in front of me, jaws ajar to reveal a dark, tunnel-like throat, long palate, and fleshy yellow gums studded with a million triangles of razor-sharp teeth.

I washed quickly and stepped onto the shore to dry myself.

Amr was quiet that evening. The day had been difficult for him, sitting for eight hours in the boat with his hangover, moving very little, drifting maddeningly, constantly tending to the tiller as to the arm of a doddery old woman, baking in the suffocating heat, and worrying about any impending disaster that he would have to answer for. He prepared our evening meal in silence, and when Wa'il opened the valve too wide on the stove and gassy orange flames shot up toward the boom above their heads, Amr reprimanded him sharply, the first display of impatience I had seen from him.

We ate our dinner quietly, and gradually Amr relaxed. Knowing that I had once been to Lake Nasser and Abu Simbel, he asked me what these places—the places his grandparents had come from—were like.

Abu Simbel, 250 miles south of Aswan and 100 miles south of the Tropic of Cancer, lay in the world's biggest middle of nowhere. Only one narrow road led from Aswan to Abu Simbel, and at the time that I visited the town, this road, for some vague security reason, was closed to all but the most necessary traffic. I made the fifty-minute flight in a small airplane full of French schoolteachers who stampeded the boarding gate and nearly poked each other's eyes out fighting for window seats so they could look out at absolutely nothing. There was not a single thing to be seen in the desert south of Aswan. From Aswan all the way to Abu Simbel and beyond, the landscape was lunar looking, a great plain of rough red sand dotted now and then with craggy little hills of what looked like lava rock. That desert had none of the elegance of the big-duned deserts of Libya and Morocco. It was all rubble and ruin. Of course, there was Lake Nasser to look at: another great, flat, mirrorlike plain devoid of any signs of life or activity—no ships, no lakeside greenery, no lakeside buildings, not even any waves. Nothing. And everywhere you looked the view ended at a hazy, sour-yellow horizon.

The town of Abu Simbel reminded me of a western American ghost town: it was made up of one or two streets, with a few skinny men walking idly up and down them plucking at their crotches. Others in bulky, ragged head wraps big as hatboxes sat crouched on their haunches at the side of the road, watching tumbleweeds roll by and taking refuge in the scanty shade of shrubs dwarfed by thirst. The heat was borderline equatorial; it asserted a heavy downward pressure. Dogs and humans looked under duress here, flattened and exhausted and flayed. When I removed my hat, the sun had made the top of my head sting in a vivid, concentrated way—it was like having a freshly baked nail driven into my skull.

The houses there were mostly single-story brick boxes, and there were many small construction sites that could easily have been confused with ruins; in Egypt it was often difficult to tell whether the half-formed houses one was always seeing were going up or coming down. There were few women on the streets of Abu Simbel and no vegetation surrounding the town. It was the driest, most barren place I had ever seen. A handful of houses had been painted a pretty Caribbean pink and orange, and on the main street there were a few restaurants that had the impromptu air of concession stands at a country fair: aluminum structures with sizzling griddles, conical logs of compressed beef sweating and rotating in front of an electric broiler, and sudden violent eruptions of greasy smoke billowing up under their torn awnings. A string of tiny shops sold tin pots and rubber buckets, Bic pens, potato chips, and cigarettes, and at the edge of the town sat a stone building with a sign on it that said, in lettering that resembled the hastily clipped and pasted characters of a ransom note, "Sanitry, inteyraTion, hoSpitaL, at, abu Simble toreST , Cety."

And of course in Abu Simbel there were the usual trinket stalls down by the temples of Abu Simbel, the only place tourists ever went in this town. The trinket sellers here were more rapacious and hard bargaining than they were in other parts of Egypt because there was so little business—few tourists stayed overnight in Abu Simbel, as there was only one thing to see and few hotels. The hawkers were bitter and cunning. Above all, they were immensely bored. It would be difficult to say which made them more aggressive, their boredom or their poverty. Every one of them sold exactly the same meticulously arrayed collection of artless trinkets as the man next to him, and there were something like a dozen stalls in all. Living in Abu Simbel during the best of times must have been trying, but when tourism was at a low point it was no doubt an existence of borderline starvation. I was careful not to touch a single trinket in Abu Simbel that I did not intend to buy, for to finger a piece of merchandise in that town was to encourage an unstoppable geyser of salesmanly blandishments, reckless urgings *(Make enjoy the eye, my lady! I would stay with you for all eternity!),* and a surge of hope that would be cruelly dashed the moment you returned the piece to its slot within the glittering rank of junk. Then the proprietor, with a sickly grin and a gelatinous gob of spit on the ground, would register his contempt for the stinginess of the Western infidel.

At this place I bought seven tiny glasses for approximately three dollars—the original price I was quoted was forty-five dollars—and the man I bought them from was so overjoyed at this sale that he offered me a bite of the melted ice cream he was eating. When I mentioned to the market manager that the men here seemed angry, he flashed his metal teeth at me and adjusted his headdress and said cheerfully, "Yes, because they are very poor and have many children." Like a number of men in Aswan and Abu Simbel, the manager had Bosnian blue eyes, kinky flame-red hair, and a wash of orange freckles across his nose.

Abu Simbel was such a strange and terrible town that I was compelled to stay overnight there in the Nefertari Hotel, a few hundred yards from the temples of Abu Simbel. The hotel was a dusty, single-story structure with many empty rooms, each with its own door leading to the outside, like the rooms of a motel. The place smelled of plaster, and every wall in the hotel seemed to have a fire extinguisher hanging on it like a technological talisman against the incendiary force of Abu Simbel's sun. Just above the banks of Lake Nasser was the hotel's tiny swimming pool. (Apparently no one ever swam in the lake, for the crocodiles in it were said to be nineteen feet long and the water was an awe-inspiring pus-green color.) The green matting around the pool was faded and curling at the corners, and the poolside cabana, which had "Merry Christmas" written in its window, was a wreck—all twisted metal, and broken glass, and water stains on the ceiling, and splinters of wood, as though a flood or a tornado or a frat party had passed through it.

The hotel was empty, but for me and four men who appeared at the table beside mine for dinner—three Egyptians and one Belgian. I gleaned from the technical nature of their conversation (conducted in English for the sake of the Belgian) that they were engineers working for UNESCO or some other international engine of progress. I had seen Egyptian men like this on trains all over Egypt, middle-class officials in Western dress with cell phones and a self-important, superior air. They were often plump and distracted and made an ostentatious show of reading their portable pocket-sized editions of the Koran, which reading consisted of a lot of hectic flipping of the pages, liberally interspersed with minute inspections of their fingernails and watches, and extended periods of gazing out the window while the book lay open and ignored on their well-pressed thighs.

When I spoke to the waiter in my stumbling Arabic, the three swarthy Egyptians lifted their mustaches from their soup bowls and stared at me. The smooth-faced, sandy-haired Belgian looked wan and tiny and somewhat apprehensive next to his three manly colleagues. I ate vegetable gruel and a salad of lettuce, cucumber, tomato, and crunchy olives from Siwa

Oasis and listened to the four men talking about marriage. I couldn't help listening, for the Egyptians spoke very loudly and were sitting a mere arm's length away from me.

The oldest and fattest of the Egyptian men said, "It is good to be apart from your wife for some time each month. Marriage works better that way."

The Belgian sipped daintily at his soup and said with uxorious sincerity, "Yes, because she can do what she wants while you are gone." The Egyptian, stricken with disbelief and disdain, reared back in his chair. "No!" he roared. "Because *you* can do what *you* want while you are gone. You are free. You don't get tired of her."

The startled Belgian, realizing too late the tenor of the company he was in, attempted to cover his mistake and match this Arabic machismo by lowering his soupspoon and stuttering, "Oh, yes. Right, right. That's true of course." And then he cleared his throat and searched for some dismissive thing to say about women. "Women are at their best *before* you get married," he said unconvincingly, and he followed the statement with a theatrical snort, an indication that he was entirely with his colleagues. Relieved, the three Egyptian men said "Ha-ha-ha" hollowly and wiped their mustaches and picked their teeth and went back to staring at me.

The next day in Abu Simbel I met a smart, skinny Egyptian tour guide who had studied comparative religions for several years in southern Virginia but had finally returned to Egypt because, he explained, he loved his wife too much. "My Egyptian friends couldn't understand that," he said, leaning against a tree skinnier than he was. "They thought I was stupid to give up my opportunity in America for a woman."

He told me that one day in Virginia he was sitting in a café with an American friend drinking orange juice and discussing women. The American asked him if he had ever considered marrying an American woman. The Egyptian said he would consider it but only if he loved the woman. In fact, he would be willing to marry a Christian or a Jew or any other brand of woman that he loved. The only woman he could not marry, even if he loved her, was a woman who was not a virgin. The American asked why a woman's virginity was so important. The Egyptian said, "Put your finger in your glass of juice." The American did as he was told. The Egyptian ordered him then to drink the juice. The American drank. The Egyptian said, "Now, if I put my finger in your glass of juice, would you still drink it?" The American said that he would not.

"My point is clear."

I asked the guide if he would kill his sister if she lost her virginity.

Without a pause, as though this was a reasonable and even a common question, he said, "I, for myself, would not kill my sister. But I would put her out of the house and disown her because she had shamed the family name."

The guide went on to tell me that some Egyptian men didn't want to go to America to avail themselves of the opportunities there because they feared they would see women in states of undress and would not be able to control themselves. "And then God would be angry with them," he said. "They believe so much in God."

When I suggested—gingerly, my voice humming with hesitation and tender hypothesis—that perhaps Egyptian men didn't respect women, the guide stuck his fingers down the open throat of his shirt and fished up a silver locket on a chain. In the locket were tiny photographs of his veiled mother and wife. "Here," he said proudly, "is the proof how much I respect women."

"They're your relatives," I said.

"I have no pictures here of my father!"

He explained why Egyptian men are allowed to have more than one wife: if a man's wife doesn't get pregnant, and he wants children, he can take another wife. I wondered if the same applied in reverse, would a woman be allowed to take another husband for the same reason.

"Of course not!" he said.

I had walked alone along the edge of Lake Nasser, which struck me as a seriously unnatural body of water. Neon green, it looked poisonous. It looked like a desert flooded with antifreeze. I stood on the shore, stared at the water in wonder, and had the feeling that if I fell into it my flesh would dissolve instantly from my bones. The heat was wounding; I had to narrow my eyes to slits to protect them from it. As I walked along the edge of the lake, I saw, every so often, a tiny patch of green, a withered clump of bushes, or a feeble stripe of grass. I saw lizards and clouds of sand fleas on the beaches, dragonflies and tiny anthills, all of which suggested that only the most minuscule life forms could thrive in these harsh conditions.

Abu Simbel and Lake Nasser were at their best when the rabid sun was gone, and then it struck me as one of the best places in the world. I sat alone in the dark by the pool and listened to crickets and the rhythmic purring of frogs. I stared at the sky for an hour. Far from any city, far from anything at all, a town so small that its artificial light had no effect on the atmosphere, Abu Simbel's night sky was a metropolis of its own, an enormous velvety parabola embracing the earth. Venus shone long on the water in a way that mimicked the moon, and the Big Dipper sat very low on the horizon. The whole place was a deeply swirling mass of stars. I felt short of breath and utterly insignificant looking at its hugeness and depth. This was a night sky you didn't have to raise your eyes to. It began below the horizon and was always right in front of you, wherever you turned. When I looked at it, the vortex of stars seemed to be lifting me off the ground, and I had to look down at my feet now and then to see that they were firmly planted. And then, looking down, I half expected to see stars there too. It was a sky so masterly and dizzying, I imagined myself having to crawl back to my hotel room on my hands and knees to keep from being bowled over by it and, more, by the endlessness that lay beyond it. This sky could make you feel comically small; you might as well crawl like the ant that you were.

As I described the night sky of Abu Simbel for Amr, he lifted his face toward the sky above us and, with the kind of fatalism that believes that everything is better elsewhere, he said, "Abu Simbel much better 'n this."

We all went to sleep early, and that night, like that day, was long. A seemingly endless parade of cruise ships passed us on their way to Luxor, each one stirring up a new barrage of waves that rocked us in our vulnerable spot and made the mast buck and teeter so that Amr and Wa'il had to jump out of their sleeping bags and—like attendants in an insane asylum—hold the moaning mast in a bear hug to keep it from juddering out of its socket. The mast was thirty feet tall, nearly the circumference of a basketball hoop at its base, and was tightly fitted into its foundation hole with a collection of cedar shims. If it toppled in the night, Amr would be in terrible trouble, not to mention the possibility that we might all be crushed under the weight of that enormous telephone pole.

Sitting up in my sleeping bag, I watched a few ships go by—at night their glowing lights made them seem cozy and noble. There were three hundred cruise ships on the Nile between Luxor and Aswan at any one time—a fleet that in daylight was just a moldy collection of buoyant buildings, bland and in need of paint. The ship I had traveled on with a hundred European tourists was tawdry and tired and had about it a melancholy air of lost luxury and promise. It was equipped with a sunbathing deck, a stagnant swimming pool with a torn one-pound note lying at the bottom of the deep end, a bar, a flashing disco dance floor, and a grinning crew of overfamiliar Egyptian attendants making lame jokes about mummies and tombs and pharaohs.

We left our camp at Silwa early the next morning, and when I reached Silsileh alone, I knew I was there just from the look of the place. I had read about this famous spot in countless books. Gebel Silsileh, the "Mountain of the Chain," was also known in Arabic as the "Place of Rowing" because it was the narrowest spot on the entire length of the Nile, and, lacking room in which to tack their sailboats comfortably, captains and their crew often had no choice but to row their boats through the defile. Here the river was hemmed in by high cliffs of red sandstone that concealed the famous quarries that had provided the stone for the temples of Karnak and Luxor, Esna and Edfu. In past decades, Silsileh had been a popular mooring place, but now tourist ships never stopped here. The cruise boat I had traveled on had passed by it at night.

I found it beautiful and a little bit frightening to see these close walls of cliff dotted with caves and cracks and small tombs rising straight up out of the water, looming above me and my tiny boat, their reflection in the water running red beneath me as I rowed. From the east cliff to the west, the river was said to be only 260 yards wide; passing so close between them was like entering a grand, high-ceilinged ballroom. Geologists have theorized that at some point these cliffs were joined into one stone barrier—the name Silsileh is believed to have come from the Coptic word for "stone wall"—and that, blocked by the wall, the Nile had pooled behind it into a lake. Only with aeons of overflowing had the water eaten through the stone and set its modern course toward Cairo.

I stopped rowing and let myself float, trying to prolong my stay between the two close cliffs. When I came to a safe spot where I could leave the boat on the shore, I climbed out and went up to the rock-cut Speos of Horemheb, with its five little doors, and peered in. The thing, like a stone chicken coop, was approximately three and a half thousand years old. The ground was dusty, reddish, and dry, and the place was empty and smelled of bat dung. The stones were slowly crumbling. I followed a narrow footpath high up the hill to the south and found more tombs. I was the only person here. Because the spot was isolated and so ridden with little tombs and shrines it felt like the oldest spot I had yet been in Egypt. I felt for the first time the thrill—and the mild anxiety—of being alone in a strange and slightly forbidden place. Little tombs and niches and stelae had been cut into the rock of the cliff; they were like abandoned prison cells now. Amelia Edwards had noted in her diary that her guides had pointed out a sort of table rock here, "fantastically quarried in the shape of a gigantic umbrella, to which they pretend some king of old attached one end of a chain with which he barred [the] Nile." I saw the very rock, still implacably standing and looking more like a half-nibbled mushroom than an umbrella.

At the top of the cliff I looked to the west and saw the enormous desert, a fearsome stretch of cooked earth, of nothing. When I saw Amr's sail approaching the gorge from the south, I scurried back to my boat and pushed off, not wanting him to know I had gone ashore.

As I approached Edfu in the late afternoon on the third day, a crowd of boys swimming off the Edfu dock tried to climb into my rowboat. I feared they would sink me and shooed them off by swatting at their heads with my cotton hat, which they found terribly funny and which only inspired them to try harder. They laughed and showed their white teeth as they slapped at the water with their skinny arms, their wet black heads glittering in the sunlight. I eluded them and waited on the dock for Amr, Madeleine, and Wa'il, who were still trailing behind me. We had made it here in three days.

Sitting on Amr's felucca, packing up my possessions, and

emptying the rowboat of my water bottles, sandals, and food, I felt both sad and excited. I was happy to have come this far but conscious that having Amr behind me had distracted me. I had spent much of my trip thinking about him, worrying for him, hoping not to displease or alarm him. We had made it here without undue difficulty. There had been no disaster, no robberies or drownings. The mast had not come unhinged, the police never showed up to protest my presence, I had met no crazy fishermen, had not tipped over, and I hadn't ruined Amr's rowboat. Now that we were here, Amr seemed very happy. He congratulated me on having rowed all this way and confessed that he was astonished to see how fast I had moved. I didn't tell him that I had deliberately drifted a good deal of the time to allow him to keep up with me or that I had actually twice rowed back upriver to keep in sight of him.

Before we left Aswan, I had agreed to pay Amr two hundred pounds. Now, moved by gratitude and affection, I gave him three times that—still it seemed too little. Amr was so surprised by the money that he didn't protest. He stood on the deck of his boat in his white gown, barefoot, the late afternoon sun illuminating his square and prematurely white head, his muddy brown eyes squinting at me. His lower lip quivered beneath his white-flecked mustache, and he clicked his tongue in that way that I knew meant he was speechless. Six hundred pounds—though it was six times what Amr usually made per month—was less than two hundred U.S. dollars. It was nothing; it had been worth it. My time in Egypt was short, and Amr had made it possible for me to begin my rowing trip. He had been unobtrusive, supportive, patient, and generous. He hadn't ridiculed my desire to row on the river or doubted my ability to do it.

Madeleine and I both gave Wa'il a tip and said good-bye to him, and Amr climbed into a horse carriage with us to accompany us from the dock to the taxi stand. Madeleine and I had agreed that Luxor would be the best place for me to find another boat and continue my trip. We would go there immediately, and I would start my search all over again. Driving to Luxor would mean missing the stretch of river between Edfu and Luxor, which I regretted, but I felt that my chances of finding my own boat here were even slimmer than they'd been in Aswan. And this way I would avoid the lock at Esna, which I was certain the authorities would never allow me to pass through.

I didn't tell Amr that I planned to continue on the river by myself. He would worry, would tell me all the reasons I shouldn't do it, and I would do it anyway. It was better not to tell him.

All the horse carriages in Egypt had funereal black bonnets, like the sunshades on old-fashioned baby carriages, and the insides of the cabs were lined with photographs of foreigners who had previously ridden in them. As we rode through the crowded streets of Edfu in this dark little box on wheels, young barefoot boys raced past us on tiny barebacked horses, whipping the horses with palm branches; then they turned and raced back again, shrieking their welcomes at the tops of their tiny voices. Back and forth, back and forth, they accompanied us in this frenzied way, the horses frothing and sweating, their hooves clattering and sliding on the hot pavement.

At the taxi stand, a driver said with the severity of an executioner, "No foreigners can ride to Luxor without bolice convoy!" then, ignoring what he had just said and without any pleading or cajoling from us, he opened the rear door of his car and shouted with the same severity, "Get in! I take you to Luxor. You give me forty bound."

I hated to say good-bye to Amr. When I told him that I felt lucky to know him, he said, "Luck for me too." There was no sufficient way to thank him for the help he had given me. I knew that he would endure ribbing and even ridicule when he returned to Aswan, towing the empty rowboat behind him. He wouldn't care. He was strong. He was also good company, and he was trustworthy. I would miss him. I wanted to hug him, but that was out of the question—such a display of affection between a man and a woman could simply not take place on a public Egyptian street without unpleasant consequences. We shook hands instead, which seemed pale and formal and deeply insufficient. It was unlikely that we would meet again.

As Madeleine and I climbed into the taxi, Amr began picking his way on foot through the throng of people jostling for taxis and carriages or waiting for the local bus. I watched the white head and the rounded shoulders so readily given to shrugging as they disappeared into the crowd, and felt very sad. I thought of Amr's life in Aswan, the home into which he had welcomed me, the housebound mother and sister he had to support with his meager income, the new house he dreamed of finishing so that he could leave his claustrophobic village and live in freedom. He was ill suited to the job of felucca captain—not aggressive enough, not coy enough, not eager enough for the money, not enough of a clown or a cad to elbow his way to the front of the crowd of Aswan felucca captains in order to attract the attention of the foreign tourists. He didn't fit in. Because he didn't fit in, his life was difficult.

Luxor

WE SET OFF FOR LUXOR, half an hour's ride, and immediately it became obvious that something was seriously wrong with the taxi. Every five minutes or so, the car would suddenly break into a feverish trembling and bucking, like a draft horse expiring, and the driver, leaning forward in his seat as if to coax it forward, would begin muttering anxiously to himself and gesticulating with his hand over the steering wheel, as though trying to reason with the demented engine. Each time he leaned forward, the sun illuminated a bald spot at the back of his head. A trip to Luxor at the price of forty pounds was a boon to him. He didn't want to lose us. He drove too fast. The car trembled and shuddered. The driver muttered and sighed, ground his teeth, frenetically shifted the gears up and down in a way that seemed wholly experimental. There were no seat belts in this car.

I looked out the window. In this middle of nowhere, a group of women draped from crown to toe in flowing black robes walked barefoot along the edge of the road, with baskets balanced on their heads. They looked otherworldly, almost demonic in the blinding light, their shadows slithering across the desiccated ground. Chickens and children straggled in and out of the open doors of mud-and-straw houses. Dry irrigation ditches with cracked mud bottoms sprouted weedy grass. Flat fields of alfalfa rolled endlessly by. A van overcrowded with turbaned men sped past us at ninety miles per hour, honking and teetering wildly.

Egyptians drove in a fashion that could only be described as chaotic. They seemed compelled to position their car in front of the one ahead of them at any cost. At night they drove with their headlights off until an oncoming car approached, at which time they helpfully blinded the opposing driver with a sudden flash of the high beams. And Egyptian highways were minefields of disaster. There were always skinny figures leaping across them at just the wrong moment, entire families sitting down to picnics in the middle of them, cars speeding along them in the wrong direction, men stopping their cars to pee in the fast lane, sudden pointless barriers stretched across the road, or wayward oil barrels, or boulders, or a huge herd of hobbled goats. Every ten miles or so the hideously crushed hull of a truck or car would appear at the edge of the road, the rusting, twisted remains of past accidents, and yet these gruesome and shockingly numerous reminders never seemed to chasten Egyptian drivers. They raced and careered and honked their way along with the heedless abandon of people who believe either that they are invincible or that life has no value whatever.

The problem with our taxi gradually grew worse. We were now traveling a mere ten miles per hour while the car shuddered and pitched and fumed. Smoke billowed out of the exhaust pipe. The driver seemed to be praying over the steering wheel.

In her patient, tactful fashion, Madeleine asked in Arabic, "Is there a problem with the car?"

The driver giggled anxiously. His bald spot was damp with perspiration. "There is no problem. No problem." Realizing that our attention was on him, he disguised the crazed, clutching motions of his gesturing hands by setting them to rolling his shirtsleeves higher on his hairy forearms.

The car suddenly ground to a halt. We sat still and silent in the heat and dust for a minute, staring through the bug-spattered windshield. The late afternoon sun slanted through the windows and made the car an oven. Finally the driver got out of the car.

Madeleine rolled down the window, leaned out, cleared her throat, and said, "Sir, excuse me, is there a problem with the car?"

I looked at her. Was she being facetious? She was speaking Arabic, which made it hard to tell.

"No problem. No problem."

The driver lifted the hood. We heard a lot of bashing and clanking, felt him tugging violently at something, and then the hood closed with such force I thought the windows would shatter. The driver walked slowly toward an isolated tin shack across the road and banged on the door. A man appeared in a navy blue monkey suit; a mechanic by the looks of him. He had smudges of grease on his forehead and a tire iron in his hand.

There is in Egypt a weird kind of storybook serendipity. In the middle of the desert, a lone bedouin always appears with nothing in his bag but precisely the sort and size of socket wrench you need to fix your Jeep and escape death. And though their state factories generate products of often questionable quality, Egyptians as individuals have a great genius for fixing things. They are capable of repairing anything at all with whatever happens to be at hand. They could coax a sundered axle into spinning another million miles with nothing but a piece of dental floss positioned just so.

The two men ducked under the hood of the car, and, after bashing at the engine for ten minutes, we were on our way again.

The next morning Madeleine and I sat on the porch of our Luxor hotel and watched five young men in plastic sandals washing the marble paving stones at the entrance to the brand-new Mummification Museum across the corniche. They used enormous squeegees to shove the soapy water around; from where we sat the process looked like a watery game of shuffleboard.

Luxor—which was ancient Thebes and the great cemetery of the Valley of the Kings—had a melancholy beauty and a haunting history that seemed almost thoroughly overshadowed by the commerce that had been built on its famous pharaonic back. There was, effectively, no business in Luxor but tourism, which gave the local men license to speak to the foreigner with immediate intimacy—they knew in advance what the visitor wanted. Packs of sunburned foreign tourists spilled out of cruise ships and paraded through the streets of Luxor in shorts and floppy sunhats and were immediately besieged by the local touts. Carriage drivers slowed their jaunty black vehicles alongside them on the corniche chirping, "Calash? Calash? Five bound!" in a way that sounded almost lewd. The Luxor horses were uniformly tiny and delicate, overwhipped, and forced to canter frenetically up and down the hard hot pavement of the corniche, laboring under the weight of cargoes of beefy German businessmen on their way to the temple complex of Karnak, their dainty hooves slipping on the oily blacktop. Felucca captains descended from the docks saying, "Felucc? Felucc? Go boat?" And at the entrances to the scores of souvenir shops, young men stepped in front of you and said, "Come in, have look. Drink tea. Just for welcome," while the subtler ones sat outside their shops with dog-eared postcards written in English and asked you to translate them as a way of getting you to stop and engage. They knew what the postcards said; they had had them translated countless times before. If they could get you to speak to them, they might also get you to give them money. With an Egyptian man, there is never any such thing as a simple or straight answer. If you ask, "Where is the post office?" he will squint at you, rake his mustache with his fingers, and answer, "Oh, lady, what you need to buy?" If you tell him that you want to post a package, he will say, "Big backage? Small backage?" Unable to see how the size of the package could make any difference whatever, you ignore his question and ask again where the post office is. "I can help you!" comes the answer. Yes, I'm sure you can help me, but where exactly is the post office? "Bost office closed now at this o'clock." Yes, fine, but can you just tell me *where* it is? "Too far," he will say ominously, because if he risks telling you that the post office is just around the corner, you'll leave him and dash his chance for a tip or a business transaction.

The Luxor men cracked silly jokes, made silly puns, said "Welcome to Alaska!" and "How now brown cow," and "See you later, alligator," and a million other English phrases they learned from the tourists and repeated with the uncanny accuracy of parrots. They had a talent for mimicry. They could do Bronx, Liverpool, South London, and Melbourne accents, all with ventriloquistic precision. Amelia Edwards caught the essence of Luxor when she wrote in 1878:

> Our arrival brought all the dealers of Luxor to the surface.
> They waylaid and followed us wherever we went . . . And now
> there is a rush of donkeys and donkey boys, beggars, guides,
> and antiquity dealers . . . the children screaming for backshish;

the dealers exhibiting strings of imitation scarabs; the donkey-boys vociferating the names and praises of their beasts; all alike regarding us as their lawful prey. "Hi, lady! Yankee-Doodle donkey; try Yankee-Doodle!" cries one. "Far away Moses!" yells another. "Good donkey—fast donkey—best donkey in Luxor!"

Edwards noted that the men of Luxor, whether Coptic or Arab, were all "polite, plausible, and mendacious."

Little had changed. The Luxor guides and shopkeepers had a genius for human psychology, for the holidaymaker's mind-set. They knew how to inspire guilt in the wealthy visitor and had constructed a colorful array of hand-tied verbal flies with which to hook the foreign fish. The shopkeepers put on a humorous, amorous, energetic show, but when you caught them off guard they always looked forlorn, paring their nails, scraping dried horse manure from the bottoms of their flip-flops, or sleeping slumped in the dust in front of their shop with their mouths hanging open. It was only when they saw you coming that they hopped up and put on the mask of bravado and romance, a mask that after just one day in Luxor grew tedious. *You are looking for me, lovely lady? Come and look my shop. For free. We go dancing tonight. Smile, you are in Luxor. Welcome back. You remember me? Here I am, Miss Lady. Miss Madame. Mrs. Madame. Mrs. Lady.*

Once in Luxor two Egyptian men had approached me and asked me to buy them a bottle of whiskey in the duty-free shop, the only place that sold hard liquor. Egyptians were not allowed to buy in these shops. One of the men peeled seventy pounds from a thick wad of bills and held it out to me. "Blease, madame," he said. He was handsome and strong. He had a wooden leg and held the top of one crutch skillfully tucked under his gesturing arm like a rolled-up newspaper. When I asked the men if they were going to drink the whiskey they said, "Us? No! We is Muslim. We do not drink. We will sell it to hotel." Or they would sell it to some unsuspecting tourist for twice the going rate.

I agreed to buy the whiskey, to see what would happen. When I went into the duty-free shop, there were four British women there, shopping loudly. They were bare shouldered in sundresses, and had fat, sunburned knees, and they jollied up their skinny, beleaguered Egyptian guide with jokes and sexual innuendo and cajoling pokes in the ribs. It was fascinating to see this unusual reversal: an Egyptian man for once overwhelmed by the overbearing, even bullying attentions of foreign women. The women bought gin and cigarettes and one of them held a can of German beer up to her face and said, " 'Ow much alcohol is in these beers?" and her bosomy daughter, without looking at the can, shouted expertly, "Five point three percent! The Egyptians invented beer!" When the cashier gave them the price of their goods in dollars, one of the women yelled, " 'Ow much is that in British? Ask 'im, Mabel. And fetch us another bottle of gin."

Behind them in line stood a tiny, fragrant, Italian man in a white sport coat who was speaking broken Arabic to no one. He was drunk. "Luxor is my paradise," he said over and over, until the British daughter turned to him and said authoritatively, "It's my paradise too, love. I been 'ere ten times in two years!"

There were, indeed, Europeans who loved Luxor obsessively. It was cheap and easy and down at the heels; the weather was always good; and there were enough cruise ships docked along the river that the sight of a foreign woman in a bikini was less shocking here than elsewhere in Egypt. In the days of Flaubert and Nightingale, it required money and time to travel to Egypt. Now, anyone could afford to come and spend a few nights in a hotel. They came as much for the constant sun and cheap beer and papyrus souvenirs as for the ancient monuments. British truck drivers, Dutch farmers, French shopkeepers, Australian secretaries. Young European women flounced up and down the Luxor corniche in clothes not much more concealing than underwear. The felucca captains stared and followed them.

It was generally known that many European women came to Luxor expressly to buy sex from the young Egyptian men, that homosexual prostitution thrived here, and that all this went on, seemingly unchecked, in the stern and censorious shadow of Islam. One afternoon in Luxor, outside a trinket shop on the corniche, I had had a conversation with a garrulous young man who worked in the shop. His name was Ahmed. He was tall, strong, and remarkably handsome, with a slender waist, powerful arms and thighs, and big eyes the color of raw honey. He had sharp cheekbones and a square jaw, and his golden eyes were shaded by long, dewy, black lashes. He wore jeans and loafers and a tight white T-shirt. With no trace of shyness, no trace of self-consciousness, no natural sense of pudency or decorum, this young man stood on the street in the hot sunlight smoking a cigarette and telling me everything he knew about sex, everything he knew about those sex-crazed European women, mostly middle aged, who jumped off the cruise ships and went running through Luxor hunting for Egyptian men half their age.

I had been to Luxor three times and knew that what he said was true. It was not unusual in Luxor to step out of the blinding sunlight into a dark little trinket shop to find a bare-limbed, middle-aged, tousle-headed German woman sitting sunburned in the lap of a panting teenage shop boy. It was not unusual to see these strikingly mismatched couples walking hand in hand along the corniche. I had seen it with my own eyes, but for the sake of the conversation I told Ahmed that I didn't believe that any of that took place here. I wanted to hear him tell it.

He laughed loudly at me. "You don't believe? I can show you

myself!" He pointed his cigarette across the river to a row of apartment buildings at the edge of the ferry landing on the west bank. "You see those buildings? Many French and German women, they keep apartments there so they can come here and fuck the young men. They pay them money. They come to Luxor five and six times every winter." He slapped his own chest. "They pay me!"

I asked why these women needed to come all the way to Egypt to find men.

"They like us because they know we strong. We get hot easy. We is Arabs. Not like pansy white men. We is Egyptian. Big men. Strong benis."

He sucked on the cigarette, blew smoke over my head, looked up and down the corniche at the tourists tottering down the gangplanks of the big white ships parked three deep along the edge of the river. Taxis trawled slowly up and down the street, the drivers hollering out the windows at potential customers.

Ahmed waved his arm at three white women crossing the street in shorts and T-shirts. "A lot of these women they married, but the husband is no good. Weak benis. Or some husbands is gay. Sometimes the French husband he come to my shop and he tell me, 'You can have sex with my wife only if you have sex with me first.'"

"And do you have sex with the husbands, Ahmed?" I said.

He spat on the dusty pavement to show his distaste. "I don't make sex with men. I don't need to. All the women they love me. But there lot of gay men in Luxor. Mostly English."

As we stood there, four young French girls went by. Ahmed interrupted the conversation to leer at them. His mouth hung open. He stared unabashedly. "See that fat one?"

He was whispering almost collusively at me, as though I was just another Egyptian fellow with like sentiments. I saw the woman; it would have been difficult not to see her: high heeled,

double chinned, in a short skirt so tight I could see the outline
of her underwear, her bra straps intertwined with the spaghetti
straps of her red halter top, peroxided hair dangling in spears
down her back. Her fat and freckled upper arms jounced and
jiggled as she walked. I had been in Egypt just long enough that
this woman, dressed as she was, looked nearly naked to me. I
was as surprised and fascinated as Ahmed.

"I like her ass," Ahmed said.

"Really," I said.

From the easy way Ahmed spoke, it was obvious that I was
not the first foreign woman he had talked with this way. He
expected no rebuke, no rebuff, no affront; he never stopped to
wonder whether I might take offense or be scandalized or annoyed or even bored by all this salacious patter.

"That kind of ass I like. Big. But she got too much tits. I
don't like tits so big. Anyway, I don't like the young women as
much as the old. I love any women that is older than forty.
They have more experience. They better in bed."

The first woman Ahmed had ever had sex with was German.
He was seventeen; she was forty-two. And just last week he
had a French woman who was fifty. He approximated her figure with his hands, sighed wistfully, and rolled his eyes. "She
was fucking great!" He spent three days walking around Luxor
with this woman, and on their last day together he asked her if
she wanted to sleep with him. She said yes, of course, and invited him to visit her in her cabin on the cruise ship. "But I
never go to the ships. I invite them to my apartment. That why
I don't live with my family. I have my own place so I can bring
the women there. Once I made sex with a woman seventy years
old. I drink a lot of alcohol, then I can do it."

"Do your parents know that you have all these women?"

He winced and frowned at me as though I were insane.
"Fuck, no! They would be angry. They would kill me and tell
me I am not their son anymore."

"Are you Muslim?"

He was silent a moment. He crossed his big arms on his chest and nibbled at his lower lip. He lowered his voice. "Well Muslim, yeah. But I don't do Islam things right now. I don't do Ramadan. I don't read the Koran. Later, when I'm older, I will do those things."

"Why later?"

"To make good with God."

I asked him if he ever had Egyptian girlfriends.

"Shit, no! I hate the Egyptian women! They talk too much. I work all day, get home at eleven at night, and she would be talking talking talking like a crazy lady. And they is all religious. They want a baby, a nice house, spend money on nothing." He spanked his hands together as if to rid his palms of dust. "Never. No Egyptian girls!"

Two British women went by, one in a sleeveless blouse. He ogled the woman's arms, looked her up and down, wrung his hands, sighed with desire.

I asked Ahmed if he ever met a foreign woman who was offended by his advances.

He smiled. "Yeah! Lots of them they don't like it. One day I'm sitting here and a pretty German lady she walks by. I say to her, 'Don't walk away! You break my heart if you leave!' She turn around to give me a punch. Like this"—he grimaced and raised his fist—"and she say, 'I break your heart? How you like I break your neck, you bastard!'"

He giggled at the recollection. "I talk to every girl who go by. I want to catch them. I make them stop and talk to me. Egyptian men, we know that all these foreign women they are prostitutes."

I looked at him, trying to decide whether to laugh or protest. "I am a foreign woman, Ahmed," I said.

He raised his palms at me and backed up on the sidewalk, realizing he had made a mistake. "Yes, I know, lady, but not you." He waved at my long trousers, my boots, my long-sleeved blouse buttoned up to my throat. "You is not prostitute. That's obvious."

"How is it obvious?"

"You dress careful. I can't see what you look like except your face. You got pride. You got nice face too. You looks like bird. But lot of them, lady, believe me lot of them is prostitutes."

The boy was not stupid, just crude and a blabbermouth. I asked him if he knew what the word *prostitute* meant.

He gave a proud little shrug to indicate that the question was too easy for someone whose English was as good as his. "Yeah. Of course. *Prostitute* mean somebody who take money for sex."

"From what you've just told me, Ahmed, it sounds as though these European women you're talking about aren't taking money for sex. It sounds like they have sex with Egyptian men because they want to. In fact, it sounds to me like it's the Egyptian men who are taking money for sex."

Ahmed stared at me, his long lashes blinking rapidly, his golden eyes shining with confusion in the sharp afternoon light. Suddenly the handsome boasting chatterbox had nothing to say. His big face seemed to have shut down. He was still as a stone. I helped him along. "I mean, you said that yourself, right? European women come here and pay the Egyptian men for sex?"

Ahmed was speechless for a long time. And then, slowly, he began to giggle nervously in recognition. "You're right, lady," he said, absorbing the irony of it. He tossed his cigarette into the dusty gutter. He looked wounded and embarrassed. "You are right." He plucked his lower lip in thought then turned to go back into his shop. "I got to go now," he said with a wave. "I got some customers here."

It was just another modern development: at the turn of the

twenty-first century, Western woman had managed to turn the Egyptian man into an exotic prostitute, much the way Western men had done with Egyptian women for years. It was perhaps damaging to the pride of the Muslim man to be bought by the Western woman, nevertheless the transactions took place with willingness from both sides. Women had been selling themselves for ages. "It may be a perverted taste," Flaubert wrote, "but I love prostitution, and for itself, too, quite apart from its carnal aspects . . . The idea of prostitution is a meeting place of so many elements—lust, bitterness, complete absence of human contact, muscular frenzy, the clink of gold—that to peer into it makes one reel." Sex could be a commodity; everyone knew that. But now the flow of the transaction had been revised and reversed. In Luxor, it was now women who clinked down their gold for men.

So many young Egyptian men approached me on the street in Luxor and whispered, "You want make sex with me?" that it grew tiresome and annoying, and when, in irritation, I knocked the baseball cap off the head of one of these boys, he looked utterly shocked by my unexpected protest and hurried away in fear. A nearby policeman who saw me slap the boy's head came running to my assistance. "What that boy do, madame?"

I didn't tell the officer what the boy did, for I knew that if I complained, the officer would arrest the boy, beat him, and put him in jail—far too harsh a punishment for such a thing.

Across the Luxor Nile there was the Ramesseum, the Temple of Ramses II, and the Valley of the Kings, the enormous pharaonic cemetery. Just as at Elephantine Island, walking across the desert on the west bank of Luxor became an exciting adventure when you realized that all that crumbling rubble under your feet was composed of bits of ancient pottery, human kneecaps, strips of linen winding-sheets, and scraps of painted wooden sarcophagi. You could walk across the open plain below the Temple of Hatshepsut and stumble on the mud-brick walls of the dwellings of ancient tomb builders. Strewn about the crumbling walls lay the builders' broken teacups, pot handles, and bits of painted jugs. The dust was pink with the powder of crushed pots. Like Amelia Edwards and that whole band of nineteenth-century travelers, the more I found of these colorful chunks of crockery and wood, bits of plaster painted in yellow and red, the more I wanted to find. The ground here was not protected, enclosed, or part of any government museum, and the sight of all these ancient scraps scattered freely about underfoot was thrilling. I once spent an entire afternoon wandering in the dust of the west bank discovering human jawbones and femurs and ancient rubbish. Holding these fragments in the palm of your hand is a way of connecting to the distant past. Some potter had made this now broken cup three thousand years ago; the fine lines that his fingertips had left on the clay were still visible. He had held it in the palm of his hand, exactly as I was holding it. When he looked up at the night sky, he had seen virtually the same stars I saw now. The thought of it made me realize that the potter and I were not so different; I could almost hear him breathing.

A Boat of My Own

MADELEINE AGREED with me that the best place to try
to buy a rowboat discreetly in Luxor was slightly downriver beyond the town, where we would be more likely
to find fishermen and less likely to be hindered by the web of
shopkeepers. The following morning we rented bicycles and
rode north along the river, past the Temple of Karnak, until we
came to a roadblock manned by young soldiers. We would not,
they said, be allowed to pass through. Why? Because it was
not safe for foreigners to venture out of the city. But, we said,
we only wanted to go a little way and see what the countryside was like, what a real Egyptian village was like.

Madeleine charmed the young men with her very good Arabic. She assured them that we would go, have a look, and
come back in ten minutes. "I promise by Allah," she said, and

the soldiers laughed. Miraculously, they waved us through.

On we rode past mud houses and mango groves and a place that looked like a power plant or a military compound. We turned down a rutted dirt road toward the river, riding beneath enormous palm trees until we came to an empty stone ghat. We saw fishermen working in the middle of the river, bending over the gunwales of their boats, hauling in nets like hanks of wet hair. We sat on the ghat and waited for one of them to pass close by, which, although we were in an insignificant and secluded spot, would inevitably happen, and we discussed how we would approach our delicate task, rehearsing what we would say.

Eventually, a young man appeared behind us on the riverbank and asked us the usual questions. We told him we wanted to buy a boat. We told him about the sleeping husband in the hotel, the surprise birthday gift, and all the implausible rest of it. Another young man appeared, and when a fisherman in just the right sort of rowboat came around a bend in the river, the two young men cheerfully yelled for him to come over and told him that I wanted to buy his boat.

The fisherman was young. He stared at us, grinning rigidly in surprise and wonder. Like many Egyptian peasants, he had three or four front teeth encased in a chrome-bright metal; his grin glinted like a teaspoon in the sunlight. I asked the fisherman if I could try his boat for a minute. He paused for a few puzzled seconds, and then he nodded. But I could only try the boat if he came with me. The two self-appointed agents wanted to come too. They were all amiable and eager to be part of the adventure.

Madeleine spoke to them. "She knows how to do it. She must try the boat alone." And the sound of her accomplished Arabic seemed to reassure them that this was true and that I was trustworthy.

I climbed into the boat and rowed it upriver a hundred yards, parallel to the bank, spun it around, and rowed back again. The boat was ideal. It was light, easy to row, and just long enough to lie down in. The men stared as I worked the oars.

I pulled up to the ghat and got out of the boat. When Madeleine asked the young fisherman if he would sell me the boat, he didn't laugh. He scratched his head in thought, then set the price at seventeen hundred pounds (about six hundred dollars).

I was nearly faint with happiness and hope.

Madeleine said, "But she could buy a brand-new boat for only one thousand pounds. Your price is too high."

It was true that the fisherman's boat was far from new. Like most Egyptian fishermen's rowboats, it was steel, painted marine blue, and was twelve feet long and just under three feet wide. It was dirty. It was dented in several places, and the paint on the hull was peeling and showing signs of rust. The oars were the usual clunky balks lashed to pegs with twine; they too were painted blue. The oarlock pegs had been roughly fashioned from tree branches. The seat and floor were covered with plastic imitation grass matting of a brilliant green and riddled with holes made by cigarette burns. The boat had a tiny storage cabin in the bow with a latched door. It had red and green hand-painted trim, an Islamic design of triangles. A few Arabic phrases, mostly involving the praise of Allah, had been painted in pink in choice spots around the boat, and there were some bulbous red hearts painted on the prow. Hearts seemed a requisite decoration on Egyptian boats, the sort of hearts drawn by schoolchildren on Valentine's Day.

I thought the boat was beautiful. I wanted it, but I could afford only nine hundred pounds. I took off my watch and silver earrings and bracelet and held them up and said, "I'll give you nine hundred pounds and my watch and this jewelry."

Madeleine translated. The man stared at me, fascinated and tempted, but he said nothing. Fearing he would say no, I reached into my bag and brought out a Polaroid camera I had with me. "And I'll give you this camera too."

I lifted the camera and snapped a picture of the young man. When, with an important plaintive whine, the camera instantly vomited up a stiff square photograph, the men's faces registered alarm. Like many Egyptians, they had never seen a camera quite like this before. They huddled around me, a mass of sweating heads, and held their breath and watched the image developing in its ghostly way.

The fisherman took the picture between his delicate fingertips and stared at his face with a look of both fear and delight. He stared a long time, then pointed at his teeth, as if surprised and a bit disappointed to find that his natural beauty was marred by all that garish metal in his mouth.

The men began to talk excitedly all at once, each one telling the other what should be done. They raised their palms to each other's chests in emphasis; they grinned and grimaced and blinked in the sunlight. The fisherman said nervously, "But I have to ask my father if I can sell the boat."

"Where is your father?"

He waved across the river to the west bank. "Far across."

We agreed to wait for him while he went to ask his father.

He tucked the photograph carefully into the pocket of his gallabiya, climbed into the boat, and rowed quickly away. I hated to see him go; I feared he wouldn't return.

The two young men sat on the steps with us at the edge of the river. As we waited, I realized that I might have felt a bit like a manifestly destined Massachusetts Pilgrim sneakily tricking the American Indians with novel trinkets and booze, but for the fact that I was still offering the man far too much cash for the boat. The camera was cheap and so was the watch, but they were all I could spare.

A third man in a lumberjack's flannel shirt joined us on the ghat. It was terribly hot in the sun. The steps of the ghat

radiated waves of heat. We drank water and listened to our
Egyptian companions conversing excitedly. They were pleasant. They spoke no English. They all talked at once, loudly and
at length, a very Egyptian habit. One of the men had a hammer
and kept tossing it up in the air excitedly like a majorette's ba-
ton. Another inspected my bracelet and then giddily fitted it
over his ear and let it hang there like a crazy earring.

I was nervous, hoping not to be thwarted or told no by anyone, hoping that something good was going to happen. Across
the river, the red string of hills above the Valley of the Kings
was faint in the afternoon haze.

The time passed quickly, and before long we saw the boat
returning across the water, this time with four men in it,
which made me doubly nervous. Who were they all? What bad
news would they bring? One of the men squatted precariously
on the high little deck at the rear of the boat. Two others were
standing up in the boat, like George Washington crossing the
Delaware. Why weren't any of them falling over? The fisherman rowed quickly against the heavy current.

In a moment of forethought and firmness, Madeleine turned
to the three chattering men sitting on the ghat with us and
said, "Gentlemen, please. Please promise me that when they
arrive you will all try your very best to remain silent for at
least five minutes."

The men laughed hysterically and slapped their knees and
tapped their watches and said, *We promise, we promise. Five
minutes exactly, madame. We shall time it!*

When the boat arrived, a tall man in a white gown stepped
forward with the Polaroid photograph in his hand. The young
fisherman had been unable to find his father and so had
brought his uncle, who looked not much older than the
nephew. The uncle's name was Shazly Fouad. His intelligent
eyes locked immediately on my camera.

I made my offer again to the uncle—the money, the supplementary watch, jewelry, and camera. He said, "No. Just the money and the camera I will take."

"You will sell her the boat?" Madeleine said, surprised as I.

"Yes. Nine hundred pounds and the camera."

I was beside myself with relief. I wanted to hug Madeleine for her skill. In my excitement I threw into the bargain the two boxes of Polaroid film I had with me and promised Mr. Fouad that if he gave me his address, I would send him four more as soon as I got home.

Never expecting I'd find a boat so quickly, I hadn't brought any cash with me. I would have to return to Luxor to get the money. We agreed to meet an hour later at a dock on the other side of the roadblock, closer to the Temple of Karnak. Madeleine translated briskly for me, a lot of fast talk back and forth. Every now and then through the mush of unaccustomed sounds, the gulping vowels and glottal stops, a word would bubble up that I recognized, each one creating the weird effect of a door clicking shut, pushing me farther outside the circle of this fuming conversation. Finally, with Madeleine as our bridge, Shazly Fouad and I sealed the deal by shaking hands, and the men immediately began clearing out the boat, gathering up its clutter of burlap bags and plastic buckets, cigarette butts and fish bones.

As Madeleine and I prepared to leave and go back to our bicycles, the young man with the hammer held the hammerhead in his hand, pointed the butt of the handle at my nose as if it were the barrel of a gun, and said, "Bam!" in a way that spooked me. When he saw the unsettled look on my face, he shook my hand and smiled and patted my shoulder to show it was only a joke.

The men reappeared at the dock at the prearranged hour—all of them: the fisherman, the uncle, the three bystanders, as well as several more who had come along for the spectacle, and when Madeleine and I arrived they clamored around us, chattering at full volume.

Madeleine took charge, and after a great deal of pleading and howling and frantic exchanges among the men, she managed to silence them. I wanted a written receipt from Shazly Fouad to carry with me on my trip. I wasn't eager to go off down the Nile in an Egyptian boat without some proof that I had paid for it. For the same reason, Shazly Fouad wanted a receipt for the camera. The transaction was unusual enough that we were both worried about the Egyptian authorities. Madeleine wrote up a makeshift legal document in both Arabic and English, and as Shazly Fouad was reading it aloud, a man in the crowd stepped forward and said, "I am a lawyer. That is not the correct and proper language. You must use the correct and proper legal language."

I could see Madeleine growing uncharacteristically impatient. Egypt was ridden with self-proclaimed lawyers mincing on about proper phraseology. Madeleine snatched up the notepad and began to rewrite the contract. The crowd—now fifteen people—surged against us, peering over our shoulders, jostling us, jockeying to get a better view of the foreign woman writing in Arabic.

A big village woman all in black appeared with her three naked children. The children were wet from swimming in the river and were covered in sand. The four of them pushed their way into the middle of the crowd and began moaning, baksheesh, baksheesh, in that mournful, pleading way, pushing against our hips. The woman held an unflinching naked baby on her broad shoulder, and with deep suspicion she watched Madeleine writing. Flies crawled across the baby's cheeks, attracted by slick trails of snot. The fuzzy heads of the other children bobbed beneath our elbows; they turned their curious, woeful faces up at us and clamored for money. I gave the mother a ten-pound note and the children a pen, hoping they would leave us alone, but one of the children began to wail because I hadn't given him more. His mother, delighted with the ten pounds, mimicked his wailing, laughed for my benefit, and gave me a chummy poke in the arm.

Madeleine wrote what the self-important lawyer had dictated to her:

In the name of Allah the Merciful and Compassionate, I the undersigned declare that I bought a fishing boat from El Shazly Fouad from the town of Luxor from the neighborhood of Azaneyya Il-Qibly for the amount of 900 pounds Egyptian only. And here I declare that.

Signed:
The seller: Shazly Fouad
The buyer: Rosemary Mahoney
The first witness: Madeleine Stein
The lawyer: Ahmed Mossad

I handed the camera and the money to Shazly Fouad, and Madeleine snapped a photograph of us shaking hands while Shazly held the nine hundred pounds up in the air.

When the sale was completed, the village woman came up beside me, wrapped her arm around my head in a kind of half nelson, and with staggering force she yanked hard until my ear was pinned to her shoulder, an indication of her congratulations and her deep affection. Her hold had the biting power of a carpenter's vise. When I opened my eyes, all I could see was the ovoid black curve of her belly and the bluish henna tattoo on her thick wrist. The woman had a pleasant smell, like fresh oats and cinnamon. Her shoulder was wet and gritty from the sandy bottom of the baby who had recently occupied the spot. She wouldn't let go of me. From beneath her forearm, I asked Madeleine to ask her to set me free. The woman pointed at herself, then pointed at me, then pointed at the boat and emitted a startling *zagareet,* that famous Arabic ululating sound that Arab women make at weddings and parties and on the occasion of important purchases, or when anything at all good happens. The woman wondered, did I want her to perform a traditional celebratory blessing, for which, she was happy to report, there would be only a very small fee?

I declined the formal celebration. I would be leaving Luxor early the next morning in my new boat and had many things to do before I left. I feared that all this jolly chaos would go on indeterminately if we didn't bring it to a close. I gave the woman another few pounds and she drifted happily away, trailed by the naked children.

I realized that I needed a place to keep the boat safely overnight, and I wanted to leave it here, away from the busy eyes of downtown Luxor. If I rowed off down the river the next morning from this spot, there would be less chance of hindrance. A nearby restaurant had a dock in front of it. We asked a waiter who worked there whether we could leave the boat at the dock for the night. He went to get his boss.

The boss was a heavy, dark, officious man who spoke English very well. Dramatically he informed me that I could leave my boat at his dock but that he, for one, washed his hands of all responsibility for it. He brushed his hands together repeatedly to illustrate the meaning of this. I said I would hire someone to watch the boat all night, and the waiter gladly volunteered. I offered him thirty pounds, which made his eyes bulge with happiness.

"Fifty bounds," said the busybody boss.

"Forty," I said.

The waiter, hardly able to believe his good fortune, stepped forward and said, "OK, madame. It's good. Forty," before the boss could queer the deal with his greed. The waiter's name was Muhammad. I told him I would return the next morning at 3:30 to retrieve the boat and hoped no one would ask why on earth I wanted to pick it up so early. I wanted to leave Luxor under cover of darkness. The two men thought I was taking the boat to Cairo in a truck. When the boss asked me who would help me remove the boat from the river, I said lamely, "Some nice men. Don't worry at all about that. Everything is fine."

No one asked another question about this weird arrangement. This could never have happened in Aswan. It was as if the Luxor people were so familiar with foreigners they simply didn't care what crazy hijinks we got up to.

Madeleine and I said good-bye to Shazly Fouad. He was worried about getting his extra Polaroid film in the mail. He gave me his address and asked Madeleine, "Is this lady trustworthy?"

Madeleine said, "Very. Very. She will do everything in her power to get that film to you. It may take some time but, God willing, you will get it."

Shazly peered skeptically at her. "By God, you say this?"

Somberly Madeleine said, "By God, I say it."

"Praise God."

Madeleine nodded and offered the proper response, "Praise God. Praise God."

When Shazly Fouad had gone, the restaurant owner commanded us to come into his restaurant and drink lemonade. I didn't want to drink lemonade. I wanted to go and buy the supplies I would need for the rest of my trip; it would take three more days at least, and this time I would be on my own without Amr to cook for me. But I didn't want to alienate this fellow who had agreed to harbor my boat on his dock.

We sat with the man at a long table in an empty dining room, and immediately he informed us that the "accident" the previous year in Luxor—the massacre of fifty-eight tourists, many of them hacked to death with machetes—was not the work of Egyptian terrorists, that this horrible act of violence was the work of some foreign troublemakers.

"Egyptian people can never do this kind of thing," the man said. "If you kill my father, my sister, my brother, I can shoot you for this, of course. OK. But I never can use an ax to cut a person that way. Egyptian people never can cut another person with blades. Some other foreign countries do this terrible thing."

Why, we asked, would some foreigners come to Egypt and do such a thing?

He pushed out his lower lip and said with brisk certitude, "Jealous of our tourism. The Entity, Spain, Europe—they want us to have bad press so that tourists do not come to us. Mostly the Entity."

"The Zionist Entity" was the way Egyptian newspapers referred to the state of Israel, for to use the word *Israel* was to honor the existence of that state, something Egyptians could not abide. Most Egyptians were eager to see Israel and its people disappear from the face of the earth. Whenever a terrorist attack took place in Egypt, Egyptians found a way to blame it on Israel, though the terrorists, when apprehended, were always Egyptian nationals and usually members of *Gama'at Islamiyah,* the extremist Islamic group. Whenever tourists got shot on their way to the pyramids, the attack was planned by Mossad, the Israeli intelligence agency. When tourists were shot at on the train to Luxor, it was of course the Israelis who had plotted the event. I had never met an Egyptian who didn't fully believe these stories.

"No other country has what Egypt has," the restaurateur said with a summarizing sip of his lemonade. He told us he had been to many places around the world. When I asked him which country was his favorite, he thought for a conspicuously long time, then, shutting his eyes, he pronounced with a slow, indifferent wave of his hand, "They are all the same those countries. Nobody in the world has what Egypt has."

A few hours later, Madeleine left Luxor to return to Cairo and her job at the university. As she climbed into the taxi that would take her to the airport, she warned me, "Don't row any farther than Qena." North of Qena there was political and religious unrest, riots, shootings, Christians and Muslims killing each other. To travel any farther north than Qena was dangerous. Though I wanted to row much farther, I promised that I would go no farther than Qena.

That night I sat alone on the balcony of my hotel room and looked down on the Nile and practiced the Arabic phrases that Madeleine had taught me, phrases I might need when finally alone on the Nile:

Di markebti. This is my boat.

دي مركبتي

Faahim? Do you understand?

فاحم

Guzzi udaami. My husband is ahead of me.

جوزي قدامي

Guzzi waraya. My husband is behind me.

جوزي وريا

Gaayeen dilwati! They are coming now!

جاين دلوقتي

Ma'aya sikeena. I have a knife.

معية سكينة

Andi tasriih. I have permission.

عندي تصريح

Mashi. Mafeesh mushkila. OK. There's no problem.

ماشي مفيش مشكلة

Emshi! Go away!

إمشي

I thought about my new boat. After all my failures in Aswan, it had been shockingly easy to get what I wanted here. I
sat in a state of surprise. I was ready now, finally, to begin
rowing on the Nile by myself. I was nervous and had to keep
getting up to check my luggage, my supplies, and my map.
That afternoon I had bought enough water and provisions for
four days. Qena was forty-five miles north of Luxor. I guessed
that if I rowed at a leisurely pace, it would take me approximately three days to get there.

I had bought bread, apricots, raisins, peanuts, a couple of tins
of sardines and tuna fish, olives, cheese, and fruit. I had found
a hardware store near the train station and bought some hand-
made cotton rope in case the twine that bound my oarlocks
broke. I bought a length of thicker rope as a spare painter or anchor line. In the dark and dusty hardware store, I had rummaged amid the huge spools of rope, and when I lifted one large
spool to have a look at the spool beneath it, the shopkeeper ran
over and lifted the rope out of my arms. When I told him I didn't
mind doing the lifting myself, he smiled and wagged his head
at me. "Oh no, my lady, it is too heavy that work. You would get
tired from it. I do not want any lady to get tired."

I had found it impossible to explain to Egyptians that even
though I was a tourist, I enjoyed hard work, that I liked doing
things for myself, that I didn't mind carrying a heavy bag or
chopping wood or walking a long distance. Once, when I told

the driver of the Luxor ferry that I had walked from the ferry landing to the Temple of Hatshepsut and back again, he laughed loudly. "No. Impossible. No one do that."

The walk was only five or six miles. "Yes," I told him. "I did do that."

He pursed his lips defiantly, his mustache twitched. "No, lady. I don't believe. No one do."

It was true that very few tourists actually walked from the ferry landing to the Ramesseum or the Temple of Hatshepsut, but I couldn't understand why. It wasn't far and the walk was interesting, with its mud huts and dusty palms and ancient-looking plows being dragged along by enormous water buffalo. I had walked along the tops of irrigation mounds through the green fields of wheat and alfalfa and sugar cane and had met farmers and bullocks and children along the way. The two Colossi of Memnon rose up on my left with their huge fractured hands resting primly on their huge thighs; they sat straight backed, like two bad boys sent to sit in the corner of a classroom. A big-eyed eleven-year-old girl hugging a wooden doll in her arms had walked along with me for a while, and we had had a brief conversation in Arabic. With her warm brown hand laid flat on my forearm she asked me my name. I said, "I am Rose." She nodded with sisterly interest and approval and asked where I was from. I told her I was from America. Her brown eyes widened generously in recognition and support. "And I," she offered with one hand pressed to her heart, "am Aïda!" Then, lest there be any confusion as to her provenance, she added regally, "From here" and pointed at the cracked black earth beneath her bare feet—eight thousand years' accumulation of Nile silt. Aïda wore a yellow robe and a purple scarf tied tight against her head, like a pirate. She had enormous golden eyes and a dainty little mouth. I gave her a piece of candy, and she offered me her wooden doll in exchange. I declined the doll as too extravagant a gift; instead she gave me the pink ribbon that held the doll's hair in place. We said good-bye by very formally shaking hands.

I would rather walk to the Valley of the Kings and have the privilege of meeting Aïda from the floodplain of Luxor than sit in a rattling taxi listening to a lot of familiar banter from a shouting, smoking, mustachioed driver. I would rather lift a spool of rope myself, just to see how heavy it is, than have a fellow do it for me. But this was Egypt, where a woman was never allowed to get "tired," where, in fact, a woman was never allowed to do much of anything but cook and scrub.

That afternoon when I went to the Thomas Cook office to get some money, the man behind the counter had said to me, "Which country you from? Holland?" No. "Swiss?" No. "Belgium?" He was clearly enjoying the guessing game, but like so many Egyptians he never guessed America. "You speak like Holland!" he said.

"No," I said. "English is my language."

"Spain you come from!"

"No."

"You are very beautiful." He picked up a telephone that had been lying off the hook on his desk and said, *"Allo, Italiana? Momento,"* and then to me he said, "I am speaking to an also beautiful Italian woman."

"Have you met her?"

"No."

"Then how do you know she's beautiful?"

"Ha-ha," he said, "I likes the Holland's people!"

In my hotel I took inventory of my possessions for the third time. I had maps and a sleeping bag and a flashlight. I had a knife and a notebook. I had mosquito repellent and matches and some money. I had rope and a good boat. What more did I need?

I went out to my balcony to look at the Nile once more before I went to bed. The evening was warm, and the air had a gentle weight to it, like a light cotton blanket. Across the river the Temple of Hatshepsut was illuminated by floodlights—a somber, solid, rather rigid structure built into the side of a mountain. As I looked at the glittering river below, the hotel owner's son appeared in the shadows on the next balcony. His name, I knew, was Adel. After a long silence he said to me, "You are very beautiful."

Nice words, those—words that anywhere else in the world one would be pleased to hear, but in Egypt you hear them and your heart sinks a little in boredom and apprehension. Exactly twelve Egyptian men had said the same hollow thing to me that day. I told Adel that. He didn't seem to care. He stepped closer.

"I guess that you are an English," he said, "because you have small nose."

A few days before a man had told me that I looked Argentine, and another had said I looked like a cat, and another had said I looked like a bird. I was prepared now for comparisons with anyone or any thing.

Adel was twenty-six years old, tall and slender, a lawyer. Unable to find a suitable job, he worked here in the hotel for his father. It was difficult to see his face clearly in the dark. "In Egypt," he said sadly, "many people don't living like human. They is living like animal. No good water, no shoes, no electricity. No reading nor writing. Like animal. The government do not caring about the people."

I listened and sympathized and waited for the next topic to catch up with him. Inexorably it did.

"And," Adel said, "relationship between men and woman is not good." He had, he said, never seen a woman naked. He had a friend of twenty-four who was so ignorant about sex that he didn't know what to do with his wife on their wedding night. "No one tell him. Until now I don't know too, but then I saw sex films. In sex films they have men and women doing many things with the body that I am surprised. Not normal things. Is true they do these things?"

Adel was looking at me, that much I could see, but the exact nature of his stare was obscured by darkness. I could hear him breathing, could see the tip of his cigarette flare when he puffed at it. I was at a loss for something intelligent to say. A dim streetlight cast its sallow light on the big leaves of the plane trees below us. Horse carriages clacked by on the corniche. Men in bent postures were still fussily working on the entrance to the new Mummification Museum. "I suppose, yes, they do."

"Egyptians people don't do these things," he said.

"How do you know?"

"I don't thinks Egyptians men do. They only lift up the dress and—excuse me, madame—fuck her. Americans people they do these things?"

Once again I had landed in the middle of a surreal conversation with an Egyptian man. The aggrieved tenor, the content, the choice of words—they never seemed to vary in these conversations. I could fairly predict how this one would go. I weighed whether I wanted to continue with it. "Well, I think people all over the world do them," I said.

He asked me if women actually enjoyed sex, a question I was not expecting. It was so direct and surprising and apparently naive that I could think of nothing to say. Into the silence that ensued Adel said, "In Egypt, we say sex is only for the men and that when men do it to the women the women would be angry."

I was reminded of a group of wealthy Arab women—probably Saudi Arabian—I had once seen leaning eagerly over the balconies of the new Globe Theatre in London watching *As You Like It,* their faces hidden behind full black veils, and how they clapped their hands and screamed with delight at the bawd's licentious behavior, and how their laughter struck a note of screeching hilarity and their hands flew to their faces when, in an unscripted and unprecedented development, the leading lady's trousers (she was at that particular moment disguised as Ganymede) suddenly came untied and fell to her ankles, revealing her thoroughly bare white bottom to the audience. "I don't believe that," I said.

Adel sat down in a chair on the balcony and told me he had asked an Egyptian woman, a friend of his, whether women enjoyed sex. The friend's answer was "I don't mind it because I am strong."

I knew that clitoridectomy, or female genital cutting, was widely practiced in Egypt; it was an ancient method of controlling a woman's interest in sex, of assuring faithfulness, of curbing promiscuity. Maybe it was true that Egyptian women didn't enjoy sex; I had no idea. The French naturalist Charles Sonnini had witnessed a clitoridectomy while in Egypt in 1778 and reported that the woman who performed the surgery had told him that if the clitoris was allowed to grow unchecked "by the age of twenty-five the thing would exceed four inches in length." Sonnini believed this and attributed the phenomenon to an "Egyptian ethnic development." To Louise Colet, Flaubert wrote of the Egyptian women, "As for physical pleasure, it must be very slight, since the well-known button, the seat of same, is sliced off at an early age."

I tried to disabuse Adel, said most women do enjoy sex, but that sometimes it was a difficult subject to talk about. The young man was so open about his own sexual ignorance that at certain points in our conversation I suspected him of putting me on. We were in Luxor, the trickery capital of Egypt, where the shopkeepers, sailors, and carriage drivers skillfully seduced the custom of tourists with elaborate schemes and stories.

Adel was long legged and sat slouched so low in his chair that he was almost lying down. His face was pointed at the moon, which was just beginning to show over the roof of the hotel. He shifted his legs and searched earnestly for the proper English words. His voice was soft and low. I listened for a false note in it, for the tightening sound of a smirk or a grin. "Yes, Egyptian women you cannot talk to about these things," he said.

"What about your close female friends?"

In a gesture of disgust he threw his cigarette down into the street; sparks trailed from it as it tumbled. "I have no female friends." There was a pause, and then, as though this fact naturally followed, he said, "Sex films are expensive."

He spoke in a burdened, sorrowful, frustrated way, and at times he lowered his voice to a half whisper, as if he knew he shouldn't be discussing these things with me, and yet he plowed on frankly. Was it a trick or was it a guileless quest for information? Both, I decided, and that was what made Egyptian men so vexing. You never knew whether to give them a brisk slap for their impertinence or to welcome the irreproachable trust they seemed to offer. It was also what made them interesting. They were skillful liars but also gullible. They were emotional and quick tempered but could be easily mollified with a few kind words. They were greedy, yet they could be very generous. The Egyptian men I had encountered, because they worked with tourists, knew that foreigners had money and sex and freedom; their reaction to all that fell just short of resentment and contained a great deal of curiosity. Even the Luxor hucksters on the corniche with their bags full of tricks were so unworldly that their ploys always stopped just short of being truly offensive or harmful.

Adel's tone was confiding. "When I touch a woman's hand, I feel something like electricity, but I don't think this happens for foreigners."

"Why not?"

He shook his head. "They already have too much seckiss."

I leaned toward him, trying to catch his eye in the faint light. I needed to see his face to determine whether he was serious. I wanted to detect an ulterior expression on his face. He had the beautiful, fine, elongated features of the pharaoh Akhenaten. It was impossible to tell what he was thinking. But my doubt about him was rising.

"I never have saw this thing that woman wear on her breast. What it's called?"

This was the unmistakable giveaway. In every Egyptian city there were entire window fronts full of bras and girdles and slips, women's clothing stores that sold a surprisingly sexy array of underwear. If Adel had truly never seen a bra before, he was blind.

"Can you send me one in the mail?"

"Would you ask an Egyptian woman to send you a bra?"

"Never!"

"Why?"

"Haram!" Forbidden.

"Then why ask me?"

He leaned toward me in the darkness; I could see he was frowning. "It's different for you," he said plaintively, his voice rising with irritation. "You are free!"

Alone

AT 3:30 THE NEXT MORNING, I went out into the street in front of the hotel, where taxis sat lined up at all hours of the day. A few drivers lay curled on the front seats of their cars, wrapped in shawls and hugging themselves in the cool night air. I shook a driver awake and asked him to drive me to the sandy beach beyond Karnak. He blinked wearily at me, sat up, straightened his loosely wrapped turban, and turned the ignition key without asking why I wanted to go to the sandy beach beyond Karnak at this ungodly hour. Like most of the Luxor drivers, he was used to strange requests from foreigners—as long as you paid the fare, they would take you anywhere.

I climbed into the car with my bags, and the driver headed off up the corniche without turning on his headlights. That pleased me—the less attention we attracted, the better. I was trembling with anxiety, certain that someone or something would stop me before I could climb into my boat and row away. But for an occasional brownish light glowing dimly in the windows of houses along the way, the town was black and still beneath the starry sky.

We arrived at the beach. I paid the driver and lugged my bags of supplies and water around the fence to the restaurant. There, in the dark, I saw the figure of Muhammad, the waiter, snoozing in a wicker deck chair on the damp dock. The rowboat sat bobbing in the spot where I had left it the day before—the sight of it there was reassuring and exciting. One dim light on the porch of the restaurant illuminated the restaurant door at the far end of the dock. I jostled Muhammad's shoulder and he leaped awake, violently tossing up his hands as if in self-defense and looking wildly around to see where exactly he was. He squinted at me through the dark. When he spoke, his voice was muffled. I gave him his forty pounds, fearing that he would insist on helping me with the boat.

He followed me to the edge of the dock, stumbling and yawning, counting his money, talking, and rubbing his eyes. "You work for company, madame?" he said. "Your husband works for company? Where you are going now? You want me to help you take its boat from the river? You want me to row its boat up to the beach? Where is your husband, madame?"

Anxiously, softly, I reassured Muhammad that everything was fine, that all the nice men who were going to help me load the boat onto the truck were waiting just downriver around the next bend, that I would row the boat the mere hundred yards down to them, and we would have absolutely no problem whatsoever removing the boat from the water ourselves and taking it on to Cairo for my dear husband's big birthday surprise.

The story was absurd. It was completely ridiculous. If I

hoped to remove the boat from the river, this would have been the best place to do it, and if there were in fact a bunch of men helping me, why weren't they here? Why did I have all this luggage with me? Above all, why were we doing this job at three o'clock in the morning in the dark? If I had been Muhammad, I would have been deeply suspicious. I told him that he could rest his mind, that he was very kind, very generous, a nice young man, had done a wonderful job guarding the boat, and that I was comforted by his concern. My anxiety and my eagerness to get away had inspired in me an Egyptian unctuousness.

The sky was showing the slightest suspicion of light, its heavy black transforming perceptibly to a deep navy blue, and the stars were fading fast. I moved toward the boat, tossed my bags into it, lost my footing on the steep dock, and promptly slipped into the tepid river up to my knees.

Muhammad gasped in alarm, his dark figure swaying on the dock. "Madame! I worry for you!"

I placated him with false laughter, thanked him again, and climbed into the boat. He raised his hands at me.

"Don't worry, Muhammad," I said.

He took a step closer. "You work for company in Cairo, madame? You know beeble in Cairo? What you are doing in Cairo? I can do any job in Cairo, if you know some beeble who need my work."

I untied the lines and pushed off from the pier. Muhammad was still talking at me as I lifted the oars into place. "Madame, I can drive the car. Look!" He pulled out his wallet and plucked something from it. "I have driver's card."

I began to row away. Muhammad stood at the edge of the dock leaning over the water toward me, waving his driver's card in the dark. "Can you get me job in Cairo, madame?"

I wished that I could get him a job. "I don't think so," I said through the darkness.

"But you can try?"

"I can always try."

"Can you call me? What your telephone number?"

I knew I was safe now. He was not the least bit curious about this weird mission of mine. Unlike Amr, he could not have cared less about my safety or about what I was really up to. All he wanted was for me to help him, to get him out of Luxor and his dreary job working for that know-it-all of a boss. I felt for him as I rowed away.

I was so nervous setting off alone that I had trouble establishing a steady rhythm with the oars. I rowed fast down the middle of the river, trying to get clear of the cluster of houses and restaurants at the end of Luxor, praying that no one would notice me or come after me, praying just to get out of the reaches of the Luxor police and people. I was rigid with stress and kept catching the blade of one of the oars in the water on the backstroke. I hardly remembered to breathe. I pulled the oars gingerly to keep them from making too much noise in the water. I could hear myself panting. Then, shockingly, out of the mist-enshrouded mud-brick houses on the eastern bank I heard a voice shouting thinly, "Madame! Blease! I can help you! Madame!"

I recognized the spot the voice was coming from; it was the same place where I had met Shazly Fouad and the three young men the day before. "Madame! Blease!" It was one of the young witnesses from the sale of the boat. He was leaning recklessly far out a second-story window of a house above the ghat, but I was far enough away that I couldn't tell which man it was, and that made it easier to ignore the pleading shrieks.

I kept rowing, resting only once to remove my hat and wrap a white cotton shirt around my head like a turban, tucking my hair up under the cloth to hide it. It was a feeble disguise but better than nothing. I was dressed in a white linen shirt and white cotton pajama pants, a combination that looked vaguely like what an Egyptian fisherman would wear. I had seen scores of fishermen from a distance, and I knew that from a distance I now looked more or less like one of them. Without Amr's protection, I knew I should try to hide both my foreignness and the fact that I was a woman. If I were to be discovered now, I would have no Egyptian acquaintance to help me. It was one thing to have had Amr trailing close behind me but another thing entirely to be going it completely alone. Foreigners didn't often travel on this part of the river. Few tour boats went downriver from Luxor. I felt that if I stayed in the middle of the river as far from the banks as possible, I could, with the help of this simple costume and vernacular boat, avoid undue notice.

I rowed with a little bit of fear and a great deal of joy. I was alone, finally, with no one to protect me. I wanted to sing for happiness—a rare, raw, immediate sort of happiness that was directly related to my physical situation, to my surroundings, to independence, and to solitude. The happiness I felt that morning had nothing to do with the future or the past, with abstractions or with my relationships to other people. It was the happiness of entering into something new, of taking the moments simply for what they were, of motion, of freedom, and of free will. I loved not knowing what would happen next, loved that no one here knew me. I felt coordinated and strong, and the world seemed huge and vibrant. It was a relief to be alone, and I was accustomed now to the feel of the river and to the fact that I was actually pulling myself along it to a new destination, turning new bends that gave me new vistas, leaving behind what I had already seen. I felt optimistic. And I relaxed enough that my mind could wander. That was always the best part of rowing—the repetition, the simplicity of the physical task, the slowly and constantly shifting surroundings that inspired free thought. My happiness was a feeling of physical lightness, of weightlessness, like drifting on air.

Months later when I read Flaubert's travel notes, I recognized the same kind of happiness with a shock of surprise. He wrote, "I felt a surge of solemn happiness that reached out towards what I was seeing and I thanked God in my heart for having made me capable of such joy: I felt fortunate at the thought, and yet it seemed to me that I was thinking of nothing: it was a sensuous pleasure that pervaded my entire being."

Sunrise came, concentrated above the short spiky palms on the east side of the river. I thought of Florence Nightingale's description of a Nile sunrise: "It looks not lurid and thick, as very brilliant colors in an English sky sometimes do, but so transparent and pure, that one really believes one's self look-ing into a heaven beyond, and feels a little shy of penetrating into the mysteries of God's throne." Though I was surprised at the accuracy and currency of the bulk of Nightingale's Nile observations, I couldn't share her heady enthusiasm about the Nile sunrise. Years of industry and its attendant pollution had given this particular dawn a beefy, congested hue. It began in a muddy, livid way and grew to the color of uncooked bacon. The sky was full of soft gray smoke from garbage fires and brush fires that had smoldered all night amid the trees along the banks. At the edge of the river I could see fishermen laying down nets or rowing their boats slowly upriver among the reeds. The river steamed gently in the sunlight; soft yellow twists of vapor lifted off its surface and disappeared in the cool morning air.

A big grassy island in the middle of the river forced me closer to the shore, and as I passed near a rowboat that looked empty along the bank, a small boy suddenly sat up in it. He stared at me, squinting into the sunlight with freshly opened eyes, looked confused, and lay down again. I was close enough that he could see my face. Ten seconds later, the boy sat bolt upright again and stared harder at me; I could see that he sensed there was something unusual about me. He shaded his eyes with his tiny hands and peered, his mouth set in a figuring grimace. Then a heavy hand reached up out of the boat—the hand, I assumed, of the boy's still-sleeping father—and roughly pulled him back down. They had camped there in the boat for the night.

At eight o'clock I stopped rowing, drifting on the current, to eat some bread and cheese and a few oranges. I checked my map and guessed that I had passed the village of Garagos and was now near Nag el-Madamud, which in ancient times was known as Madu. In the Twelfth Dynasty, during the reign of Sesostris III, there had been a temple here dedicated to Mentu, the god of war and sun who wore three feathers on his head, like an American Indian, and always had a spear in his hand. That temple was gone, replaced by a Greco-Roman temple, but I had no need or desire to see any of it. I had the water and the sky, the sun and the palm trees. That was enough. I lifted the oars and rowed on a little slower to make my trip last longer. Rowing for the sake of rowing was my only purpose. I wanted only to feel the water passing close beneath the hull of my boat, to hear it swilling around my oars.

Beyond Luxor there were surprisingly few boats on the river. There were no powerboats, no feluccas, and very few fishing boats. In six hours I had seen just two barges, burdened with raw lumber and steel, and two cruise ships. I had seen heavy farm animals being pushed into the river and men washing in that methodical, careful, graceful way. I had heard children shrieking with delight on the banks. I had seen men working the fields, bending and hoeing, hauling and pulling. In a few places along the Nile, they were still using the primitive *shaduf* to lift water from the river into their fields. The contraption was thousands of years old in design, the same tool the pharaonic *fellaheen* had used, a bucket on a string tied to a long swinging arm suspended between two poles. One end of the arm was weighted with stones to counterbalance the weight of a full bucket of water. In this way, they hauled water up over the riverbanks. How many bananas, how much alfalfa had this land produced over six thousand years, I wondered.

These working men never looked twice at me. The boat, the turban, the white of my clothes, and my standard rowing style were enough to suggest that everything was as it should be. My alien female presence in this particular boat in the middle of the Egyptian countryside was so unexpected that I passed through the farmland unnoticed. I perturbed nothing and no one. The only odd thing about me was that I was actually traveling; I appeared to the farmers on the southern horizon of the river and disappeared on the northern one. I was clearly going someplace, was not a local person, not one of them. Most fishing boats stayed within range of their villages, rowing back and forth across the river, or up and down the local banks, like horses in a corral. They always moved slowly; their goal was nets and fish. Few boats went off on journeys like mine. If I had been a farmer, I would have wondered at this skinny stranger rowing down the middle of the river so intently.

I had seen notably few women on the river. There had been a couple washing clothes or walking along the banks with baskets on their heads, disappearing in and out of clumps of trees in their long black gowns, but I had seen many more birds than women. I saw herons, egrets, kingfishers, black-and-white hoopoes with harlequinesque markings and fanning red crests, green bee-eaters, hovering kestrels, and scores of unidentifiable buteos soaring high above the river. The Egyptian sandpipers were so pretty that once, sailing with Amr, I had exclaimed at the sight of one, "Oh, what a good bird!" and Amr had responded, "Yes, that bird is delicious!" It shocked me that anyone could eat a bird so beautiful, but the people in Aswan would eat just about any bird they could catch, including the foul cormorant.

One afternoon at the edge of the Nile in Aswan, at the foot of the high sand dune that led to the Tombs of the Nobles, I had seen four young men crouching behind a low stone wall intent on systematically trapping sparrows in a fine net. One man would hurl a stone into a bush full of birds, the startled birds would fly up over the wall, and just at the right moment the other men would raise a long net directly across the birds' flight path, ensnaring seven or eight at one time. They had shown me the sum of their catch: fifty or so tiny sparrows tossed into a cardboard box, a mound of bodies and feathers, damp and matted with blood. How did they kill the birds? They showed me the bloody steak knife they used to slit the birds' throats. Did the sparrows taste good? They pointed their thumbs at the sky: *Very delicious!*

The birds I saw that day moved about the riverbanks and in the shallows of the river with the freedom and authority of long-term residents. They never seemed frightened when I approached, just curious. They stared at me, walked a little, pecked at the ground not two feet away from me, and stared some more. They had none of the skittish nervousness of the birds I saw regularly at home.

Clumps of water hyacinth had suddenly begun to appear north of Luxor. Ripped from their vines along the edge of the river, they floated quickly along on beds of their own broad leaves, carrying high their swollen rust-colored buds. The buds looked like the inflated fingers of a brown rubber glove, and if there were four or five buds on one plant, the whole thing looked spookily like a bloated hand rising up out of the river. The first time I saw one like that, I gasped in fright, thinking it was a drowned body drifting beside me. On the riverbanks I saw ancient mud houses painted mustard yellow and sky blue, power lines, thin spires of smoke rising straight into the windless sky, acacia trees and tamarisks, oxen pulling wooden carts through the mud. In the middle of a small grassy island, a lone donkey stood scratching his side on the trunk of the tiny tree he was tethered to. Everything passed by as in a slow-rolling film, perpetually moving, each scene gradually replaced by another. Floating pump stations appeared now and then, and sometimes the banks of the river were built up with stone ghats.

That afternoon I stopped at the edge of an empty island and let the boat hang in the shade of the reeds. I lay down in the bottom of the boat to rest and watched the cloudless sky. There were rarely any clouds here at this time of year, yet it was amazing to me how the shifting sun could make this seemingly blank plain look so many different ways in the span of just one day. The Egyptian sky was not simply blue—it had color and great depth, shading, and moods. Sometimes it was pink, other times yellow, late in the day it turned lavender, then purple.

Water pumps muttered on the far shore, and tiny sparrowlike birds flitted in the reeds all around me. The boat rocked gently, and I realized that the Nile never had the swampy smell that some urban New England rivers have: a musty, rotting odor with a chemical tincture, like dry-cleaning fluid. Even in Cairo, with all its urban waste and probable toxicity, the Nile had no unpleasant smell.

Like the sky, the river, too, responded to the sun; it never looked one way for long. Here the water was quiet, opaque, and had the creamy coffee color of the Seine. "The water of the Nile is quite yellow," Flaubert wrote, "it carries a good deal of soil. One might think of it as being weary of all the countries it has crossed, weary of endlessly murmuring the same monotonous complaint that it has traveled too far. If the Niger and the Nile are but one and the same river, where does this water come from? What has it seen? Like the ocean, this river sends our thoughts back almost incalculable distances."

I had wondered often about the source of all this ever-flowing water. The countries it had crossed were ten in all: Burundi, Rwanda, Tanzania, Uganda, Kenya, the Democratic Republic of Congo, Sudan, Ethiopia, Eritrea, and Egypt. Flaubert, like many people of his day, believed that the Niger and the Nile were the same river—they aren't and never were, but no one understood that until the late nineteenth century. Technically, the real source of the Nile is the rain that develops from the South Atlantic Ocean through the process of evaporation and condensation. The rainfall drains into the Nile basin and feeds the lakes of east Africa. The Egyptian Nile is a combination of water from the White Nile and the Blue Nile. The White Nile effectively has its source in the Luvironza River in Burundi, which flows into the Ruvubu River, which flows into the Kagera River, which in turn flows into Lake Victoria, where it is then known as the Victoria Nile for the next two hundred miles until, in Uganda, it flows into Lake Albert. From Lake Albert, the White Nile continues northward into Sudan, where it's called the Bahr el Jebel, and in Sudan the river enters the Sudd, the vast and infamous swampland of southern Sudan—a mess of floating islands composed of mud, papyrus, aquatic plants, and reeds. The islands, some a mile square, drift and shift and interlock. The Nile as an identifiable river ceases here for a time as its waters filter slowly through the reeds in a million different streams. The historian Emil Ludwig wrote of the Sudd, "Here it is as though the Nile were a rope frayed in the middle, the solid bulk teased and parted into a hundred strands." Judging from the accounts of numerous adventurers and explorers, the Sudd must be one of the most inhospitable places on earth. In 1908 a horrified Winston Churchill wrote in his travelogue *My African Journey* that the Sudd was:

> at once so dismal and so terrifying that to travel through it is a weird experience . . . For three days and three nights we were continuously in this horrible swamp into which the whole of

the United Kingdom could be easily packed . . . To travel
through the Sudd, is to hate it forevermore. Rising fifteen feet
above the level of the water, stretching its roots twenty or even
thirty feet below, and so matted and tangled together that elephants can walk safely upon its springy surface, papyrus is the
beginning and end of this melancholy world. For hundreds of
miles nothing else is to be perceived—not a mountain-ridge
blue on the horizon, scarcely a tree, no habitation of man, no
sign of beast. The silence is broken only by the croaking of innumerable frog armies, and the cry of dreary birds.

I was fascinated by the grim power of the Sudd—a place so
dense and choked with vegetation that the Nile waters almost
fail to pass through it. In his book *The Nile,* a detailed anatomy
of the river, Robert O. Collins writes of the Sudd, "The river
can hardly move at all in this Stygian swamp, so it sits, and in
the steamy heat near the equator, more than half of the water
of the Bahr al-Jabal evaporates away into the atmosphere." It
was the impassability of the Sudd that for millennia had pre-
vented the discovery of the source of the Nile. Neither pharaohs nor emperors had been able to cut through that swamp.
Because of the shifting movement of clumps of growth, it was
impossible to cut a permanent channel there. A ship would
move upstream a bit, only to have drifting islands close in
behind it, blocking any possible retreat back to civilization,
while more drifting islands from upstream would float down
and press against the ships until they were trapped, unable to
move in either direction. Collins writes, "To abandon ship
meant certain death in the Sudd, with its swamps stretching
endlessly beyond the horizon. Relief expeditions did not always arrive in time to save the occupants of a stranded vessel
from starvation. There are reports of fragile steamers being
crushed by the implacable pressure of the river, building its
block of sudd, and legends of cannibalism when rations came

to an end." Fish, crocodiles, and even the enormous hippopot-
amuses in the Sudd are often literally crushed to death by
the swamp's enormous floating islands. In 1839 Muhammad
Ali sent the Turkish naval captain Salim to break through the
Sudd. Salim failed on his first try but returned a year later and
successfully cut the first passage. But once a cut was made
through the swamp, it was impossible to keep it clear. In 1869
Muhammad Ali sent the British explorer Samuel Baker to the
Sudd with twelve hundred soldiers, but Baker, too, failed to
break through permanently.

The much-diminished White Nile trickles out of the Sudd
and, fortunately for northern Sudan and Egypt, gets replen-
ished at Khartoum by the Blue Nile flowing into it from the
Ethiopian highlands. For all the old associations of Lake Victoria as the source of the Nile, the truth is that more than four-
fifths of the water of the Egyptian Nile comes from Lake Tana
and the monsoons in Ethiopia. North of Khartoum, the Nile
meets the Atbara River, its last tributary, and travels on through
the deep desert of Sudan and on into Egypt in a slow, steady,
unaltered state, yet with enough volume and force to have
been able to kick dust into Amr's parents' cup of water at Elephantine before the construction of the High Dam.

The water, or some small part of it at least, that was passing
beneath my boat had traveled slightly downhill for approximately one hundred and fifty days from its source near the
equator. It had traveled more than four thousand miles and
had been running its modern-day course for over twenty-five
thousand years. How many eyes had looked at the same water
I was looking at? How many people had drunk from this water, rowed on it, swum in it, or drowned in it?

As I lay daydreaming in the bottom of my boat, I heard with
striking clarity the familiar sound of a public address system
being switched on, the flickering static, the clumsy finger testing the microphone with a click, a pause, and then a low voice

launching into the call to prayer. A breeze from the east blew
the singer's voice directly over me. *Allah hu akbar!* The voice
had a plaintive catch in it, a thrilling break that seemed to ex-
press great emotion. Soon, a second voice drifted from the
other side of the river, singing the same words, but the new
voice was high and tiny as it struggled against the breeze.

I was exhausted. There was still some light left to the day,
and I could feasibly row another hour or two, but I decided to
stop here for the night. I had slept poorly the night before in
nervous anticipation, and now I could hardly lift my arms.
This seemed as good a place as any to spend the night. It was
quiet, secluded, and therefore relatively safe. It wasn't that I
feared being harmed as much as I feared the clamoring attention of local people—too much attention could bring my trip
to an end. If I spent the night closer to a village, I would benefit
from a greater civic protection but raise my chances of being
discovered. I decided to stay where I was.

By five o'clock the moon was a pale disk over the eastern
shore of the river, and distant voices babbled beneath it in
the banana groves. By ten o'clock Venus would be gone and the
nearly full moon would be high overhead. I climbed out of the
boat and wandered around the little island, stretching my legs.
The island was another barren hump of sand and grass and
stunted shrubs in the middle of the river. I sat on a warm patch
of sand near my boat and made a small fire just for the pleasure
of it. My sunburned face, ankles, and hands responded to the
heat of the fire with a stinging that felt almost cold. I was still
wearing my makeshift turban on my head and had come to find
it more comfortable than a hat.

I amused myself by burning twigs and eating peanuts and
watching the beauty of the place change with the changing
light, the blue and green, the gold and ochre and violet slowly
transforming to other softer colors. The sun was hidden behind the red stone cliffs in the west, but the sky and the east

bank were still blindingly bright. This, I thought, was how ho-
bos lived, and it was easy to see the appeal of that freedom
and irresponsibility. I heard the sound of a tractor coming
from some indeterminate spot across the river, then realized it
wasn't a tractor at all but the purring of frogs tuning up for the
evening in the grasses all around me. Egypt was full of audio
and visual tricks like this. In Egyptian towns and cities, what
you think is a beautifully colored bird in a tree is really a plastic trash bag caught on a twig. What you think is the sound of
crickets is really somebody's chirpingly off-centered fan belt.
At an ancient temple, what you think is the whistling of some
rare bird is really a soldier trying to get your attention. And
then when you arrive in the country, what you think is a
lumpy heap of trash floating down the river is really four knobby-
headed water buffalo crossing from one side to the other. What
you think is litter snagged on a tree branch is really a beautiful bird. What you think is a man hissing and clacking at
you is really the rattle of the ubiquitous maculate kingfisher.
It seemed to me there were a limited number of sounds on the
planet, and nature and humans borrowed them from each
other.

Kingfishers plopped into the river. A raft of pelicans floated
by. A red-legged stint gingerly picked his way through the water
hyacinths. When a long metal barge came motoring upriver toward Luxor, I felt a hobo's urge to hoot and throw a stone at it.

Darkness came quickly. I huddled around my fire and ate
some bread and tuna fish and two apples. This was a strange
place for a foreigner to be sitting alone. You couldn't call it a
wilderness, for there were people less than a mile from here in
every direction. But it was an empty spot at the edge of the
river and I was alone. That thought made my pulse quicken,
made my head snap around to see who might be approaching.
Anticipating the night ahead, I was undeniably nervous.

I kicked sand over the fire, repositioned my anchor in the

mud, and lay down in the boat with my sweater as a pillow. As I lay down, a handful of cockroaches crawled out from under the fake grass on the bottom of the boat and scurried along the gunwales and over my hands and shoes. They had been there all day, hiding. Under any other circumstances, I would have been disgusted by the sight of them, but here I didn't care. I was tired and had no choice but to sleep in the boat with whatever unsavory creatures were in it with me.

The river's current gently bent the reeds around me, and the sand three feet from my boat gave off vents of warm air. Venus and several bright stars cast long trails of light on the water. I watched the movement of the stars, sliding east to west. Eventually the moon, just short of being full, was so bright it dimmed the stars, and I found that by the light of it I could write in my notebook without a flashlight. Cast onto the land, the light of the moon was greenish—it glowed and made the grass look black and the sand look like heaps of snow, just as all the travelers before me swore it did. Eventually I closed my notebook, positioned my flashlight and knife beside my head, removed my turban, and lay there staring at the sky.

Why I read three books about crocodiles before taking my trip to Egypt I don't really know. I had been told many times that there were no crocodiles in the Egyptian Nile, but like a child who dreads being frightened and yet begs to hear the awful ghost story again and again, I had to know what a crocodile could do, how it thought, what it ate, size of teeth, greatest enemy, and so forth, and therefore one horrible book led compulsively to another. That night as I lay on my back, separated from the Nile by an eighth of an inch of hammered steel, crocodiles were on my mind in a way they had not been in the light of day. Let me just say that only two types of crocodilians are considered to be maneaters: the saltwater crocodile and the Nile crocodile. Beneath me was the Nile. I knew that there were no crocodiles here, but it had not escaped my notice that when people spoke of the Nile crocodile and its disappearance from Egypt they always used qualifiers. They said, "By 1870 the Nile crocodile had *practically* vanished from all of the Nile below Aswan," or they said, "The Nile crocodile *virtually* disappeared," or "the crocodile is *almost* completely gone," or "*for all intents and purposes* the crocodile has been eradicated." Now, lying here on top of the river, I of course had to think about those one or two crocodiles that for all intents and purposes had surely survived, couldn't help imagining a large lurking thing bumping roughly against the bottom of the boat. After a few minutes of recalling every terrible thing I knew about the Nile crocodile, I stopped simply imagining the rough bump and began fully expecting it.

I sat up in the boat, looked around at the bright water shimmering and swirling beneath the moon. Seeing nothing unusual, I lay down again.

You probably know that crocodiles don't sleep much—a few intermittent catnaps during the day after they've eaten a few cats—and then at night they go hunting, floating quietly, with only their eyes and ears above the water level, which makes them not only hard to see but hard to hear. What exactly would I do if that elongated crocodile snout with its jutting mandibular teeth just now presented itself on the coaming of my boat and gave me a leering lipless smile? "Life is never more intense and worth living than when death lurks around the corner." That was the epigraph to one of the books I read about crocodiles. From this terrifying little book, *No Tears for the Crocodile* written by one Paul L. Potous and published in 1956, I learned that around that time—not so long ago—crocodiles were responsible for a greater number of human deaths than any other wild animal in Africa. In addition, the crocodile was able to do all that damage even though graced with a brain not much bigger than a shot glass. A crocodile can remain submerged for a full twelve minutes, as compared with a hippo's trifling eight, and he can see awfully well underwater. He has at least sixty teeth, and if he knocks one of them out, another one grows back in its place, and if he knocks *that* tooth out, another replaces that one, and on and on that way endlessly, which is a big part of the reason crocodiles can live so long—two hundred years they've been known to last, chewing their way through the decades with ease. It's not unheard of for one crocodile to zip through two thousand teeth in a lifetime. In addition, the crocodile never stops growing. At birth an infant crocodile is about the size of his mother's nostril, yet he can manage almost immediately to trot off and take care of himself. When they're feeling threatened, crocodiles clap their jaws together. If they're hungry enough, they'll run across dry land to snatch up their next meal. They can run almost thirty miles per hour on land on those short little twisted legs and are said to be capable of running at a kind of gallop, speeding through the sugar cane like a low-flying missile. Mr. Potous informed me frankly that the crocodile does not have to be provoked in order to attack, "for it hunts man by instinct, lying in wait for its victims at the places where it knows they must come to draw water or where they go down to bathe and wash themselves [or where they are lying in their preposterously small boat not too far from Luxor]. Men, women, or children—they are all a meal to the saurian."

I sat up a second time and looked across the water. My hands were so bright in the moonlight that they were distracting. I looked north and south. I didn't see anything bad—just water, the black sky, the moon, and the banks of the river. I lay down again, the boat rocked, and though I tried to think of other things, I had to remind myself that the Nile crocodile has a varied array of hunting habits, from the sudden lunging rush to the coy, sneaking trap. Most of all he seems to like to come up behind you, following you with his periscopic eyes, and then at an opportune moment he knocks you clean off the

riverbank and into the water with his enormous tail, an experience that I expect is probably not unlike getting struck by a
moving cargo van. Or, if he's in a hurry, he simply lunges all at
once out of the river, grabs you with his jaws, pulls you into the
water, and drowns you. In general, the crocodile seems to go
for the head or the leg, perhaps finding easier purchase there.

Despite all those large and replaceable teeth, crocodiles
have some difficulty chewing, so they whirl their catch around
and around in the water until they break off a choice piece
that they can swallow whole. In his *Handbook of Alligators
and Crocodiles,* Steve Grenard explains this: "Crocodiles have
no way to anchor their prey once it is dead, so to get a mouth-
ful of meat, they bite the animal and roll over and over on
their long axis until they twist off a hunk of meat. Then they
bring their heads above water, flip their food into the air and
grab it again, each time getting it further and further down the
gullet. They usually need to rest for a few minutes before taking another bite." Sometimes they even fall asleep in the middle of a meal and can be found snoring away on a beach with
a ragged hunk of animal flesh perched on a back tooth, "which
they have been unable to swallow but which they retain as a
snack until such time as they awake." And if the crocodile
finds its meal too tough to rip apart, it simply stores the whole
maimed mess in the mud at the bottom of the river and waits
for it to rot a little. Grenard also let me know that while crocodiles can apply "many tons of pressure with their bite," they
have very little strength when opening their mouths, and so it
is therefore easy to disarm a crocodile by simply clamping his
snout shut with one's hands. (Mr. Grenard did not tell me how
one would safely get away from the crocodile and resume normal life once one grew tired of that particular posture.)

By the way, never expect to meet just one crocodile, because
where there is one there are usually others. They live in com-
munities, though actually the only thing they like to do as a

community is stage a feeding frenzy, attacking another living thing, a hippo, say, or a human, and pulling it to shreds in great harmony.

Mr. Potous, who during his life spent a truly creepy amount of time with crocodiles, was in the habit of cutting them open just to see what and who they had eaten. "The stomach contents of crocodiles," he says, "are at times interesting although often gruesome, and I have found the remains of metal bangles, human and animal bones, native beads, baby hippo tusks, teeth and many other objects . . . The original owners of these beads were women and girl children who wore them as ornaments and who had been taken and devoured by the crocodiles."

I lay on the Nile in my boat under the glare of the huge Egyptian moon. The boat swayed. The black water swirled beneath me. I turned onto my side, closed my eyes, and changed the subject: scorpions, which according to Charles Sonnini, "here grow to a very large size," had a sting that "occasioned acute pain, swoonings, convulsions, and sometimes death." And then I put my shirt over my head, trying to block out the moon and that terrible picture I had once seen of a Nile Malapterus, an electrical fish that looked not unlike a very large snake and whose touch, according to reports, made men convulse and go stiff with the electric shock.

Eventually, out of pure mental and physical exhaustion, I fell asleep and, mercifully, did not wake until dawn.

Fear Afloat

THE NEXT DAY passed much as the day before. Again the heat was a powerful presence long before the sun ever lifted itself over the tops of the banana trees. Again I rowed, saw the same sort of palms I had seen the day before, the same sort of villages, the same exotic birds, the tall green grasses at the edge of the river, and the vaguely threatening beige desert beyond. Still cloudless, the sky went through yesterday's mood shifts as the sun inched across it; fragile at dawn, wounded at noon, intoxicated in the evening. Now and then an island appeared, or a barge lumbering down the middle of the river, or a herd of oxen drinking at the water's edge. I saw a party of flamingos on the riverbank teetering on pink stilts, stabbing their beaks at the water, their feathers a pale whitish pink, their beaks the size and shape of a lobster's claw. A child waved boldly at me from the riverbank, and I waved back, but few people seemed to notice me, let alone detect that I was a woman. I spoke to no one.

I rowed more slowly that day, more calmly. From time to time I let the boat drift. I made notes in my notebook but discovered that there was little to write except that I felt a constant combination of fear and exultation at my present situation, that I was making progress, that the rowing was easy, and that the river was—as it had been the day before—very flat and wide. The Nile and its banks changed little from one bend to the next. Floating on the Nile in the 1980s, William Golding wrote with a touch of bafflement and rue, "It is symptomatic of the sameness of the Nile that I found myself struggling to find variety to put into my journal and without much success. I decided to list any stuff there was floating in the water, but there was nothing but the odd clump of *ward el Nil*." I, too, saw little in the river but clumps of *Ward el Nil,* the ubiquitous water hyacinth, which the Egyptians called Rose of the Nile. Aside from the hyacinth, the only thing I saw in the water was the reflection of the palm trees and the occasional mud house crumbling at the river's edge, the sky, and my own burned and furtive face. Though the Nile was the longest river in the world, I often had the feeling while rowing it that I was sitting alone in a sparsely furnished room. The flat blue sky was the ceiling, the light brown river the floor, the omnipresent glare and the two narrow panels of green on either side the walls. Too, the Nile was quiet. If I spoke out loud to myself, as I admit I have a strong tendency to do, my voice sounded disturbingly feeble and small.

Coptic churches began to appear, the crosses at the peaks of their spires contrasting bravely, even defiantly, with the infinitely more numerous and more popular crescent moons at the tops of minarets. I guessed that I was nearing Naqada, which in the early Christian period had been populated chiefly by Copts. Florence Nightingale, who referred to Egypt as "the birthplace of monasticism," had stopped here to look at the spot where Saint Pachomius had established one of Egypt's first monasteries. She was sorely disappointed by what she found. "Here the Christian spirit of zeal and devotion was nurtured," she wrote. "Now nothing seemed to grow here but a little Indian corn. If the inhabitants were Copts, as most of the people are about there, they had not even a church—worse than the Mahometans."

By the time I reached Qus, the day was unbearably hot. Just beyond the east bank of the river, a huge gray block of a building appeared, the biggest thing I had seen yet—bigger than the Temple of Kom Ombo. It had many tiny windows, like a prison, and tall smokestacks that sent balls of white smoke into the sky—it was a factory where they made paper from the by-products of sugar cane. Qus was the place where the Greeks had established the city of Apollinopolis Parva. In the Middle Ages it had been an important trade center and the starting point for the caravan route across the Arabian Desert to the Red Sea. It was also once notorious for the huge number of scorpions that could be found there. Now it was just another modern Egyptian city, all smoke and noise and broken streets. I rowed slowly past it and watched the factory smoke dissolving high in the sky.

Red stone cliffs had begun to appear again in the distance to the west, tapering down toward Qena, like the monumental hills in the Nevada desert. Because I had never seen an Egyptian fisherman wearing sunglasses, I had kept my sunglasses in my bag and now my eyes were stinging from the intense light.

In midafternoon I stopped on a sandy beach below an island, a wide flat place that, when the river was high, would be inundated with water. The edge of the river was crowded with water hyacinths, and for the first time I saw one in bloom—a pinkish white orchidlike cluster of flowers with a deep purple heart. It was a beautiful flower for a plant that was really nothing more than an invasive weed that had appeared on the Nile some hundred years ago and had proliferated to the point of infestation. Beyond the beach, tiny sand dunes made the vista uneven; ripples of heat rose up from the hot hollows between them. There was beach grass here and the dried brown stubble of reeds, a few thornbushes and furry acacias. Several hundred yards to the west, the line of palm trees began, and far beyond them I saw a faint string of gray smoke lifting into the air, smoke from what was surely a village. The east bank was just a low flat line of palms and greenery. The only people I saw were two fishermen far downriver, spanking the water with sticks, scaring up fish.

I anchored my boat and stepped onto a beach littered with snail shells. After sitting so long on the water, I was unsteady on my feet; everything seemed to sway beneath me. I walked the length of the beach—the length of a football field—and back again, then sat in the shade of a large bush. The shade formed an oval exactly the size of my body, and as the shifting sun forced the shade to slide around the bush, I had to slide with it. A pair of stone curlews, shorebirds slightly bigger than crows, fluttered out of the sky and landed near me on the beach; they had long yellow legs and shocked-looking bright yellow eyes as big as a human's, and they stared at me in a spooky, hypnotized way. Dragonflies floated drunkenly by. Whole rafts of water hyacinths hurried past like feathery green mattresses set loose on the current. The sky looked galvanized in the east, a broiled grayish white, though directly above me it was turquoise blue. I sat happily for an hour, drank a bottle of water, and tried to figure out where I was. I guessed I was twenty miles or so from Qena. I was exhausted. The palms of my hands were raw. I felt the heat pushing me toward the earth, and eventually I lay down in the sand, using my shoes as a pillow.

Not fifteen feet away from me, two boys walked by on a path at the edge of the river. I positioned my arm over my face thinking, *You look like an Argentine; you look like an English, a cat, a bird,* and hoped that in my white shirt and loose white pants I looked like just another barefoot Egyptian man having a nap. The boys passed by, never once breaking their steady stream of chatter, never once glancing at me. I lifted my head and watched them go. My boat parked at the edge of the river didn't attract their attention—it was too common a sight, the sort used by every fisherman in Egypt.

My disguise was working. I marveled at how easy it had been. Having recovered from my initial shock and surprise that I had found my own boat and been able to row out of Luxor in it, I was able to think now, to reflect on what I was doing. Dress in white, wrap a shirt around your head, tuck your hair up, use a local boat, and nobody would notice you were a white woman floating down the Nile through Egypt. It seemed preposterous, but I was so unexpected in this place that it worked. No one cared; no one suspected. I was so inconspicuous that I had begun to feel almost invisible. I thought of the number of Egyptians who had said to me, *It's different for you; you're foreign; you're free*, and I felt like a spy—outwardly one thing, inwardly another. I was a misfit in the best possible way. I wasn't supposed to be here, yet I was here anyway, and what was the consequence? It was like being let in on a secret. No one was offended by it, no one knew me, and I had disturbed nothing. I was masked; I had no identity beyond surface; I blended in and so was insignificant.

I looked at my torn hands and the burned tops of my feet; I looked at the boat and the desert landscape and the enormous sky. Why was I doing this? It wasn't so much to prove to myself that I could do it—I had always known that I could do it—but more to prove to myself that it was not a remarkable thing to do. This was a matter of a calm and civilized river, a boat, two oars, and a knowledge of how to use them. Those were the bare facts, and the most important to me. Everyone had said, *You can't.* But so far it looked as though I *could.* Anything, really, was possible if you cared enough and had the right tools. I have always resented imposed constraints, hated all the things people said one should and should not do. *A woman shouldn't . . . A man wouldn't . . .* People were always conjuring up a wall and telling you to stay on your side of it. More often than not, the wall was false, a cliché, an inherited and unexamined stock response to the world.

I lay back in the sand, fatigue making it hard to move, one burned cheek pressed into the hot dirt. Minuscule ants marched single file across my ankles, and three feet from my head a clamorous reed warbler lived up to its name, but then I slept as if drugged.

When I woke two hours later, I saw the moon beginning to rise over the east bank, a pale white ball lifting over the lip of the palmy horizon. The trees on the east bank were washed orange and red by the light of the setting sun behind me, and the sky just above them was pinkish white. My side of the river had fallen into shadow, yet the earth still sent up waves of hot air. I went back to my boat and decided that this was as good a place as any in which to spend the night. I was in a little cove with a four-foot dune of sand rising above me. Amid tall grass and reeds, the boat was secure and well hidden here.

I lit a small fire, again not for the heat but for the amusement of it, ate some of my provisions, took some photographs, and watched as the blue of the sky deepened to magenta and then to purple and then to navy blue. Again I was truly alone. At Abu Simbel, Florence Nightingale had written of the pleasure and "power" of being able, for once, to leave her boat and visit the temple "without a whole escort" at her heels.

I was delightfully alone now and exulting in my freedom.

No one on earth knew that I was here, and I knew no one. The river, the trees, and the sand I was looking at—it could have been a scene from almost any period in Egyptian history. A great blue heron with a wispy foulard of gray breast feathers picked his long-legged way up the shore and stood patiently in the water not ten feet from me, head lowered, shoulders raised, like an unhappy soldier standing guard in the rain. He turned his narrow head slowly toward me, stared morosely, and looked slowly away again as if to say, *There's room enough here for both of us.*

∧∧∧∧

HERODOTUS, who reckoned the Nile was about the same length as the Danube, was a ripping-good storyteller. His work is furnished with extreme characters, bizarre events, power struggles, omens, oracular epigrams, weird coincidences, phenomenal human manipulations of nature, beheadings, poisonings, and, at more than one ancient dinner party, the severed head of a son served up on a silver platter to his own unsuspecting father. Herodotus went* up the Nile in the fifth century BC and was the first outsider to write about Egypt in a systematic way. Many nineteenth-century travelers to Egypt would have read Herodotus the way modern travelers read guidebooks and, like me, would have been intrigued by his general description of the Egyptian people, who, like their river, operated in reverse:

> For instance, women attend market and are employed in trade, while men stay at home and do the weaving. In weaving the normal way is to work the threads of the weft upwards, but the

---

* He *said* he went. In modern times, there has been much debate about whether Herodotus ever set foot out of Greece.

Egyptians work them downwards. Men in Egypt carry loads on their heads, women on their shoulders; women urinate standing up, men sitting down. To ease themselves they go indoors, but eat outside in the streets, on the theory that what is unseemly but necessary should be done in private, and what is not unseemly should be done openly ... Elsewhere priests grow their hair long; in Egypt they shave their heads. In other nations the relatives of the deceased in time of mourning cut their hair, but the Egyptians, who shave at all other times, mark a death by letting the hair grow both on head and chin. They live with their animals—unlike the rest of the world, who live apart from them. Other men live on wheat and barley, but any Egyptian who does so is blamed for it, their bread being made from spelt, or *Zea* as some called it. Dough they knead with their feet, but clay with their hands—and even handle dung. They practise circumcision, while men of other nations—except those who have learnt from Egypt—leave their private parts as nature made them ... In writing or calculating, instead of going, like the Greeks, from left to right, the Egyptians go from right to left.

In defense of the value and necessity of his own account of a journey he made in Egypt in 1777 (well before the real boom in Egyptian travel and its consequent avalanche of travelogues and reports), Charles Sonnini wrote with palpable anxiety: "From Herodotus down to Volney, writers of equal celebrity ... demonstrate the curiosity which [Egypt] generally excited. But this frequence of travelers cannot exclude my pretension to a place among the rest, and I am not to be deterred from speaking of Egypt by the number or renown of those who have trodden the ground before me ... Objects do not present themselves to all observers under the same point of view."

No, true, they do not. Take, for example, the disagreement of feeling from Gustave Flaubert and Florence Nightingale in response to the Sphinx. On first sight of the monument, Flaubert nearly came unhinged with excitement. "I am afraid of becoming giddy," he wrote, "and try to control my emotion." Nightingale, however, was flatly unimpressed by it, mocked it for its state of disrepair, and wrote with characteristic erudition and contempt: "May a 'portion for seven, and also for eight' thereof be mine before I visit the Sphynx again."

Flaubert and Nightingale were not acquainted and never, as far as anybody knows, ran into each other in Egypt, though during the early parts of their trip they moved through the same neighborhoods at the same time. On Sunday morning, November 25, 1849, Flaubert recorded in his notes, "Arrival in Bulak . . . From Bulak to Cairo rode along a kind of embankment planted with acacias or *gassis*. We come into the Ezbekiyeh, all landscaped. Trees, greenery. Take rooms at the Hotel D'Orient." Two days later Nightingale reported, "Before ten we were anchored at Boulak; and before eleven . . . we had driven up the great alley of acacias from Boulak to Cairo to the Ezbeekeeyeh and the Hotel de L'Europe."

Nightingale and Flaubert visited the usual places of interest and recorded many of the same details. Flaubert on entering the passageways of the Great Pyramid: "Smooth even corridor (like a sewer), which you descend; then another corridor ascends . . . wider corridors with great longitudinal grooves in the stone." Of the same experience, Nightingale: "Down one granite drain, up another limestone one, hoisted up a place . . . You creep along a ledge and at last find yourself in the lofty groove." Nightingale described Saqqara as "a desert covered with whitened bones, mummy cloths, and fragments, and full of pits . . . strewed like a battlefield, so as really to look like the burial place of the world." Flaubert's assessment of Saqqara: "The soil seems to be composed of human debris; to adjust my horse's bridle my *sais* took up a fragment of bone. The ground is pitted and mounded from diggings; everything is up and down."

Where Nightingale was tough minded, unsentimental, and rational, Flaubert was emotional, sometimes prissily melodramatic, and superstitious. Preparing to embark on his trip to Egypt, he was careful to leave his writing desk exactly as he would were he to return to it the very next day, because, as he told his friend Maxime du Camp, "It is unlucky to take precautions!" At the start of his trip he caught a glimpse of a priest and four nuns standing at the entrance to the train station and later wrote of the sight, "Bad omen!" He was so desolate at leaving his mother behind in Croisset that at every stop on the trip to Paris, he considered leaping off the train and returning home. Thirty years later, Du Camp quoted Flaubert as having cried out dramatically in Paris, "Never again will I see my mother or my country! This trip is too long, too distant; it is tempting fate! What madness! Why are we going?" Finally, "after hours of sobbing and anguish such as no other separation ever caused me," Flaubert mopped up his tears, resolved to go through with it, and spent the next two days in Paris sedating himself with "huge dinners, quantities of wine, whores," because, as he noted, his "poor tortured nerves needed a little relaxation." Flaubert was self-conscious enough that even in the midst of a terrible fit of weeping at leaving his mother, he could pause to observe the particular quality of his own voice: "[I] held my handkerchief to my mouth and wept. After a time the sound of my own voice (which reminded me of Dorval* three or four times) brought me to myself." Flaubert's self-involvement, his touching streak of youthful vanity, appears again when he appraises with satisfaction the particular way he stood on the deck of the ship that carried him to Alexandria, "striking attitudes *à la* Jean Bart, with my cap on one side and cigar in my mouth . . . I watch the sea and daydream, draped in my pelisse like Childe Harold. In short, I'm on top of the world. I don't know why, but I'm adored on board."

* French actress Marie Dorval.

Where Nightingale was physically intrepid and unflinching, Flaubert could be surprisingly delicate. While climbing the Great Pyramid, he wilted and had a terrible struggle reaching the top. "The Arabs push and pull me," he wrote. "I am quickly exhausted, it is desperately tiring. I stop five or six times on the way up." By contrast, Nightingale skipped effortlessly up the 450 feet of the pyramid, then wrote dismissively, "As to the difficulty, people exaggerate it tremendously;—there is none, the Arabs are so strong, so quick, and I will say so gentlemanly; they drag you in step, giving the signal, so that you are not pulled up piecemeal. The only part of the plan I did not savour was the stopping when you are warm for a chill on a cold stone, so that I came to the top long before the others." When it came time to surmount the rapids of the first cataract in Aswan, Flaubert chose to disembark and travel safely overland rather than take part in that potentially dangerous stretch of the journey, whereas Nightingale, who strikes one as willing to try just about anything, hiked up her skirts and faced the cataract passage with glee. When the ordeal was safely over she observed, "The sense of power over the elements, of danger successfully overcome, is . . . one of the keenest delights and reliefs."

Nightingale wrote long (not to say almost mincing) meditations on the temples and tombs of Egypt; she was so surreally well versed in Egyptian history that she could wander about the country appraising the ancients as if they were long-lost neighbors. She referred to Moses and Plato as "the pair of truest gentlemen that ever breathed," to Cleopatra as "that disgusting Cleopatra," to Cheops as "abominable man!" and as for Joseph out of Genesis: "I never could bear Joseph for making all the free property of Egypt into Kings' property." Of Ramses II she wrote dotingly, "I feel more acquainted with him than I do with Sethos; and he was so fond of his wife."

While Nightingale rhapsodized about the art of the temples,

Flaubert confessed that the temples bored him "profoundly" and rarely mentioned them but to note the wasps' nests in their corners, the bird droppings that streaked their walls, the yellow cow that poked her head through the temple door, the man outside the entrance with a jug of milk on his head. Forgoing the temples, Flaubert focused his attention on dancing girls, hookers, and bathhouse catamites. He seems to have had a sexual adventure of one stripe or another with every prostitute in Egypt and recounted his experiences with the same elaborate devotion and intimacy of detail that Nightingale granted the kings and gods. He was particularly taken with Kuchuk Hanem, the famous *almeh* of Esna, whose breasts were "apple-shaped" and smelled "something like that of sweetened turpentine." Romantic though he was, Flaubert was drawn to the grotesque and the bitter; at times his details are almost clinical. Of one encounter he observed, "On the matting: firm flesh, bronze arse, shaven cunt, dry though fatty; the whole thing gave the effect of a plague victim or a leperhouse. She helped me get back into my clothes." And of another, "I performed on a mat that a family of cats had to be shooed off."

You would think there could not have been a more dissimilar pair of tourists than Florence Nightingale and Gustave Flaubert, except that they shared nearly as many qualities as they didn't. Both were brilliant, iconoclastic, sensitive, and impatient with hypocrisy and convention. Neither had any desire to fit the tediously clichéd expectations that society had slated for them. Both were charming conversationalists but prized solitude and generally considered most other people a tiresome distraction. Both were traveling in Egypt during a period of considerable personal uncertainty and self-doubt; both agonized over how they would use their talents and answer their natural impulses—Flaubert's literary, Nightingale's spiritual and medical.

Under pressure from his father, Flaubert had briefly studied law, an experience "which only just failed to kill me with bottled-up fury." He despised the tidy little bourgeois path he was expected to follow, and when his nervous mother wrote to him in Egypt suggesting that he take a "small job" on his return to France, he replied with annoyance, "First of all, *what* job? I defy you to find me one, to specify in what field, what it would consist in. Frankly, and without deluding yourself, is there a single one that I am capable of filling?" More than anything else, Flaubert wanted to write; indeed, sitting in his study in Croisset, he had already written two unpublished novels and a handful of short stories. But he was confused about what he would write next and how he would write anything with lasting effect. Doubt tormented him. From Cairo he wrote to his mother:

> When I think of my future (that happens rarely, for I generally think of nothing at all despite the elevated thoughts one should have in the presence of ruins!), when I ask myself: "What shall I do when I return? What path shall I follow?" and the like, I am full of doubts and indecision. At every stage in my life I have shirked facing my problems in just this same way; and I shall die at eighty before having formed any opinion concerning myself or, perhaps, without writing anything that would have shown me what I could do.

Three months later he wrote again from Esna: "I think about what I have always thought about—literature; I try to take hold of everything I see; I'd like to imagine something. But what, I don't know. It seems to me that I have become utterly stupid." At Philae he wrote, "I don't stir from the island and am depressed. What is it, oh Lord, this permanent lassitude that I drag about with me?" In a letter to his close friend Louis Bouilhet, Flaubert's frustration is palpable: "Sitting on the divan of my *cange,* watching the water flow by, I ruminate about my past life . . . Am I about to enter a new period? Or is it the beginning of complete decadence? And from the past I go dreaming into the future, where I see nothing, nothing. I have no plans, no idea, no project, and, what is worse, no ambition."

For her part, Nightingale believed that God was calling her and was confused as to how to respond. She too suffered bouts of depression and anxiety. Like Flaubert's mother, Nightingale's parents were concerned about her future and were deeply appalled when she spoke of nursing as her desired profession; most well-off, well-educated British people of the day considered nursing a lowly occupation fit only for the loose, the uneducated, and the intemperate. Yet, from her experience tending to sick relatives and neighbors, Nightingale knew without question that her heart lay with nursing. She was an innovative scientist, progressive, and firmly believed that there were vast improvements to be made in the nursing profession, that a nurse could and should be more than a passive, handholding attendant who simply kept the patient company while he faded and died.

Nightingale's parents naturally expected her to marry, but, like Flaubert, she balked at the constraints of marriage. Twice during a seven-year courtship, her suitor, Richard Monckton Milnes, proposed, and twice—to her parents' disappointment and bafflement—she rejected him. Nightingale believed that God intended her to be celibate. (Milnes, it transpires, was a comically improbable figure for such a chaste and high-minded woman as Nightingale. He was reputedly obsessed with sadomasochism, was said to be the owner of the largest collection of hard-core pornography in Britain—in *Nightingales,* her biography of Florence Nightingale, Gillian Gill calls this stash "the most extreme pornography the world had seen before the invention of film and the Internet"—had a collection of hangmen's autographs and a bookmark fashioned out

of human skin, was gay, and seems to have hosted nonstop Sa-
dian sex parties at his home, an estate he nicknamed "Aphro-
disiopolis." Whether Nightingale was aware of any of these
details at the time nobody knows, but she was not impercep-
tive. Milnes was fat, literary, good natured, influential, generous, and Nightingale claimed to have loved him, though I
think she *must* have suspected something was slightly off
about the guy.)

Nightingale claimed that God spoke to her for the first time
when she was sixteen; what exactly he wanted her to do for
him she didn't know. In a private journal she kept while in
Egypt, she recorded three or four times that God had spoken
to her again. Near Asyut she wrote, "God called me in the
morning and asked me would I do good for him alone without
reputation?" Nightingale's biggest source of anxiety seemed to
be her longtime habit of daydreaming, which in itself doesn't
sound so terrible, until you discover that the daydreams had
the quality of full-blown visions, that they were all-consuming,
and that they could come over her at almost any time, whether
she was alone or in company. Gill describes the dreaming as
"a state of absorbed reverie, when for minutes or even hours
on end she would be so absorbed in some imagined adventure
as to be impervious to what was happening around her." In
contrast to the smooth, entertaining, and lucid letters she
wrote to her family, the tortured content of Nightingale's private diary is startling. Its pages are full of shamed and dispir-
ited comments about her daydreaming. Without revealing the
subject of her dreams, she perceived the habit as corrupt, sin-
ful, described it as a "murderer of thought," an addiction
worse than opium, and thought that she was losing her mind.
She wrote, "[I] struggled against dreaming as the desert fa-
thers once struggled against erotic fantasies." Midway through
her trip, at Gerf Hussein, she remarked with despair, "Oh
heavenly fire, purify me—free me from this slavery."

If two troubled geniuses ever floated down the Nile, they were Florence Nightingale and Gustave Flaubert. Travel broadens the mind, they say. It also clears it. Among their other reasons for traveling to Egypt, Flaubert and Nightingale came, as many travelers did, as a way of clearing their minds. On completing his trip, Flaubert suddenly felt immense inspiration and wrote joyfully to Bouilhet: "A bizarre psychological phenomenon! Back in Cairo (and since reading your good letter), I have been feeling myself bursting with intellectual intensity. The pot suddenly began to boil! I felt a burning need to write! I was wound up tight." On March 9, 1849, toward the end of her trip, Nightingale wrote in her diary with calm gravity, "During half an hour I had in the cabin myself . . . I settled the question with God."

Objects may not present themselves to all observers under the same point of view, but they can sting and stroke those varied points of view to exactly the same effect. Nightingale saw chaos in Egypt; Flaubert saw harmony. Nightingale saw the misery of life; Flaubert saw the glory. Both saw clearly, and both were looking at the same thing. In the end, they saw what they needed to see. Both were devastated at having to leave their boats behind. One wrote, "Leaving our little boat was heart-rending," and the other, "We left the dear old boat wringing our hands, while we irrigated the ground with our tears all the way to Heliopolis." (I'll leave it to you to guess who wrote which.)

Asked whether Egypt had lived up to his expectations, Flaubert responded, "Facts have taken the place of suppositions — so excellently so that it is often as though I were suddenly coming upon old forgotten dreams." Nightingale, similarly, wrote, "I had that strange feeling as if I had been here before, — it was so exactly what I had imagined, — a coincidence between the reality and the previous fancy, which never comes true with me."

〰〰〰

AT EIGHT O'CLOCK I climbed back into my rowboat, rearranged my food and my water bottles by the intense light of the full moon, unwrapped the shirt from my head, and lay down for the night with my sleeping bag spread over me, and my sweater for a pillow. Less fearful and more tired this night than I'd been the night before, I fell quickly into a sound sleep.

Three hours later, lying on my right side with my face aimed north, my eyes opened abruptly at the sound of water swirling around the prow of my boat, very close to my head—the swishing of an oar. And then something solid thudded with a metallic ring into the side of my boat, rocking me a little. I knew immediately that it was another boat and that there was no way in the world that a person sitting in a boat next to mine could have missed the fact that I was lying here. I could feel whoever it was watching me by the impossibly bright light of the moon, which now was directly overhead. My hands, my white sleeves, and the tip of my nose glowed. Like a rush of electricity a paralyzing fear came over me, and the air around my face suddenly felt intensely hot. I lay immobilized, like an overturned crab unable to right itself. My heart seemed to shake the entire boat with its clacking protest. Was it better to just lie there and pretend to be asleep or to sit up and present myself? It had to be a man, for who else would it be in a boat on the Nile? The suspense was excruciating. I pretended to be asleep, my arms and legs frozen with fear. I felt limbless. A minute or so passed and then, unable to stand it anymore, I suddenly sat upright.

There in a rowboat exactly like mine sat a man and four small boys, their features clearly visible in the moonlight. At my sudden movement every one of them reared spectacularly back in fright, which caused their boat to wobble and bounce on the water.

I stared at them. They stared back at me. And no one spoke for what seemed like a very long time. Finally, though I wanted to scream, I said, "What?" in a somewhat normal tone of voice. Why I said this I don't know. What else, really, was there to say?

The man peered at me, dumbfounded, wary, absorbing the fact of my voice, my English, my hair that now, unwrapped, hung to my shoulders. He raised a questioning hand. Parrot-like he said, "What?" back at me.

Fear had robbed me not only of my little elementary Arabic but also of my English. "What what?" I said dumbly, raising my own hand.

The man's face bore a look of tense confusion. His nose and the palm of his hand were khaki colored in the moonlight. He had a luxurious mustache and bright eyes. He seemed to be staring almost in self-defense, like an animal cornered, as frightened as I. *"Bititkallim Araby?"* he said.

I said no, I didn't speak Arabic.

With that figuring Egyptian flick of his raised fingers, he said, "Which country?"

I told him. He leaned closer in bafflement, examining my hair. By now he certainly knew I was a woman. "America," he said.

"Yes."

"One person?"

All the clever phrases of self-defense that Madeleine had taught me had abandoned me now. I had completely forgotten how to say *My husband is over there behind that bush with a large gun,* or, *The police are following me and should be here in approximately two minutes.* In fact, I completely forgot to lie and said, "Yes, one person."

He gestured at the boat and asked whose it was.

"Mine."

He blinked at me, his eyelashes glittering in the yellow light. The children stared in puzzlement and fear, their open mouths four little black holes above their moonlit chins. Seeing me here under these circumstances must have been as odd for them as it would be for a Bostonian to find a crocodile trotting up Tremont Street.

The man leaned forward and looked into my boat, studying my things.

"I bought this boat," I said in Arabic. My voice sounded thin and terribly distant—an insignificant little cheeping.

He asked where I bought the boat. I didn't want to say Luxor, didn't want to tell him I had rowed all that way. I feared he wouldn't believe me, would think I was mocking him. More than that, I wanted him to believe that I had some association with people in Qena, which was not too far from here. "Qena," I said.

"Qena," he said. "You come from where today?"

"Qena. I came from Qena to here. Now I'm going from here to Qena."

"You?"

"Yes."

He was incredulous. "Too far."

Qena was probably less than twenty miles away, not far at all. "Not so far," I said.

He reached out and gripped the edge of my boat and pulled it against his in a startlingly proprietary way, and the four little boys teetered like tenpins on their perches, their shadows rocking and shifting over the moonlit water, their hands flying up and clutching at each other for balance.

The man had begun to smile, a smile that appeared to me ulterior and full of terrible confidence. His teeth were brilliant in the whitewash of the moonlight. His voice grew eerily soft, and he talked through his smile in a lilting way. "You have cigarette?"

I had cigarettes. Though I didn't smoke, I had brought a pack of cigarettes with me for the same reason I had brought a box of pens. I clawed through my luggage, my hands shaking, found the cigarettes, gave him one.

"Marlboro," he said, recognizing the package. "Marlboro. Good cigarette. *Shukran geziran. Geziran.* Sank you."

I found my matches and in my nervousness I reversed traditional roles and lit his cigarette for him, horrified at the way the match flame jittered in my trembling hand.

The way he was peering at me was awfully unnerving. He seemed to be thinking, considering his options, relishing the possibilities as he blew smoke at my forehead. I was a mere woman: no threat at all. He looked to me like a demented cat leering at an unfortunate mouse, delighting in thoughts of the painfully perverse tortures he could visit on his hapless prey. In precisely the tone of voice one would use to console a tiny, nervous child, he said, "*Good* cigarette. *Good* cigarette. Good, *good* cigarette." He seemed delighted with himself for knowing these words in English. He withdrew a packet of *sisha* from within his gallabiya and offered it to me in exchange for the cigarette.

I had no interest in this fruity tobacco. "No, thanks. Thanks a lot, though," I said. "Thanks very much." I didn't want him to sense how great my fear was. That was too much information to give away. One person's visible fear can trigger another's aggression.

A long silence followed. I was completely unable to gather my thoughts; they were the racing, repetitive, scattered thoughts of a hunted animal. I wanted to get away, to row off in a hurry, but knew that I shouldn't do anything abruptly or defensively for fear of attracting from him precisely the sort of behavior I hoped to avoid. The last thing I wanted was for him to panic. I felt thoroughly powerless and at his mercy. With false and quavering cheerfulness, I said, "What is your name, sir?"

"Mahmoud."

"Very nice to meet you, Mahmoud."

"What your name?" he said. I told him. "Nice to meet you, Mister Rose."

"Not Mister," I said absurdly, "Miss," and the little boys collapsed in a startling sudden laughter that rang sweetly in the soft light. Did they understand English?

Mahmoud put his face near mine. "You have camera?"

"No, I don't." Of course I had a camera, but no longer my cheap Polaroid.

"No camera," he said ruminatively, breathing through his teeth, taking pride in the sound of his few English words. He was smart, had already picked up a few phrases from me. His voice seemed to have assumed a gloating tone.

"Are these your boys, Mahmoud?" I said pointing at them. They were small and thin, like most Egyptian boys, and they were all dressed in ghostly white gallabiyas.

Yes, they were his boys. In Arabic, I asked each boy his name and age, and Mahmoud answered for each of them. The boys giggled, happy at being noticed, quizzed, and identified. There was a box of pens near my feet under my sleeping bag. I found the box and handed it to the boys. They giggled some more and held the pens appreciatively up to the moonlight.

"So many boys, Mahmoud," I said spryly, though my mouth was dry as limestone. I was so afraid that I was having trouble speaking.

"Yes, many boys." He had a creepy way of breathing through his teeth. He raised both hands at me and said, "I need money."

The statement struck me as so shockingly ominous that all I could do was ignore it, pretend he didn't say it. With thoroughly counterfeit casualness, I asked one of the handful of questions I knew how to ask in Arabic, *"Inta min ein, ya Mahmoud?"*—"Where are you from, Mahmoud?"—as though we were a couple of genteel travelers casually meeting at an embassy cocktail party.

"Qena."

"And you're on your way home now?"

"Home," he said, a word he clearly didn't know. Without

precursor and in a voice that sounded almost menacing in its softness and clarity he said, "I love you," and leaned back slightly as if to bring into better focus the effect of this generous statement.

It's curious how in certain circumstances those three much-desired words can sound so ominous; curious, too, how transporting are the physical effects of fear. Petty bodily discomforts—a scraped knee, a bruised toenail, blistered hands, a sore shoulder—all that is rendered nonexistent when challenged by the pain of brute fear. My heart seemed to vibrate. I seemed to have lost all motor control. My thoughts were hopelessly scattered, and what little intelligence I had once possessed had now abandoned me. With heavy dread I envisioned having to stab this man with the knife I had hidden in the bow of my boat. I had told myself the knife would come in handy for any number of daily functions, but at the back of my mind I knew I might need it for just such an occasion as this. Before lying down to sleep, I had opened the knife and placed it beside my pillow. Now, blazing moonlight notwithstanding, I was so blind with fear I couldn't see the knife anywhere in the bottom of the boat.

I raised my watch ostentatiously to the neon moonlight, faked a yawn, and with mock surprise and as much of a display of informal calm as I could muster, I said in English that he could not possibly have understood, "Wow! Look at the time! Ten o'clock! So late! Ho-hum. Guess I'd better be moving along," when in fact what I wanted was to clock the man in the mustache with the butt of my enormous oar and shriek, "Don't you fucking touch me!" My racing thoughts were studded with horrid scenes from my shattered imagination: chief among them was the picture of my own body floating facedown in the river at sunrise for a flock of flamingos to find. I wanted to tip my oars into the water and race off, but my anchor was embedded in the sand. I would have to climb out of the boat and unhook it. How to do this without alarming Mahmoud?

I feigned boredom and ease, looked idly around at the moon-lit water, tried smiling at the kids, gave their father a few more cigarettes.

"Thank you, Miss Rose," he said.

"Well," I said, to move things along, and slowly I disentangled myself from my sleeping bag, stood up, and stepped from the slender bow of my boat onto the sand. I pulled up the anchor and said something ridiculous like, "Beautiful moon," when in fact the moon I had so admired when I first lay down seemed grotesque to me now, revealing me flagrantly, betraying me, illuminating Mahmoud's eyes and teeth and lips, making the water hyacinths look grisly and the sand lewd. If it hadn't been for the moon, this man would never have spotted me.

I got back into my boat, slowly packed up my sleeping bag, and just as I began with pathetic hope to settle my oars into place and make my getaway, Mahmoud stepped lithely out of his boat and into mine, his authoritative weight jerking my boat into deep rocking.

My heart plummeted. Mahmoud sat down on the thwart. "I take you in Qena," he said, pointing at his chest and adjusting his gallabiya between his knees in preparation for rowing.

I thanked him for the offer, said it wasn't necessary. Again he informed me that he would take me to Qena, indicating with his strong hands flashing in the light that he could row very well. In Arabic I said, "No, thanks. I can do it. There is no problem."

He sat breathing and grinning and thinking. "I take," he said, pointing at himself again.

In an instant my fear was overtaken by anger. This is something that happens with me—if frightened and beset enough, I can become infuriated, and my fury fuels an almost supernatural determination and strength. I had no intention of letting Mahmoud frighten me further, no intention of letting him control me.

"Get out of my boat," I said in English.

He hesitated.

I raised my hand between us and waved at him. "Out. Out. Get out now. I'm going. I don't want you to help me."

To my surprise Mahmoud stood up and stepped gracefully back into his own boat. My boat was partially wedged against the riverbank by his. I said briskly, "Go on. Get out of the way. Good-bye. Push me off. I'm going."

"Dilwati?" he said.

It was eerie the way his smile glowed in the repulsive moonlight.

"Yes, now."

"Miss Rose."

"Push me off," I said. "Come on."

Freed from the bank, I began to row, my oars making futile slaps at the clumps of water hyacinth and the stringy river grass; the boat was mired in the shallow water. I set my bare feet against the steel ribs of the hull and yanked at the oar handles, pulling with so much force that the boat suddenly lurched into the stream of the river.

To say that I rowed frantically does my frenzy no justice. My fatigue was gone, replaced by a roaring furnace of energy. I pulled faster and harder than I ever imagined I could. The wind had picked up slightly during the night, and the river had begun to resemble a mountain lake, the surface gone jagged with tiny ripples and waves. An occasional small whitecap flared and curled into itself. The air was blood warm and the moonlight followed me in a hideous jiggling trail of yellow. With each pull of the oars, an involuntary and audible huff of effort and horror escaped my mouth, and when I realized that Mahmoud had decided to come after me in his boat I cried out, "Oh, Christ!" in a little wail of desperation that the wind instantly snatched away. I pulled harder.

I could make out the outlines of Mahmoud's boat a hundred

yards away, the silhouettes of the four boys. I was moving so fast that I was actually stirring up white wake. I saw a light amid the trees on a sizable island in the middle of the river, but I knew that Mahmoud would reach me by the time I got to it. No matter how fast I went, Mahmoud would be able to go faster. Rowing was his life. This was his river. If I was headed for a large jagged boulder just beneath the surface of the water here, I wouldn't know it, but he would. He would know every quirk and current and swirl of the river.

I had rowed six or seven hours already that day, and the palms of my hands were bubbled and shredded. I knew that no amount of raw adrenaline strength would get me out of this. And then I saw the dark form of Mahmoud's boat stop and veer away toward the shore. My heart leaped. He was relenting. He had given up. I was free of him. I rowed harder for several minutes. But before long, I saw unmistakably that he was coming after me again. He had only stopped to get rid of the boys, who had been weighing him down.

My fear, and my anger, doubled. "Goddamn him!" I said. He was determined to catch me. I knew that he would. We rowed this way for what seemed like an eternity but was surely no more than ten minutes. I rowed blindly, certain that my life was over, looking left and right toward the riverbanks for any sign of light or life. I could hear Mahmoud shouting at me through the wind, "Blease! Miss Rose, blease stob! Blease!"

I knew that my body would be found the next day in one unpleasant state of corruption or other. I have often hoped that in the last minutes of my life, I would have at least one or two profound and meaningful thoughts, but all I could decipher amid the jumble of disjointed notions that spun in my brain was that I would rather have a crocodile end my life than some crazy man. The suspense—not knowing what he wanted or what he planned to do—was so excruciating that finally I stopped rowing. I would face him. I would challenge him and get the whole thing over with. I stopped my boat and shipped the oars. Where *was* that fucking knife? My mind spun and tumbled. If he touched me, I decided, if he did anything that I felt was a violation, I would kill him. Without question, I would make every attempt to kill him. It was the first time in my life that I had resolved to take another person's life in order to spare my own, and the feeling that accompanied that decision was the lowest and loneliest and most dismal I have ever experienced.

Mahmoud glided up alongside me and grabbed my gunwale again with that catlike swiftness and determination. He was breathless.

I considered lifting one battering ram of an oar and heaving it butt first into the spot between his eyes, a blow that would certainly disable him. "What do you want?" I said. "What? What do you want?!"

"Miss Rose!" He was gasping.

"What?" I said furiously. I had a weird urge to stand up in the boat. "Money? Is it money?"

He leaned very close. I could almost smell his mustache. "Money," he said. "I need money." He held the edge of my boat with both hands. I wanted to smash his fingers. I slapped his hands off. He laughed.

I reached around for my knife. "How much money?" I said, one of the more asinine things I've ever said. Under the circumstances, why bother to ask how much? Why not just hand him my entire wallet, which was sliding around beneath my feet somewhere? "How much?" I said, hoping that money was all he wanted.

"Ten bound, Miss Rose."

The words landed against my face with the sting of a brisk slap. I stared at him. Ten pounds was little more than three U.S. dollars. Could it be that he had chased me all this way, abandoned his young boys on a darkened riverbank, gone quite far out of his way at the end of what had surely been for him a very long workday to ask me for a mere three dollars? Not possible. There had to be more. I fumbled around for my wallet and fished through it for a ten. The conspicuous thickness of the bills in the fold looked almost vulgar in the moonlight. I thought how absurd this fussy, selective formality was. Mahmoud could, if he wanted to, simply reach over, pluck the whole thing out of my hands, knock me over, and the job would be finished. He'd be rich, and I'd be conveniently dead.

But not if I killed him first. And I *would* kill him first. I'd stab him or club him or drown him.

As I clawed at the wad of Egyptian bills, Mahmoud muttered, "America good country. Good cigarette. I love America. I love you," in that monotonous way.

I plucked up a twenty-pound note. "Here, Mahmoud. Here's twenty. Take it." The bill fluttered in my trembling hand.

Mahmoud gasped at the sight of the twenty. *"Ya saalam!"* he cried. "Miss Rose! Sank you! Oh, Miss Rose!" He was breathless with shock and happiness. He took the bill, kissed it, touched it to his forehead, kissed it again. "I love you! I love you!" he said. His boat clanked against mine, rocking us both. He smooched loudly at the money between his words of thanks. "Sank you, oh, sank you, Miss Miss Miss Rose."

He was drunk with glee. I pushed his boat away and said sharply, *"Khalas!* It's finished. Go back to your boys."

"Boys, yes." He grinned. "Good-bye, Miss Rose. Good-bye!"

To my shock and dismay, he gathered up his oars and began to row upriver again, staring and grinning as he went. I watched as he hurried away, his white figure bending forward with each pull of the oars. I could hear him crying in the moonlight, "Miss Rose, good-bye, good-bye," in an almost beseeching voice that shrank to a cat's wail as the distance between us grew. He thanked me until he disappeared.

I sat in the boat in a state of confusion and disbelief for several minutes. The blood that had seemed to drain from my body during this race now rushed back in a hot flood. When Mahmoud was finally out of sight, my fear suddenly increased. I was in the middle of the river, it was midnight and now quite windy. Qena, my final destination, was approximately fifteen miles away; I could faintly see the green neon lights at the tops of the minarets in the suburbs of Qena. Far from being a comfort, the proximity of the city seemed threatening, full of Muhammads and Ahmeds, Mahmouds and Husseins, with their questions and probings, their jokes and their tricks. I was completely rattled. The world felt upside down. Which was the river, which was the sky? Despite the big moon, it all looked black to me now.

I was alone, but there was no guarantee that, drawn by the memory of all those bills in my wallet, Mahmoud wouldn't get smart and come back to finish the job.

The act of rowing now was a palliative, a distraction. I rowed steadily for another hour and a half, maybe two hours, the minarets and lights growing larger and more numerous as I went. I could hear late-night voices in dimly lit areas along the riverbanks. I didn't relish the thought of arriving at a dock in Qena now and having fifty men question me in the middle of the night. I decided to stop just before the city in a cove where I would be invisible, preferably hidden by some trees. I rowed as quietly as I could, trying not to attract attention or stir up any barking dogs.

A mile or two above Qena, I found a dense overhanging tree whose branch tips bent low into the water. It was a dry, thorny tree weighed down with dust and cobwebs and rotting moss. In daylight these trees had always reminded me of death. I wanted to be able to row out of my resting place instantly if necessary. Putting the anchor down would only slow my flight if I had to hurry off again in a chase. I got the brilliant idea of simply catching my boat securely on the heavy branches of this tree and letting the current pin the boat to them. That way

I could leave my oars in the water and at the ready in the event of another bad encounter. But the current here was stronger than I realized, and before I could stop it, my boat had been pushed deep into the tree's tangled branches, so deep that the branches formed a thorny cage around me, making an instant getaway impossible—indeed making a getaway of any kind impossible.

The boat was thoroughly stuck in the arms of the tree. I was trapped. I sat there for a minute with a weary hand over my eyes, sighing, my fingers trembling. And then I found myself standing up in a tangle of branches and cobwebs, the floor of the boat teetering beneath my feet. When I grabbed on to a branch and tried to pull myself out of my little cave of thorns and branches, dead leaves and dusty hunks of moss and lichen came showering down onto my head. In the commotion the hull of the boat clanged against a thick branch and rang out like a marimba in the dark, frightening several dozen egrets and kingfishers who'd been snoozing in the top of the tree. All the birds flew up at once, clacking and shrieking indignantly like murderous chimps in a bad zoo. The racket was so loud I was certain the police or some other form of trouble would descend on me momentarily. Every move I made kicked up another shower of debris and ripped fresh thorn holes in my shirtsleeves and hands. Finally I blundered free and into the current of the river. I was clammy with sweat, and cursing aloud in a voice wavering close to tears, and all the while the ice-blue stars glittered and the yellow moon glowed steadily and the river flowed in its lazy, undulating, eddying way.

I was bereft. I moved on, looking for coves, testing spots beneath overhanging palm trees and finding nothing suitable. And I began to question what it is in me that wants to scare myself this way. In a kind of hysteria, I sputtered out loud to myself, "You fool!"

I didn't want to be seen, but neither did I want to be too far from the comfort of the bright lights, which shone on the water just around a bend not a hundred yards from me. (I didn't know then that these lights belonged to the Qena tourist police station.) Finally I found a spot in a cove safely out of the current and hidden from above by a dense thicket. It was two o'clock in the morning. I threw my anchor into a clump of weeds and just sat there, deciding that if I had to stay awake until sunrise with my knife in my hand, that wouldn't be so terrible. I was completely enervated.

I sat for an hour, lighting cigarettes and puffing grimly at them, keeping myself company with their little red glow. Eventually, not caring anymore what happened to me, I lay on my back in the bottom of the boat. The gentle current pulled the boat this way and that, causing the stars overhead to wheel left and right like the moving image of a night sky in a planetarium. The boat rubbed against the tall grasses, making the sound of a hulking person walking through a meadow. Frogs clacked near my head, large birds let out sudden yelps in the bushes, crickets stitched and complained, and dogs let out random yips in the distance. The tree above me hummed with bugs. The water rippled and rilled. Everything seemed like a sign of an impending intruder.

I covered my face and head with a shirt to defend myself from the mosquitoes that were crazily strafing me, and finally I fell into a comatose sleep, waking every half hour to discover that I was still alive, then sleeping again, sweating beneath my sleeping bag, not caring about the cockroaches—or perhaps they were scorpions now—that skittered over my fingers.

At five o'clock I woke up and started off down the river again in the milky morning, bleary-eyed and miserable. I glided past the blazing police station, where a few young officers were just beginning to climb out of big canvas tents, and a few others in disheveled uniforms were sipping from mugs and rubbing their eyes. The station sat above the river on a small hill; I rowed by beneath them, directly under their noses. They didn't notice me.

Never having been to Qena, I knew little about the city and nothing about its waterfront. I could see the Qena bridge, a long flat span supported by enormous concrete pilings. I pulled the boat up to a flight of stone steps that led up the tall bank, and sat there watching the rising sun slowly illuminating the red line of cliffs across the river to the west. Covered with an integument of pale yellow pollen, the river looked sad and dirty here. Once it ran under the bridge, it would turn to the left and begin the great Qena curve, the largest turn the Nile makes in all of Egypt, a turn so sharp that for a brief span it actually flows southward. I could see the start of the curve just beyond the bridge.

I sat in the warm morning air, jangling with fatigue and trying, without success, to calm down. I watched a kingfisher efficiently kill a minnow by banging its head repeatedly against an iron railing at the edge of the steps. The kingfisher was a murderous bird, a kind of flying jackknife.

I shut my eyes and thought about Mahmoud, my nighttime visitor, and I felt uneasy and somehow embarrassed. What, actually, had Mahmoud done? He had asked me some questions, had said that I was beautiful, that America was beautiful, and that he loved me (I later learned that in Arabic there is little distinction between the words *like* and *love*), which was nothing every other man in Egypt hadn't done. He had chased after me when I tried to leave him behind, which was nothing every other man in Egypt hadn't done. He had climbed into my boat, and when I asked him to get out he promptly did as I asked. He had offered to row me to Qena—an attempt at an honorable way of earning a little tip, which was what every other man in Egypt would do. They would row you twenty miles for a tip of three dollars; they would walk two miles carrying your three suitcases on their shoulders for fifty cents; they would stand all day on one leg for a dime if you asked them to. Mahmoud had asked me for three dollars. He had demanded nothing. He had very little English and therefore no graceful or subtle or polite way to make himself understood, to make himself human. He had obviously had no contact with foreigners and so had no knowledge of how to charm or disarm me. Scores of Egyptian men had accosted me in Luxor and Aswan, Abu Simbel and Cairo, saying suggestive things, saying they loved me, asking me to dance, touching my arms, asking me to have sex with them, pulling a million tricks to get me to part with my money and myself. It was annoying at times, but it was all a clumsy expression of friendliness, of boredom, and of grinding poverty. It was all rather harmless, a game. And what had Mahmoud done? Less. He wanted a paltry three dollars. What was that? A pittance. I had given little Egyptian children more than that at one sweep, had countless times spent more than that on a beer or a cup of coffee. Mahmoud had four boys to support and surely a wife somewhere. He probably lived in a mud-brick hut with a dirt floor and a bamboo ceiling and spent his days hauling at fishing nets for pennies a day. Mahmoud had done nothing; he had not even touched me. In desperation he had followed me. He had wanted a mere three dollars, and yet in defensiveness and fear and ignorance of who he was, I had resolved, with a brutal fury I had never known I was capable of, to kill him.

I felt ashamed. That fear and violence had sprung from my imagination, from suspicion, from misunderstanding, from the lonely foreign setting and the absence of the sun. I think it's not unfair to say that if I had been sleeping in a rowboat on an American river—the Hudson, say, or the Colorado, or the Mississippi—my fears would have been more founded, and my morning would perhaps never have come.

When the sun was solidly in the sky and the day in Qena had begun, I gathered up my possessions and stepped onto the dock. There was no one around to give my boat to, and so I decided to just leave it there on the dock for some lucky fisherman to find. I hated leaving it. I had gone to such lengths to find it. It had carried me this far and felt like a friend now, with its goofy red hearts, its pink graffiti about Allah, its cockroaches, and its tattered lining of plastic grass. I tied the boat up beside a decrepit steamer with twisted iron rails. I had come to love the enormous oars so much that I wanted to take one home with me, but I left everything as it was and walked up the steps to find a narrow road and an empty car sitting at the curb with its motor running, its driver's door open, its hood up, and no driver in sight.

I walked away from the river in what my map recorded as the direction of the town. Qena was small and depressing. Visitors only came here to see the Temple of Dendera, a relatively minor attraction situated on the other side of the river. They stayed for a day, then went away again. The buildings of Qena were brown and dusty, with broken windows and aboveground sewage pipes connecting them. A little girl standing in an alley saw my face, and her eyes widened in fear and she ran away. Eventually I came to a hotel and found a man sleeping in a van with "Tax" written on the side of it. I woke the man and asked him if he could take me to the train station. He was so startled at the sight of me that he couldn't speak. I was probably the only foreigner in Qena that day, if not that entire week. He opened the door for me, I climbed in, and we headed off down the rutted road. The van didn't seem able to go above ten miles an hour. After five minutes or so, I asked in Arabic, "Is there a problem with the car?," a phrase I had learned by listening to Madeleine.

"There is not problem," the driver said anxiously, predictably. "Not problem."

There was, of course, a problem, but I didn't care.

I sat on a broken bench on the platform at the Qena train station waiting for the morning train to Cairo. A dozen policemen in ill-fitting tan uniforms wandered around the dust-brown train station. Their shirts were three sizes too small and their trousers three sizes too big. They wore flip-flops and tan berets made of felt shoddy. They walked in a shuffling way. A skinny man went by carrying forty loaves of pita bread in his arms, a stack of warm flat disks like a pile of old magazines. Heavy black-veiled village women with plump fingers and hennaed wrists sat impatiently on wooden benches eating pumpkin seeds, spitting the shells onto their swollen feet. They had gold teeth and flashing eyes rimmed with kohl, fat tobacco-brown cheeks and the bulky arms of professional wrestlers. They wore big golden rings and bracelets and earrings. They talked loudly.

Amr must have been nearly back home in Aswan by now, back to the leaden routine of his life. I thought of how he had said with such sadness, "That man could not make himself known," when he spoke of the American businessman who had come to Elephantine Island and insisted that his origin was Nubian. Amr had become a friend to me. Though we came from such different places, though he was an Egyptian man and I was an American woman, he had been able to make himself known. Because he had been able to tell me who he was, what he felt, what he thought, I had been able to accept him, even to identify with him. Mahmoud had had no such luck, and so he had embodied all that I feared, all that others had told me I should fear.

A tiny barefoot boy of perhaps four or five jumped off the platform into the track well below the platform, ran across the tracks, and climbed up the other side to the opposite platform. As he climbed he held the hem of his gallabiya in his teeth to keep from tripping on it. His parents didn't seem to care that he was playing on the train tracks, though the arrival of the train was imminent. He skipped around on the platform, lifting his gown over his head, gleefully revealing his tiny naked body, then jumped bravely onto the tracks again and crossed back to his family. When he sat down on the bench, his father began to slap his little head in a brutal, ceaseless way. The boy howled. His tongue was crimson in the sunlight. Tears streaked his little cheeks.

"Travel does not make one cheerful," Flaubert wrote during one of his depressions on the Nile. Travel *never* makes one cheerful. But it makes one thoughtful. It washes one's eyes and clears away the dust.

BIBLIOGRAPHY

Baedeker, Karl, ed. *Egypt: Handbook for Travellers. Part First: Lower Egypt, with the Fayûm and the Peninsula of Sinai.* Leipzig: Karl Baedeker, 1878.

———. *Egypt: Handbook for Travellers. Part Second: Upper Egypt, with Nubia, as Far as the Second Cataract and the Western Oases.* Leipzig: Karl Baedeker, 1892.

Churchill, Sir Winston. *My African Journey.* London: Hodder and Stoughton, 1908.

Clark, James M., Louis I. Jacobs, and William R. Downs. "Mammal-like Dentition in a Mesozoic Crocodylian." *Science* 244 (June 2, 1989): 1064–66.

Collins, Robert O. *The Nile.* New Haven, CT: Yale University Press, 2002.

Comb, Andrew M. "Crocodylus niloticus." Animal Diversity Web, University of Michigan's Museum of Zoology, 1996. http://animal diversity.ummz.umich.edu/site/accounts/information/Crocody lus_niloticus.html.

Copies of Original Letters from the Army of General Bonaparte in Egypt Intercepted by the Fleet Under the Command of Admiral Lord Nelson, with an English Translation, 3rd ed. London: J. Wright, 1798, 1799.

Earl, Lawrence. *Crocodile Fever.* New York: Alfred A. Knopf, 1954.

Edwards, Amelia. *A Thousand Miles Up the Nile.* London: George Routledge and Sons, 1889. First published 1877 by Bernhard Tauchnitz.

Elisofon, Eliot. *The Nile.* New York: Viking, 1964.

Fagan, Brian M. *The Rape of the Nile: Tomb Robbers, Tourists, and Archaeologists in Egypt.* New York: Charles Scribner, 1975.

Fernea, Robert A., George Gerster, and Horst Jaritz. *Nubians in Egypt: Peaceful People.* Austin: University of Texas Press, 1973.

Flaubert, Gustave. *Flaubert in Egypt, a Sensibility on Tour: A Narrative Drawn from Gustave Flaubert's Travel Notes & Letters.* Edited and translated by Francis Steegmuller. Chicago: Academy Chicago Publishers, 1979.

Gill, Gillian. *Nightingales: The Extraordinary Upbringing and Curious Life of Miss Florence Nightingale.* New York: Random House, 2004.

Golding, William. *An Egyptian Journal.* London: Faber & Faber, 1985.

Gordon, Lucie Duff. *Letters from Egypt.* London: Virago Press, 1983.

Grenard, Steve. *Handbook of Alligators and Crocodiles.* Malabar, FL: Krieger Publishing, 1991.

Herodotus. *The Histories.* Edited by John Marincola. Translated by Aubrey de Selincourt. New York: Penguin Classics, 1996.

Hopley, Howard. *Under Egyptian Palms, or Three Bachelors' Journeyings on the Nile.* London: Chapman and Hall, 1869.

Lane, Edward William. *An Account of the Manners and Customs of the Modern Egyptians.* 1860 edition. Reprint, Cairo: The American University in Cairo Press, 2003.

Lear, Edward. *Selected Letters.* Edited by Vivian Nokes. Oxford: Oxford University Press, 1988.

Ludwig, Emil. *The Nile: The Life Story of a River.* Translated by Mary Lindsay. New York: Viking, 1937.

Neill, Wilfred T. *The Last of the Ruling Reptiles: Alligators, Crocodiles, and Their Kin.* New York: Columbia University Press, 1971.

Nightingale, Florence. *Letters from Egypt: A Journey on the Nile, 1849–1850.* Edited by Anthony Sattin. New York: Grove Press, 1988.

Potous, Paul L. *No Tears for the Crocodile.* London: Hutchinson, 1956.

Pye-Smith, Charlie. *The Other Nile.* New York: Viking, 1986.

Raven-Hart, Major R. *Canoe Errant on the Nile.* London: John Murray, 1936.

Russel, Terence M., ed. *The Napoleonic Survey of Egypt: Description de L'Egypte. The Monuments and Customs of Egypt, Selected Engravings and Texts.* Singapore: Ashgate Publishing, 2001.

Siliotti, Alberto. *Egypt Lost and Found: Explorers and Travellers on the Nile.* New York: Stewart, Tabori & Chang, 1999.

Sonnini, Charles S. *Travels in Upper and Lower Egypt Undertaken by Order of the Old Government of France*. Translated from the French by Henry Hunter. Piccadilly: D. D. Stockdale, 1799.

Wilkinson, John G. *Murray's Handbook for Travellers in Egypt*. London: John Murray, 1858.

ACKNOWLEDGMENTS

I am grateful to Kate Wodehouse at the Providence Athenaeum and to Mary Warnement at the Boston Athenaeum, for their assistance with research for this book; to Zoe Pagnamenta, for her early reading; to Marie Salter of the copyediting department at Little, Brown and Company; to Pat Gentle, for the gift of Sifnos; and to Mara Samellas Taylor and her brothers, John and Demi Samellas, for their generosity in Athens. I would also like to thank Mary and Sam Parkman, Stephen A. Mahoney, Pat Towers, Shirley Hazzard, John and Nancy Mahoney, Ellen Mahoney Sawyer, Betsey Osborne, John Barnett and Isolde Maher, Vanessa Hartmann, Marcia Whitaker, A. Thomas Cole, Melina Papageorgiou, Louly Seif, Elaina Richardson and the Corporation of Yaddo, the National Endowment for the Arts, and Nikolaos Ieronymakis.

I am very much indebted to Betsy Lerner, my agent, for her tireless help with this project, and to my editor, Pat Strachan, for her support, skill, good humor, and grace.

ROSEMARY MAHONEY was educated at Harvard College and Johns Hopkins University. She is the author of *The Early Arrival of Dreams,* a *New York Times* Notable Book in 1990; *Whoredom in Kimmage,* a National Book Critics Circle Award finalist in 1994; *A Likely Story: One Summer with Lillian Hellman;* and *The Singular Pilgrim: Travels on Sacred Ground.* Mahoney received a Whiting Writers' Award. She lives in Providence, Rhode Island.

Reading Group Guide

DOWN THE NILE

Alone in a Fisherman's Skiff

ROSEMARY MAHONEY

A conversation with the author of *Down the Nile*

Rosemary Mahoney talks with Jeffrey A. Trachtenberg of the *Wall Street Journal*

In *Down the Nile,* Rosemary Mahoney rows from Aswan to Qena, a trip of roughly 120 miles. By the yardsticks of most armchair travelers, this voyage barely amounts to a ripple. The Nile in that area is heavily populated, and the river itself is flat and safe.

Yet Ms. Mahoney, who made the trip in 1999, had to overcome a challenge never envisioned by earlier explorers: nobody wanted to sell a boat to a woman. Indeed, the thought of a woman rowing her way down the Nile without male companionship and direction struck most Egyptians she met as impossible.

Still, Ms. Mahoney's determination to pursue her quest paid off. That she did so without permission of the authorities provides an additional undercurrent of excitement.

What was the initial attraction?

It was about the rowing. I know it was an unusual thing to do, but I'm drawn to that kind of challenge. I'm very curious about the world, foreign cultures. Also I wanted to prove to myself that just because it was an exotic place it shouldn't be impossible for a person to do that kind of thing. It wouldn't have been quite as difficult for an American man, but a man would also have had obstacles. You really don't see foreigners traveling alone on the Nile. They are on a cruise ship, or they hire a captain to sail them on a felucca for a couple of days.

*There's something incongruous about a rower having to con-
ceal her intentions. Were you bemused or annoyed?*

I was both bemused and amused, but I was never really annoyed. Egyptian men couldn't fathom why I would want a rowboat, or why anybody would want to row for no reason. For
them, it's pure labor. And I'm a woman. It's unheard of in Egypt
for a woman to do that kind of thing.

*A trip such as this would have likely attracted some media
coverage in the West. Do you think that local people lost out
on something because of the secrecy that surrounded your
experiences?*

Yes, maybe they could have learned something from me. But I
don't speak Arabic, and as I understood it, you needed a per-
mit to row on the river. I didn't think they would grant me
one. So I was doing it without permission. For that reason I
didn't want to draw attention to myself. It's also true that
Egyptians are incredibly friendly. When they see a foreigner
in an unusual place, they all come flocking. I wouldn't have
gotten very far if I'd been open about it. I would have had a
hundred people following me, trying to help me.

*You often appeared exasperated with the women you met, in
part because they seemed so docile. Were you ever tempted to
say: Life doesn't have to be this way?*

I wouldn't say I was exasperated. I really felt for them. I found
it depressing, the way women are forced to live in Egypt. They
are basically not respected. They are treated like children and
not allowed any independence. I found it difficult to believe at
times. It's the sense that women are property of the men.
Therefore it's a man's job to control and protect them. It's a
matter of education. And it's tradition. A lot of Egyptian

women don't know there is another way of life. The poverty in Egypt is quite serious.

You eventually compromised by borrowing a rowboat from a man who followed behind you in a felucca for the first half of your voyage. Any regrets?

No. In some ways I learned more by having spent that time with Amr, the felucca captain. He taught me a lot and he was an incredibly generous, admirable man. He became a friend. I've seen him again. I was in Egypt two years ago. He was still sitting on the dock, waiting for work. Because of the threat of terrorism, it's even worse there than in 1999. He was supporting his crippled sister and two brothers, and it was an incredible amount of responsibility.

Are there any Egyptian travel narratives you would recommend?

William Golding's *An Egyptian Journal.* It's very simple, and nothing really amazing happens. But he has a lovely style.

Although this is a first-person narrative, you reveal very little of your personal life. Was this by design?

I had just split up with a guy I'd had a long relationship with in New York. In some ways I think I took this trip to distract myself. I also wanted the book to be about the trip, less so about my personal life. I've written about myself elsewhere— *A Likely Story: One Summer with Lillian Hellman* was a much more personal book.

Jeffrey A. Trachtenberg's interview with Rosemary Mahoney originally appeared in the Wall Street Journal Online on August 4, 2007. Reprinted with permission.

Questions and topics
for discussion

1. Rosemary Mahoney describes the Egyptian government's attitude toward tourists: they are vigilantly protected from possible danger. How do you think this special treatment affects foreigners' experience of the country? How does it affect Mahoney's?

2. What are some of the primary differences between tourists' travel on the Nile in the nineteenth century and travel in the twentieth and twenty-first? Other than the adoption of some modern technologies, why do you think it has changed?

3. Mahoney relies heavily on the diaries of tourists who traveled before her. Has our modern conception of the country changed drastically from that of earlier generations? Discuss the possible reasons for this shift.

4. Do you think a foreign man would have experienced Mahoney's trip differently? What aspects do you think would be easier? Do you think anything would be more difficult?

5. As a foreign woman, Mahoney is not treated the same as an Egyptian woman or man. How is her journey affected by this? In what ways does it restrict or free her actions?

6. In a country as religious as Egypt, confrontations are bound to occur. Where do you see tensions among beliefs arise in Mahoney's account? Were there factors other than religion that contributed to these conflicts? Are the tensions resolved? How?

7. Amr is one of the few men to take Mahoney's wish to row down the Nile seriously. What makes him different from other Nubian and Egyptian men? In what ways is he the same?

8. When Mahoney departs from Aswan, she is followed down the river by Amr. How does her journey change once he has left her? How would you feel if you were alone on the Nile? Discuss the ways in which Mahoney was either restricted by her solitude or allowed new freedom.

9. Discuss how Western culture has influenced and changed the Egyptian way of life. What ideas and images have stuck in the Egyptian consciousness? How do these shape the way foreigners are viewed?

10. Does Mahoney view Egypt differently at the end of her journey? How are her expectations changed or confirmed?

When a Crocodile Eats the Sun
A Memoir of Africa
by Peter Godwin

"In telling the story of his parents—who after World War II moved from England to Rhodesia—Mr. Godwin gives us a searing account of what has happened to Zimbabwe in the last thirty-odd years. . . . A powerful and deeply affecting book about a family trying to ride the tsunami of change in a country that is coming asunder."

—Michiko Kakutani, *New York Times*

The Ornament of the World
How Muslims, Jews, and Christians Created a Culture of Tolerance in Medieval Spain
by María Rosa Menocal

"Illuminating and inspiring. . . . The book could not be more timely or more encouraging. Menocal shows us a rare moment in history when Muslims, Christians, and Jews found a way to live with each other in peace and prosperity."

—Jonathan Kirsch, *Los Angeles Times*

Back Bay Books • Available wherever books are sold

Now in paperback • Great for reading groups

Leaving Mother Lake
A Girlhood at the Edge of the World
by Yang Erche Namu and Christine Mathieu

"Gorgeously crafted. . . . Namu's discussion of the little-known Moso culture will come as a surprise even to hard-core fans of Chinese women's history. . . . It's refreshing to discover an autobiography that tells the story of a truly exciting and un-usual life."   —Linda Schlossberg, *San Francisco Chronicle*

The Bookseller of Kabul
Asne Seierstad

"Certainly the most intimate description of an Afghan house-hold ever produced by a Western journalist. . . . Seierstad is a sharp and often lyrical observer. . . . *The Bookseller of Kabul* reads like a novel and is absorbing reportage."
—Richard McGill Murphy, *New York Times Book Review*

Back Bay Books • Available wherever books are sold